AF594586

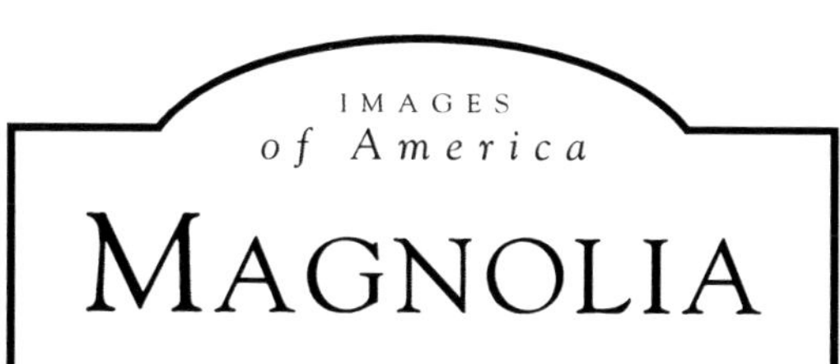
IMAGES
of America
MAGNOLIA

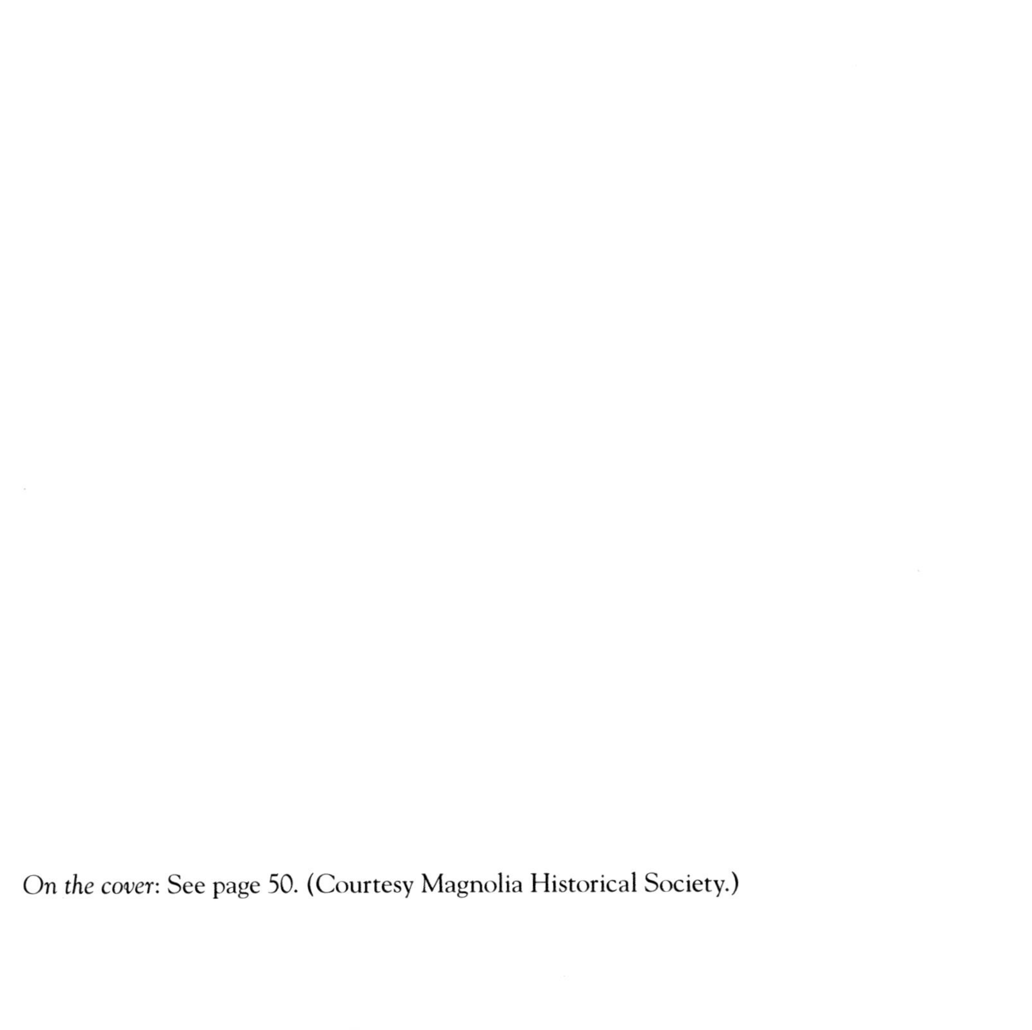

On the cover: See page 50. (Courtesy Magnolia Historical Society.)

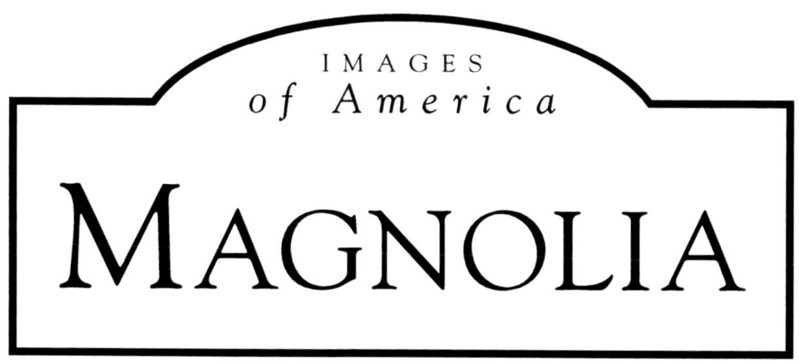

Victoria A. James and Cheryl L. Baisden

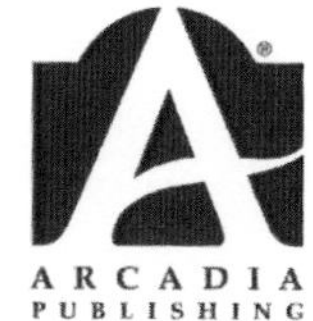

ISBN 978-0-7385-5502-7

Published by Arcadia Publishing
Charleston SC, Chicago IL, Portsmouth NH, San Francisco CA

Printed in the United States of America

Library of Congress Catalog Card Number: 2007928859

For all general information contact Arcadia Publishing at:
Telephone 843-853-2070
Fax 843-853-0044
E-mail sales@arcadiapublishing.com
For customer service and orders:
Toll-Free 1-888-313-2665

Visit us on the Internet at www.arcadiapublishing.com

Contents

ACKNOWLEDGMENTS

This book would not have been possible without the assistance of the Magnolia Historical Society, which was kind enough to provide access to its wonderful collection of photographs and documents, as well as the memories and insights of its members. A special thank you goes to Helen H. Bradley, who dedicated her time to help select the materials for this book. Her commitment to preserving Magnolia's past harkens back to her days as borough clerk, when she collected many of the items that form the foundation of the historical society's collection today.

Chartered in 1991, the Magnolia Historical Society is located in the replica train station at Evesham Road and Atlantic Avenue and is open to the public at select times for research.

INTRODUCTION

In 1682, when William Albertson Sr., a member of the Colonial Legislature, purchased a sprawling tract of land among the Lenni Lenape Natives Americans and a smattering of like-minded Quakers, he had no idea what awaited his descendants. Generations of Albertsons would raise families on the rural tract and, by the onset of the Revolutionary War, would establish themselves as the civic leaders of a small settlement dubbed Greenland, because of the greenish hue of the clay soil. In 1878, with the railroad laying tracks through the rural settlement, the station probably would have been christened Greenland had it not been for the fragrant flowering trees on the Albertson homestead, which earned the station stop the name of Magnolia.

By all accounts, the Magnolia train station was on the map in no time. With vacationers riding the rails to and from the new shore resort known as Atlantic City, business along the Magnolia train tracks was booming at general stores selling hand-churned ice cream, penny candy, and a wide assortment of essentials. And more business meant an increased interest in the quiet little village as the perfect place to build a home and raise a family. A mere 37 years after the railroad came to town, local leaders such as John J. Albertson and Harry Wolohan moved to incorporate the thriving community—by then boasting a population of about 1,000—and officially adopted the name Magnolia for the single square mile borough.

Throughout its history, the little borough of Magnolia has prided itself on its community spirit, from the local PTA raising funds to send an ambulance to France to assist the troops in World War I to the founding of the Magnolia Community Project in 1966 to help local fire and disaster victims. Whether it was Dr. Leslie Lyon accepting chickens in lieu of cash for medical care during the Depression, or "Aunt" Nell Morris arriving at the door to lend a hand with a new baby or an ailing grandmother, neighbors helping neighbors was what defined Magnolia. It is little wonder, then, that the borough selected "One Square Mile of Friendliness" as its motto after reading the contest submission written by Thomas Bradley IV in 1966.

As the photographs in this book illustrate, that civic passion and pride has served Magnolia well.

One

Paving the Way

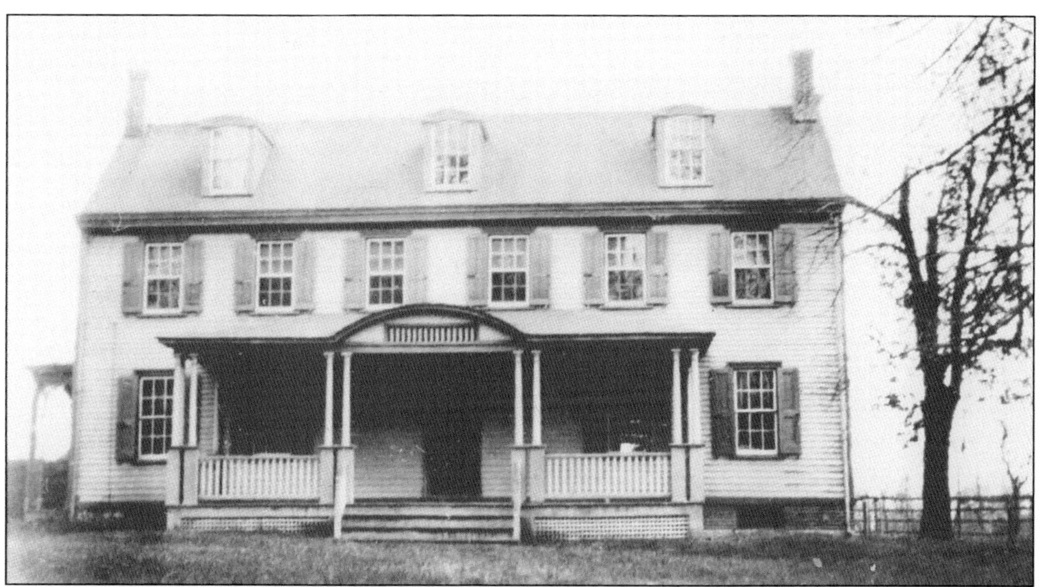

The Albertson family was the first to make its mark in what would become Magnolia, beginning with William Albertson Sr. in the late 17th century. In 1743, Josiah Albertson, a shoemaker who later established gristmills and sawmills, built this farmhouse, which still stands, possibly on the site of the family's 1709 log cabin. His son Josiah and grandson Chalkley both served on the state legislature.

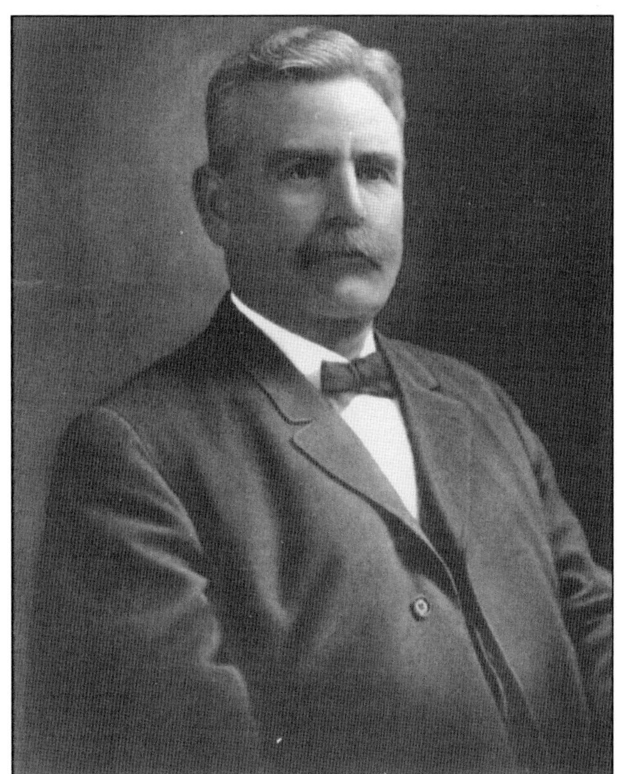

Chalkley Albertson's son John Jarrett (J. J.) also was instrumental in the development of Magnolia and its surrounding communities. An engineer by trade, he began his career with the Philadelphia and Atlantic Railroad in 1878 and later laid out the town of Haddon Heights. In 1892, he became the Camden County engineer, supervising the construction of hundreds of miles of roads and roadway bridges, a position he held for 35 years. Married to Elizabeth Swift Wills of Moorestown (pictured below), J. J. assisted in the construction of the Camden County Courthouse and designed and built the White Horse Pike. His will set aside a piece of land at Evesham Road and Albertson Avenue for the establishment of John J. Albertson Park, which stands opposite the municipal building.

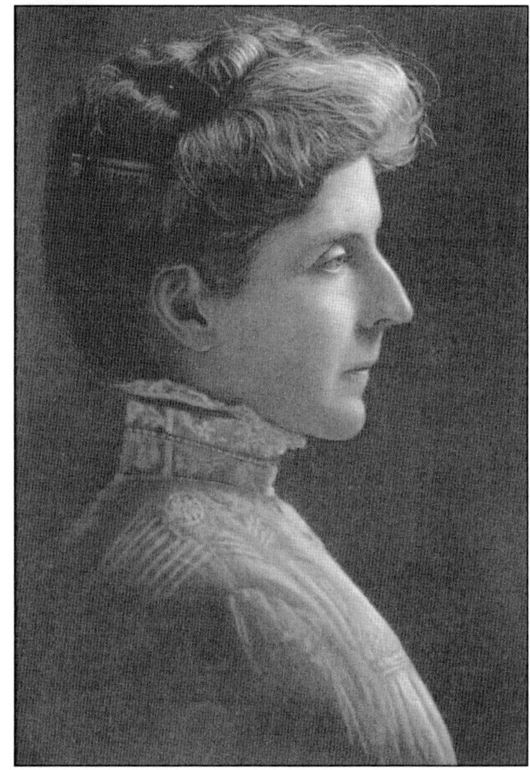

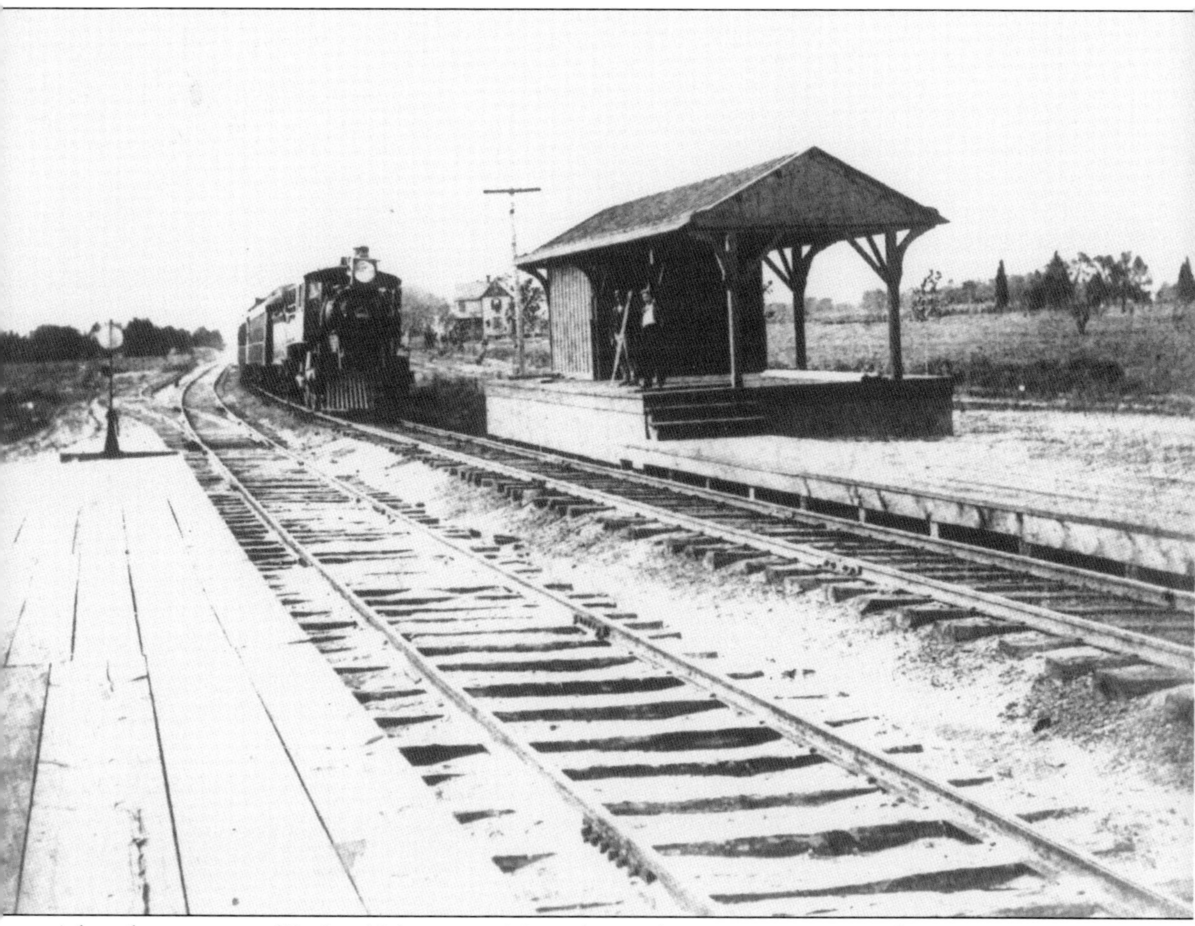

A beer brewer named Richard Massey put Magnolia on the map in more ways than one. In 1877, Massey rebelled against what he perceived to be the Pennsylvania Railroad's high shipping rates and convinced the Camden and Atlantic Railroad to build a narrow-gauge line that stopped in the region then known as Greenland and traveled to the shore. Massey stumbled upon a name for his new station, and later the borough, as he strolled down the magnolia tree-lined walkway to Chalkley's home one day. In 1883, the rail line was purchased by Reading Railroad and rebuilt as a regular-gauge line. This photograph was taken in the takeover year.

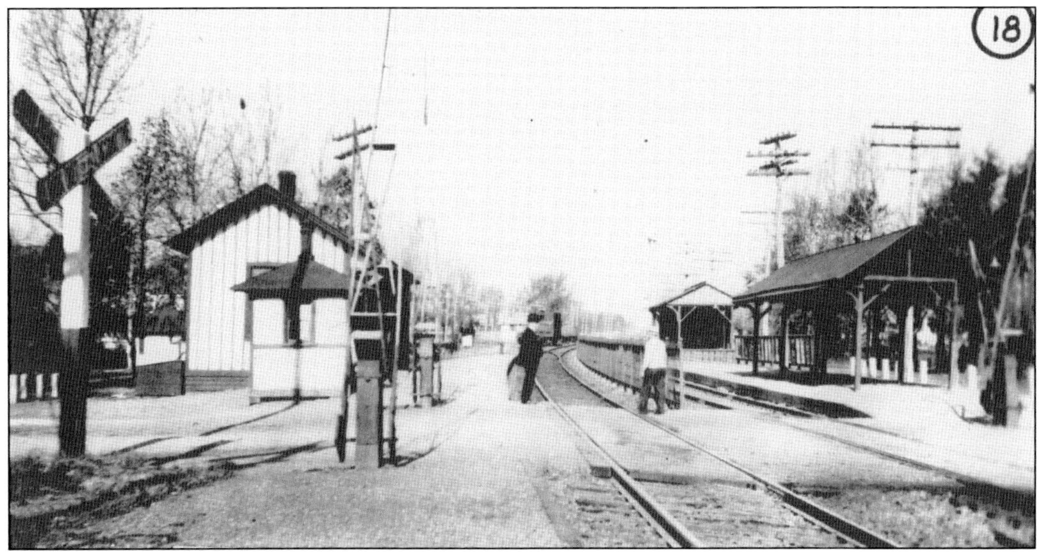

Magnolia's railroad station, pictured here in 1910, was constructed in 1890, at Evesham Road and Atlantic Avenue. As rail traffic increased, a watchtower and switching station, possibly the country's first, operated at Atlantic and Washington Avenues. Olaf Hagen, who later became the borough clerk, was the Magnolia stationmaster, and gate man Frank Bender (on the tracks in white) was employed to raise and lower the gates by hand.

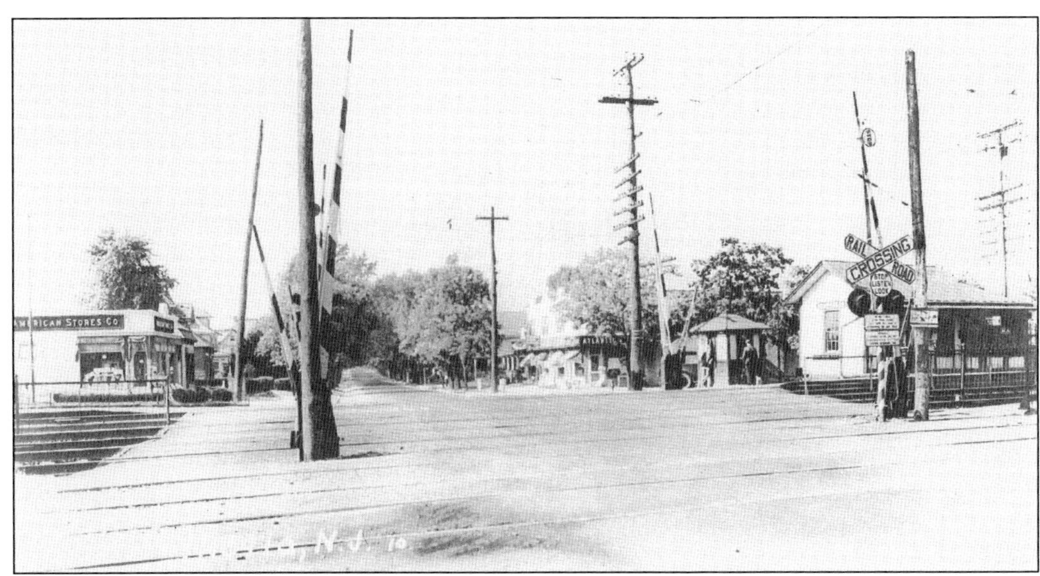

In 1903, trolley tracks (visible in the foreground) were laid parallel to the railroad tracks, to transport passengers from Camden's ferry stations to Clementon. Operating year-round, the trolley is best remembered for transporting Philadelphia and South Jersey residents to Clementon Park, a ride that took more than an hour. Once at the park, visitors could dance, swim, picnic, boat, compete in athletic contests, and enjoy movies and a penny arcade.

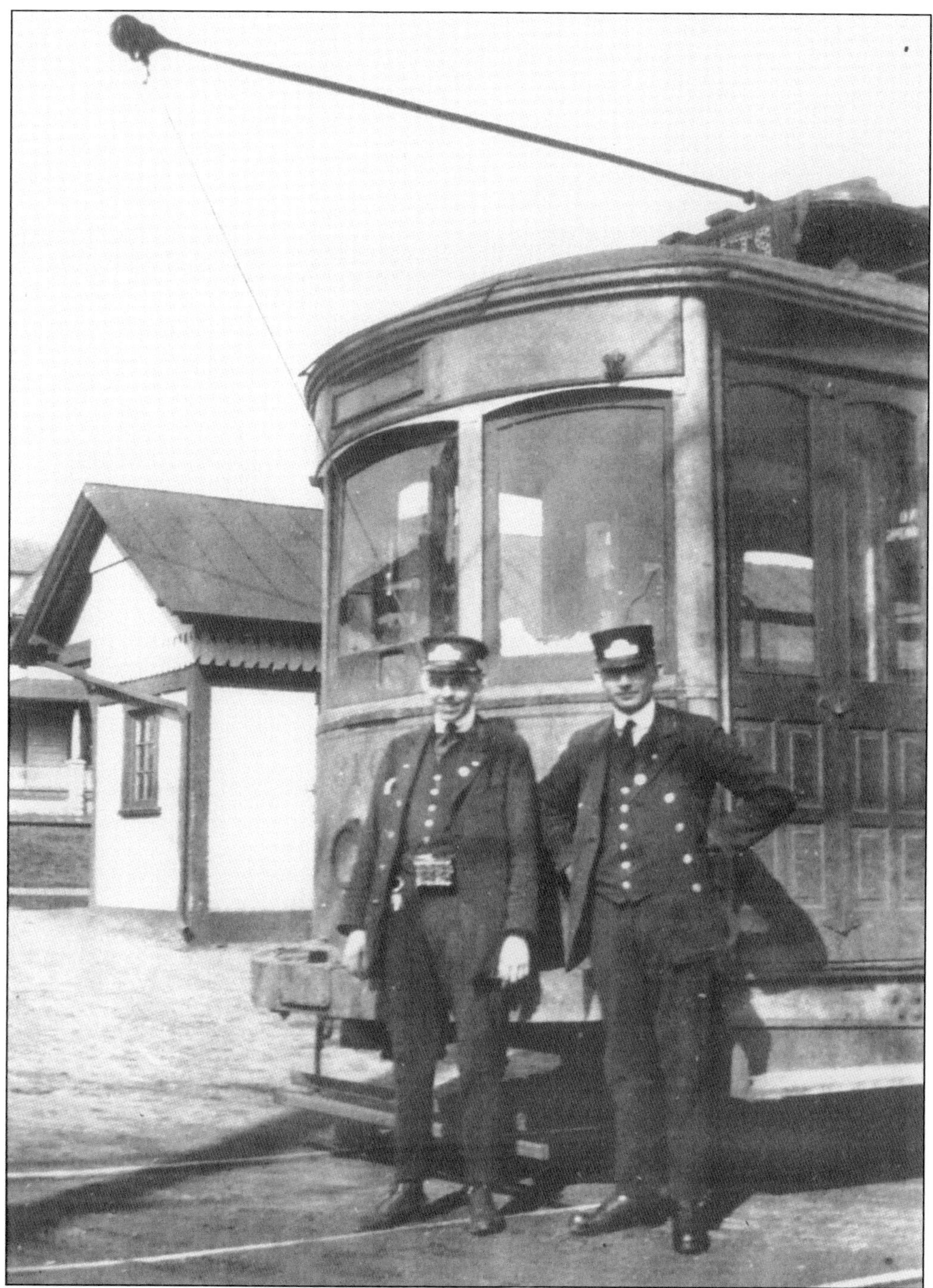

The trolley line, pictured here, was abandoned in 1937 and replaced by a trackless trolley that traveled through the same communities, using the old tracks for portions of the route and retracting its wheels at other times to cruise the streets like a bus. In addition to traveling to Clementon Park and various Camden destinations for shopping and evenings on the town, the trolley was used daily by commuters heading to and from work and students like Magnolia's teenagers, who rode it to nearby Haddon Heights to attend high school.

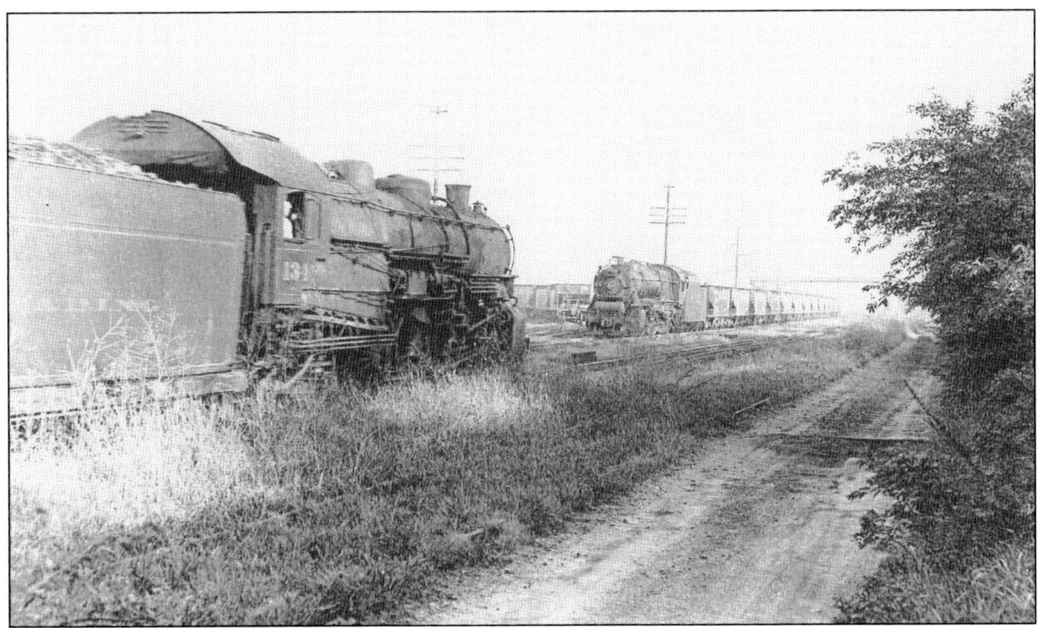

At one time, nine locals stopped in Magnolia daily, Monday through Saturday, and three trains came through on Sunday. In this 1951 photograph, the local can be seen on the left, passing along East Atlantic Avenue near Lincoln Avenue and heading toward Barrington. The last steam engine departed from the borough in 1968.

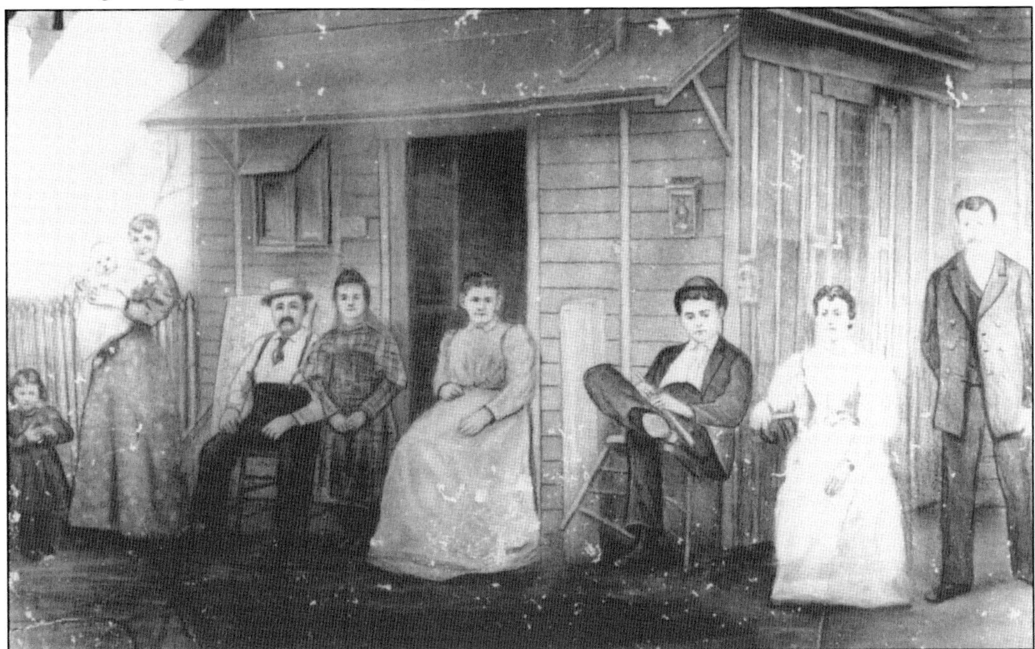

This charcoal drawing from around 1900 shows tollbooth operator Ben Mezger and his family in front of the tollbooth at the White Horse Pike and LaPierre Avenue. Mezger, who lived in the attached house with his family, collected 3¢ from every traveler headed for Haddonfield along the dirt roadway. In Haddonfield, another tollbooth was set up to collect fees from those continuing on toward Camden.

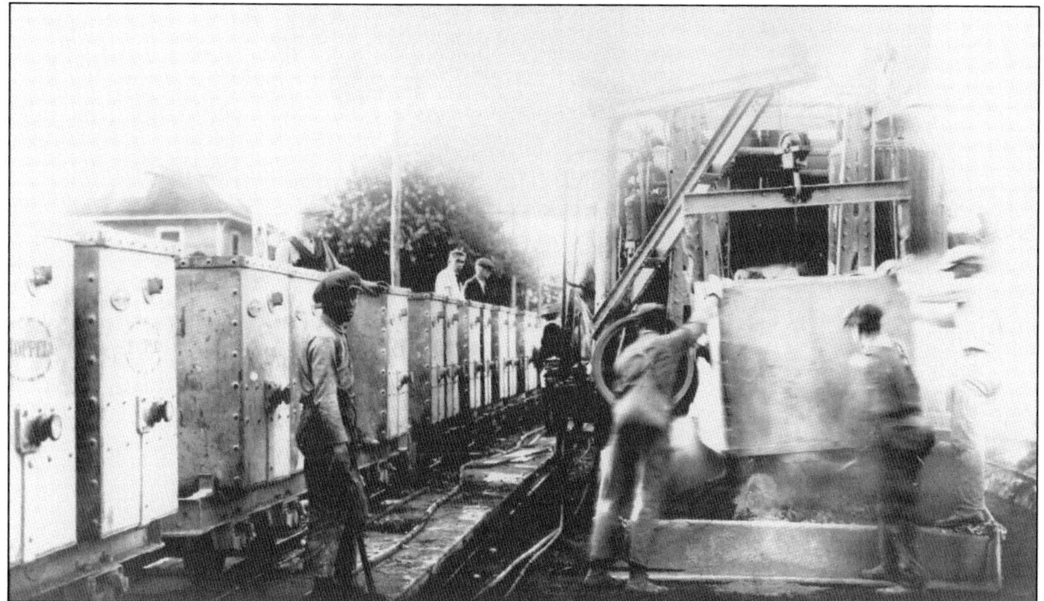

The oak-and-pine-tree lined White Horse Pike was officially established as a recognized turnpike in 1854, the result of legislation introduced by state assemblyman Chalkley Albertson with the future development of his hometown in mind. Named for the White Horse Tavern in Somerdale, it had long been used as a stagecoach route and remained a dirt road until 1922, when this major paving project began.

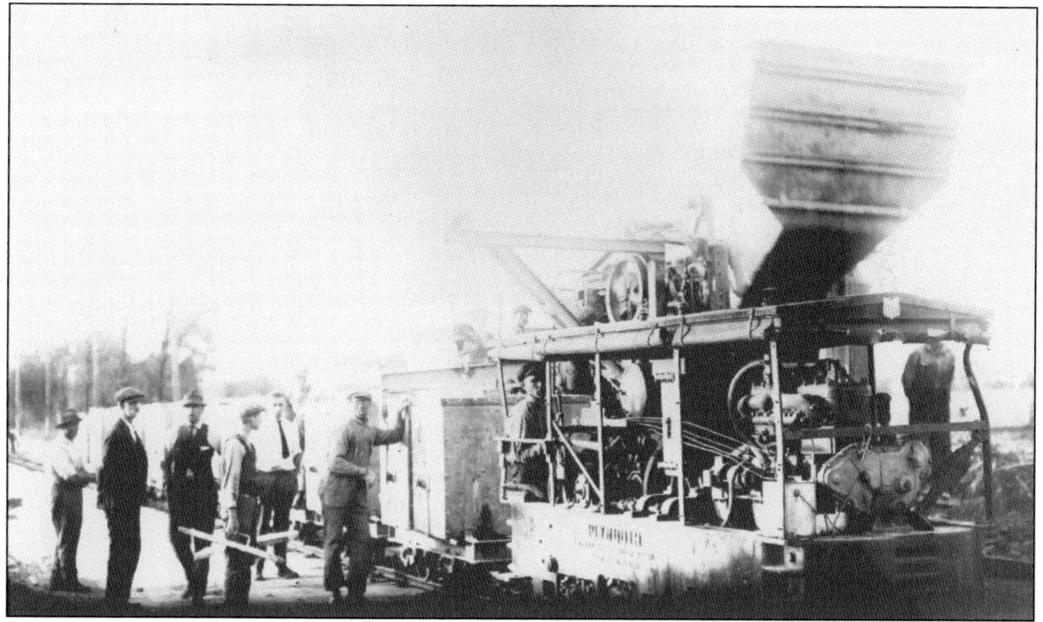

The popularity of cars and the steady increase in traffic led to the decision to pave and widen the pike, making it the state's first paved concrete road. On November 4, 1922, the newly paved roadway was dedicated, and Magnolia celebrated with a huge parade and the crowning of the first Miss Magnolia, a title created for the event. Pictured here, Howard Cliver operates a paver during the 1922 project.

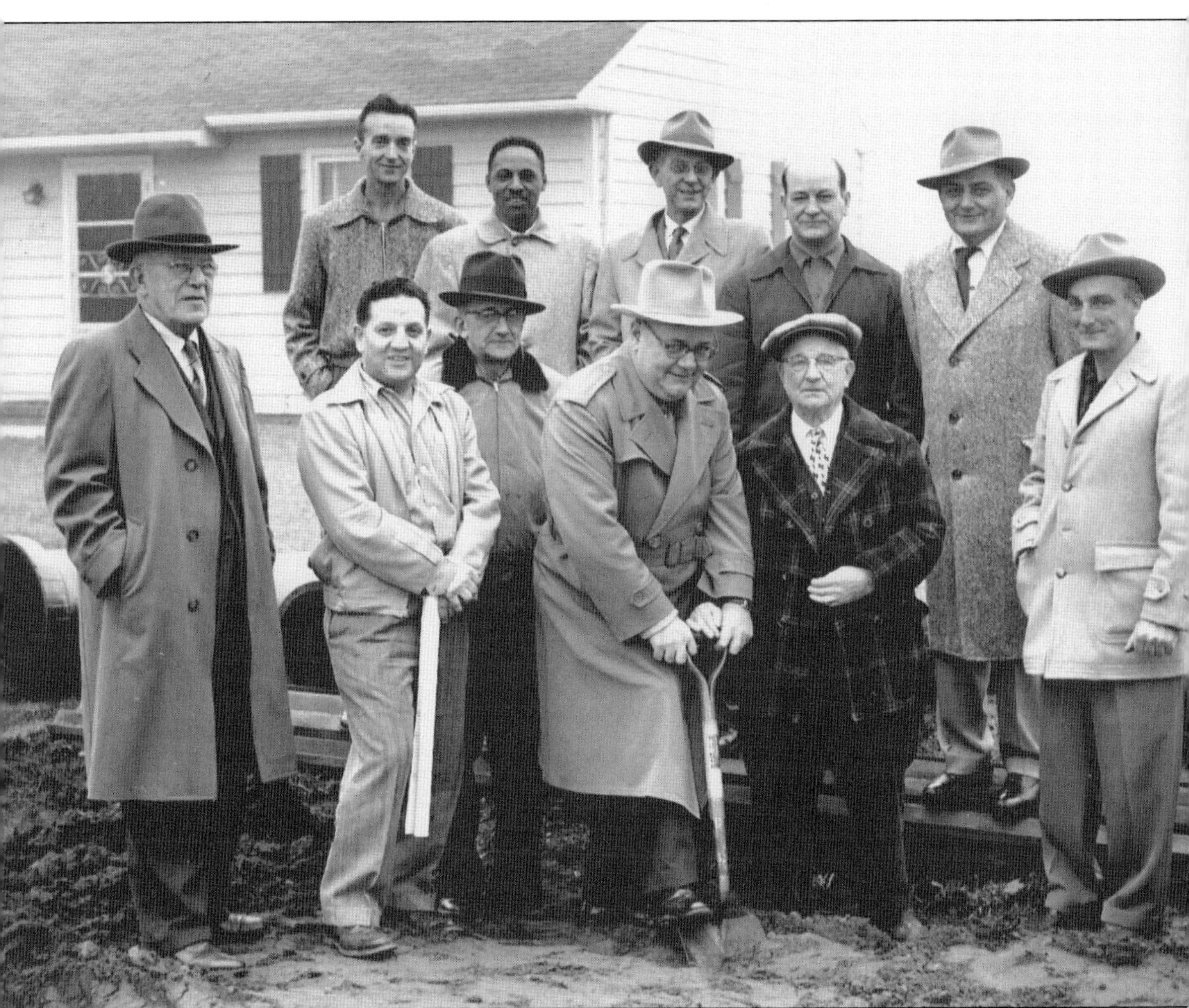

With development on the rise in the borough after World War II, the newly incorporated Magnolia Sewer Authority broke ground on its first project in February 1955. The sewer system began operating a year later. On hand for the groundbreaking were, from left to right, (first row) Andrew Cramp, Anthony Masi, Joseph Hahn, Mayor Francis Scott, Edward Winterbottom, and George Stoddart; (second row) Edward Gavin, Paul Jones, Beverly Davis, Harry D'Amico, and Samuel D'Amico. The borough's water and gas lines were installed in 1916 by Laurel Springs Water Company and New Jersey Gas, during Magnolia's first 20th century growth spurt.

Two

ALL AROUND THE TOWN

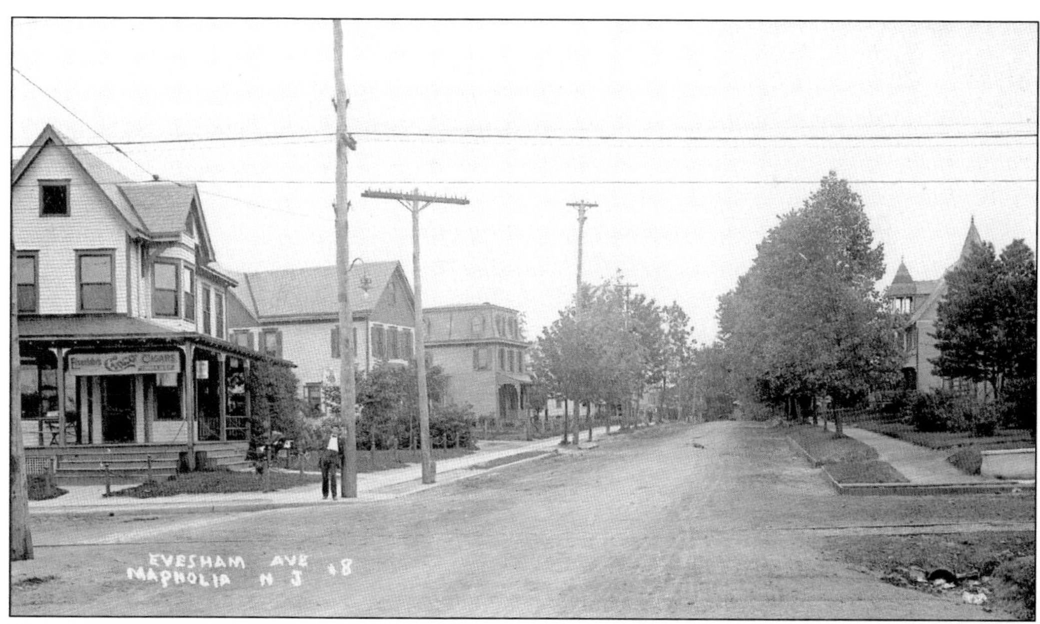

The main thoroughfare through Magnolia was Evesham Road from the time it was originally laid out in 1808. The dirt roadway, which was paved in 1916, allowed area farmers to transport produce by horse and wagon to boat landings, like the one once located on Somerdale Road at Timber Creek. The well-traveled road is seen here prior to its 1916 paving.

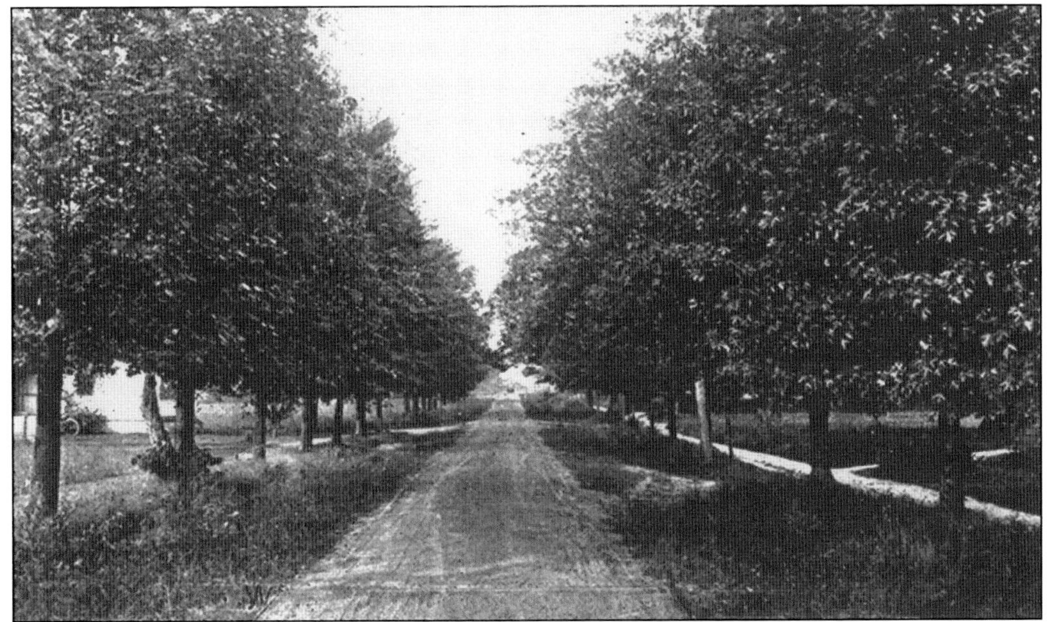

Although it was a main thruway, Evesham Road maintained a rural feel, with trees canopying the residential section well into the 20th century. This view of the 300 block of Evesham Road was taken before Eastern Telephone and Telegraph erected poles in the borough in 1903.

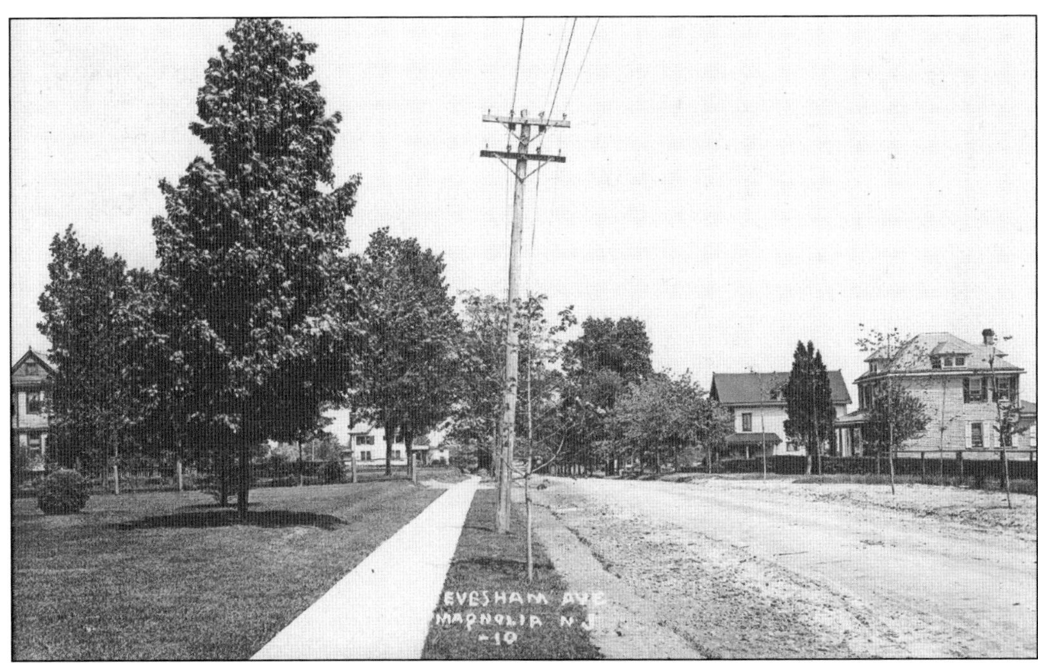

The first sidewalks were laid in the borough along Evesham Road in 1909, bringing a noticeably suburban feel to the 49 residential and commercial properties that dotted the road at the time.

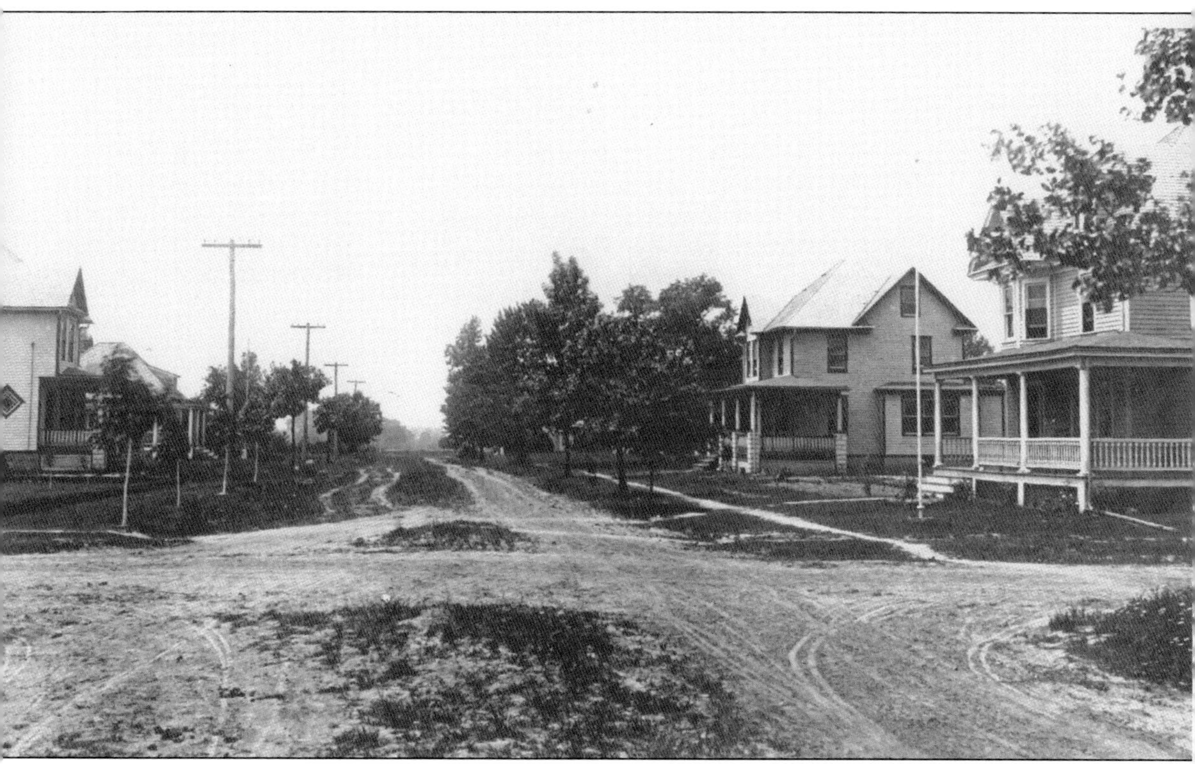

This photograph of the 400 block of Jackson Avenue shows the Dold and Lovett residences on the left and two homes owned by the Allen family, who ran a Magnolia meat market, on the right. In 1915, baseball manufacturer Wilson Shibe resided one block down, at 523 West Jackson Avenue. His brother Ben was the major owner of the Philadelphia Athletics. Wilson also owned Shibe Park, later renamed Connie Mack Stadium.

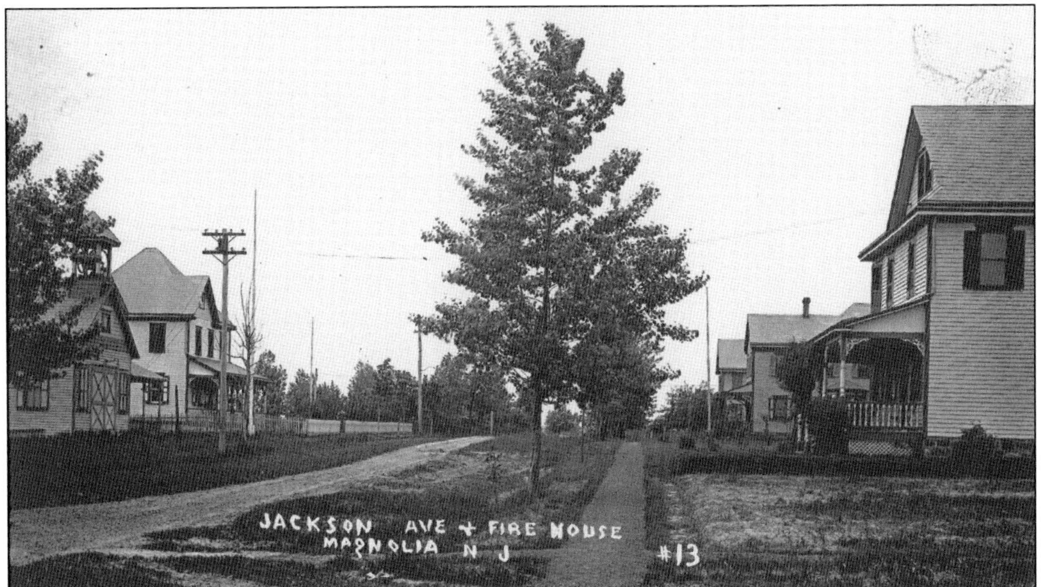

This photograph of homes in the 200 block of Jackson Avenue also shows the original borough firehouse. In the days of horses and carriages, marble stepping-stones stood at the curbs outside prominent homes to assist travelers entering and exiting a coach. Two remain in the borough—one at the Lyons' Madison Avenue home and the other, originally belonging to the Tracys of Atlantic Avenue, now positioned at the municipal building.

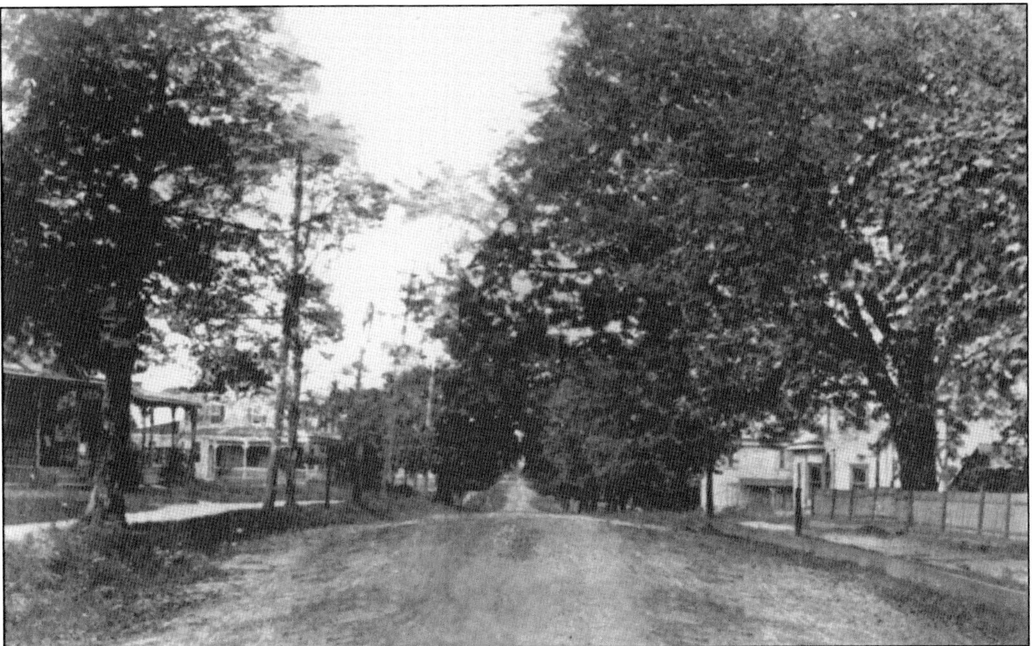

By 1917, Magnolia homes were renting for about $5 a month, and the borough had passed a law requiring every resident fly the flag to support American soldiers fighting overseas in World War I. Ignoring the local law resulted in a visit by a committee appointed by the mayor, demanding an explanation. This photograph of the 100 block of Evesham Road was taken shortly before the flag-flying order took effect.

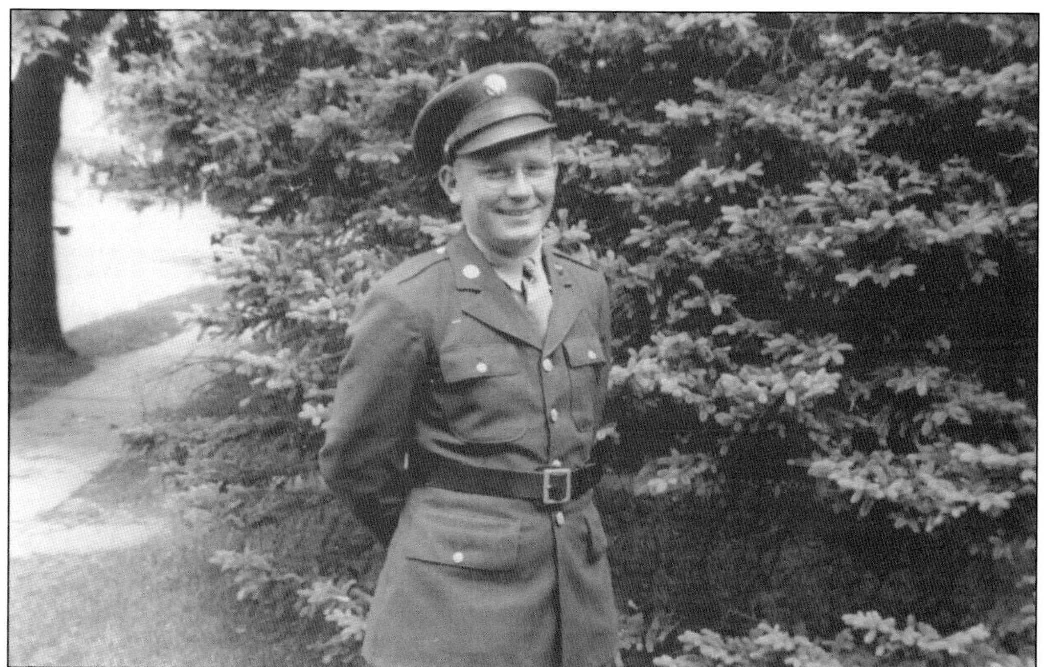

Four borough streets were named for Magnolia servicemen who died in World War II. Edwin Johnson, pictured here, was the first local wartime casualty. Killed on January 26, 1944, in Anzio, Italy, he is buried in Arlington National Cemetery. Johnson Place was named in his memory.

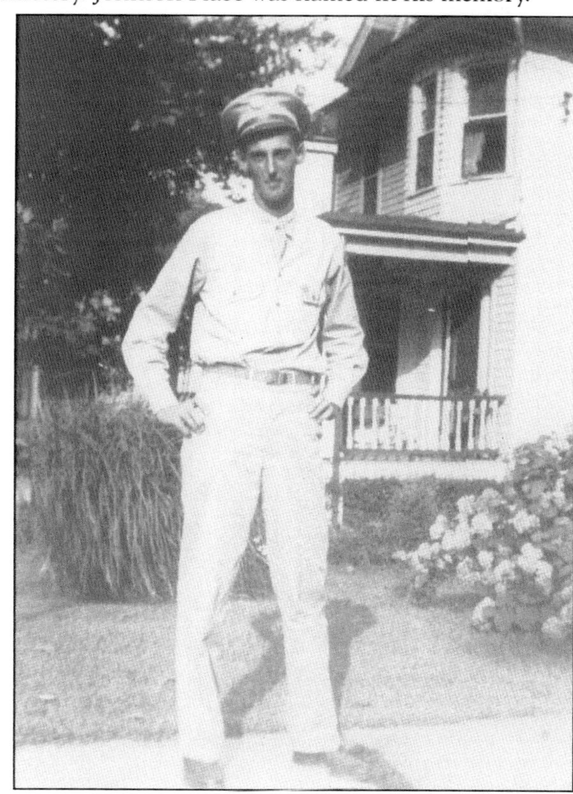

Curtis Arnold was killed just a few days later, on January 31, 1944. Arnold was raised at 422 West Evesham Road and is buried in the U.S. Military Cemetery in Nettuno, Italy. Arnold Place was named in his honor.

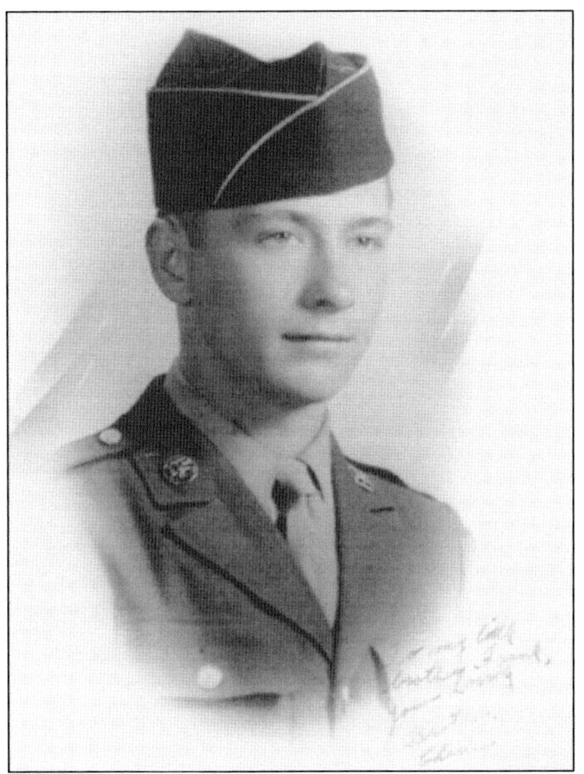

Charles Paulson, like Edwin Johnson, died in Anzio in 1944. Only 19 at the time of his death, he grew up at 227 East Washington Avenue. Paulson Drive was named in his memory.

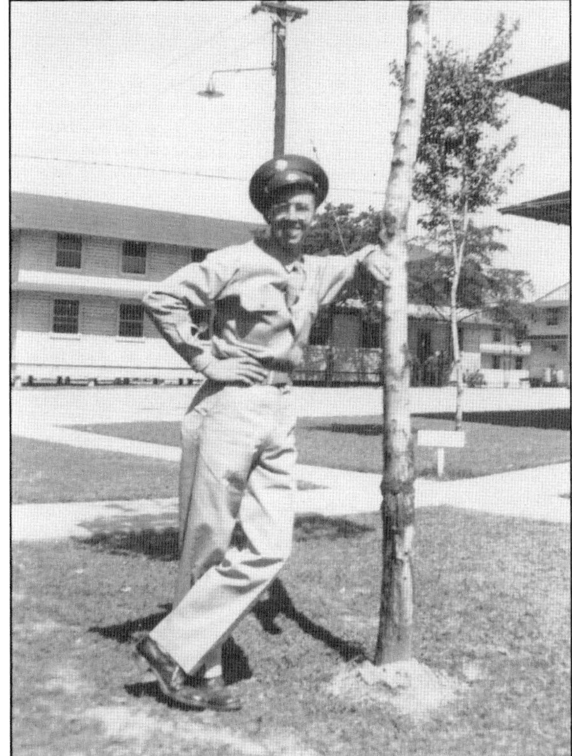

George Morrow grew up at 117 West Lincoln Avenue and was the fourth and final Magnolia boy killed in the war. He died and was buried in Anzio. Morrow Avenue and the Morrow Room of the First Baptist Church were named in his honor.

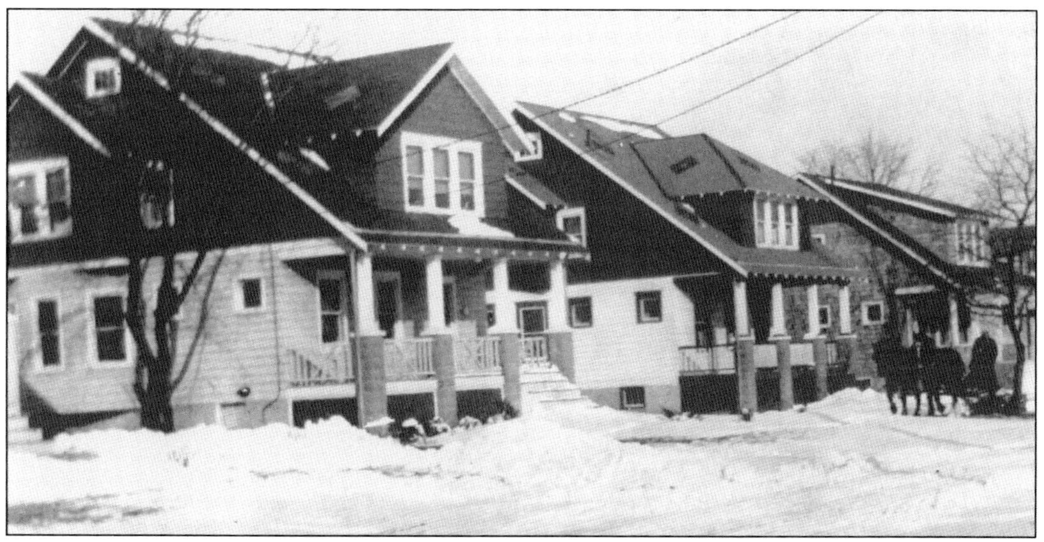

In bad weather, Magnolia residents worked together, like this local farmer (visible at right) using a horse-drawn snow plow to clear the sidewalks in the 200 block of Washington Avenue in the 1920s.

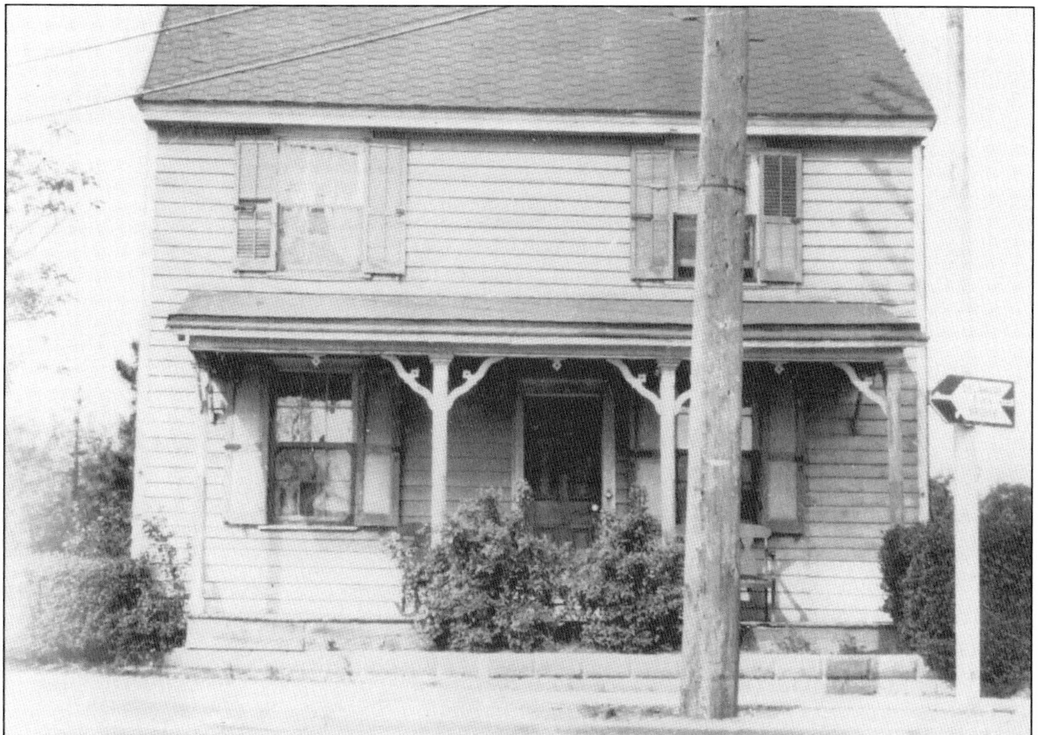

Frank LaPierre, a Camden blacksmith, moved to Magnolia in 1898 and raised six children in the borough. This photograph of his home was taken sometime after 1926. The house was located on the White Horse Pike, next to what is now Produce Junction.

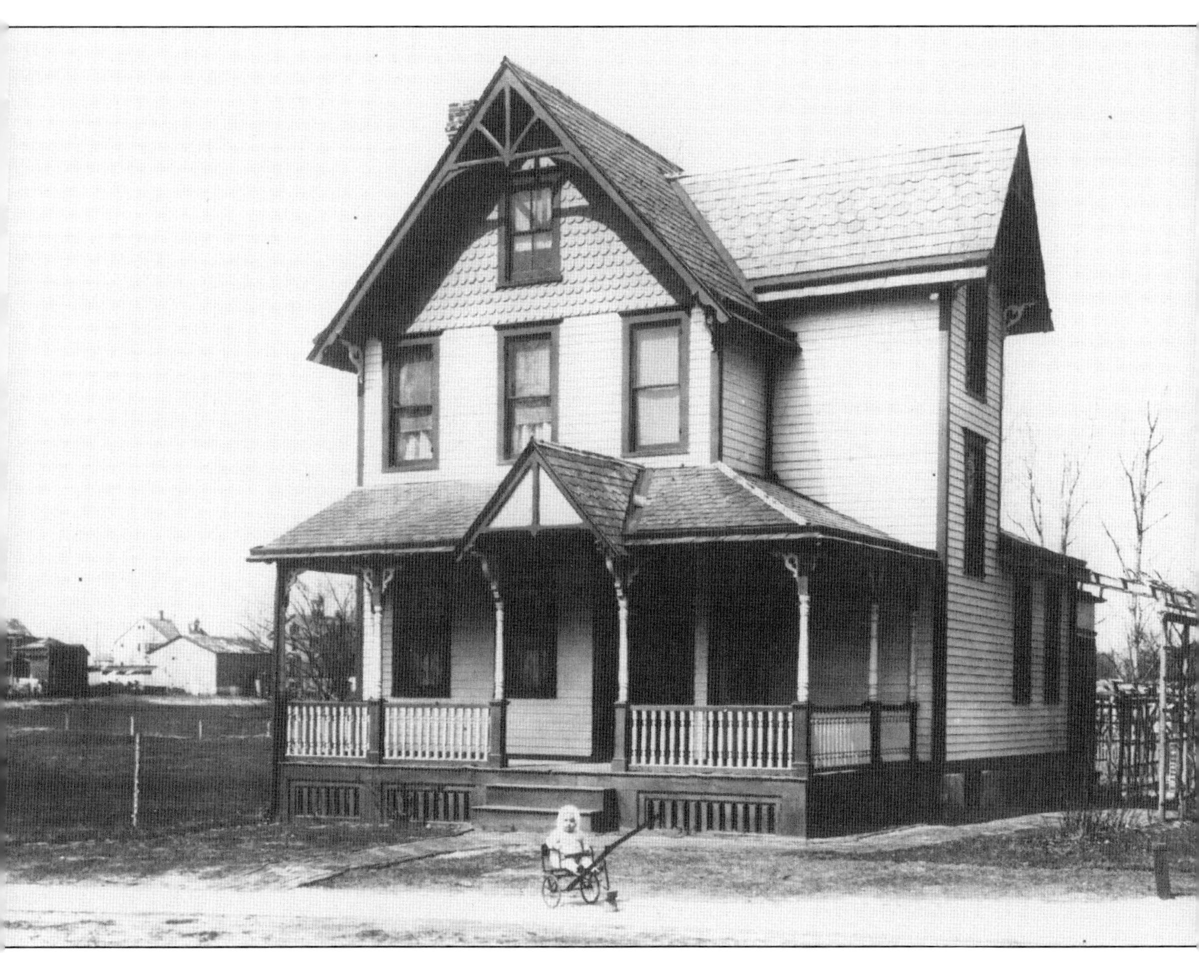

The Dean family home, seen here in the 1880s, remains at the corner of Barrett and Evesham Road and later was owned by John Spiegle and then the Hollywood family. Harry Dean opened a hardware store in neighboring Somerdale during World War II.

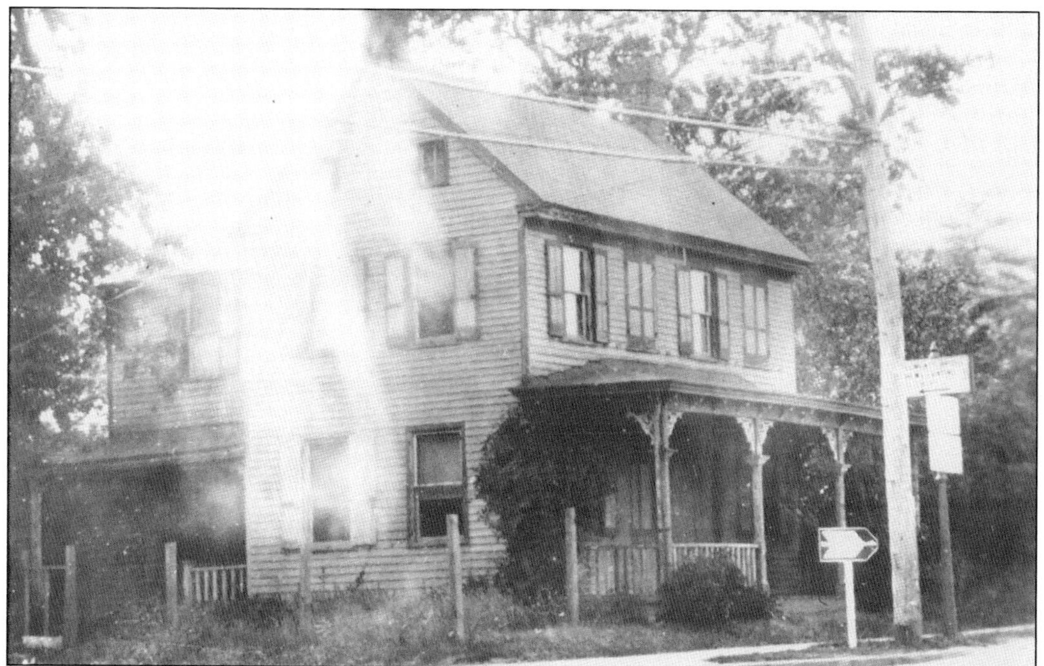

The home of Susanette Fish, pictured here in the early 1930s, was torn down prior to 1950 to make way for a gas station, and is now the site of Walgreen's at the corner of the White Horse Pike and Evesham Road. In addition to this property, Fish owned the large tract of land where St. Gregory's Church now stands.

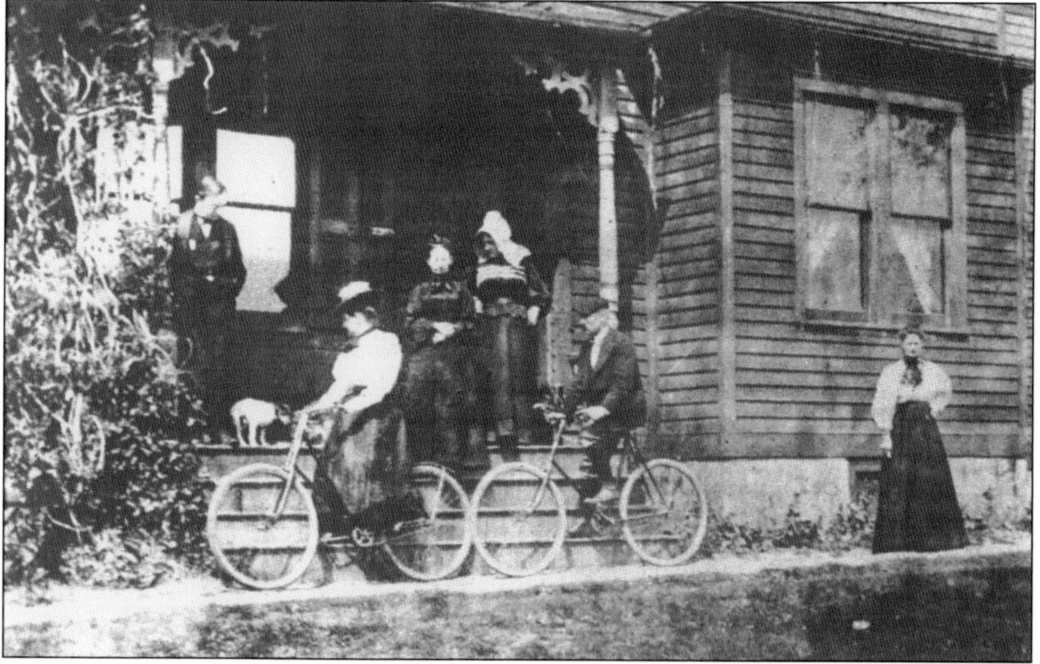

Bicyclists and members of the Maxwell family gather at the Maxwell home on 331 West Madison Avenue around 1900. Claude Maxwell, who was raised in the house, served as chief of Magnolia's special police force.

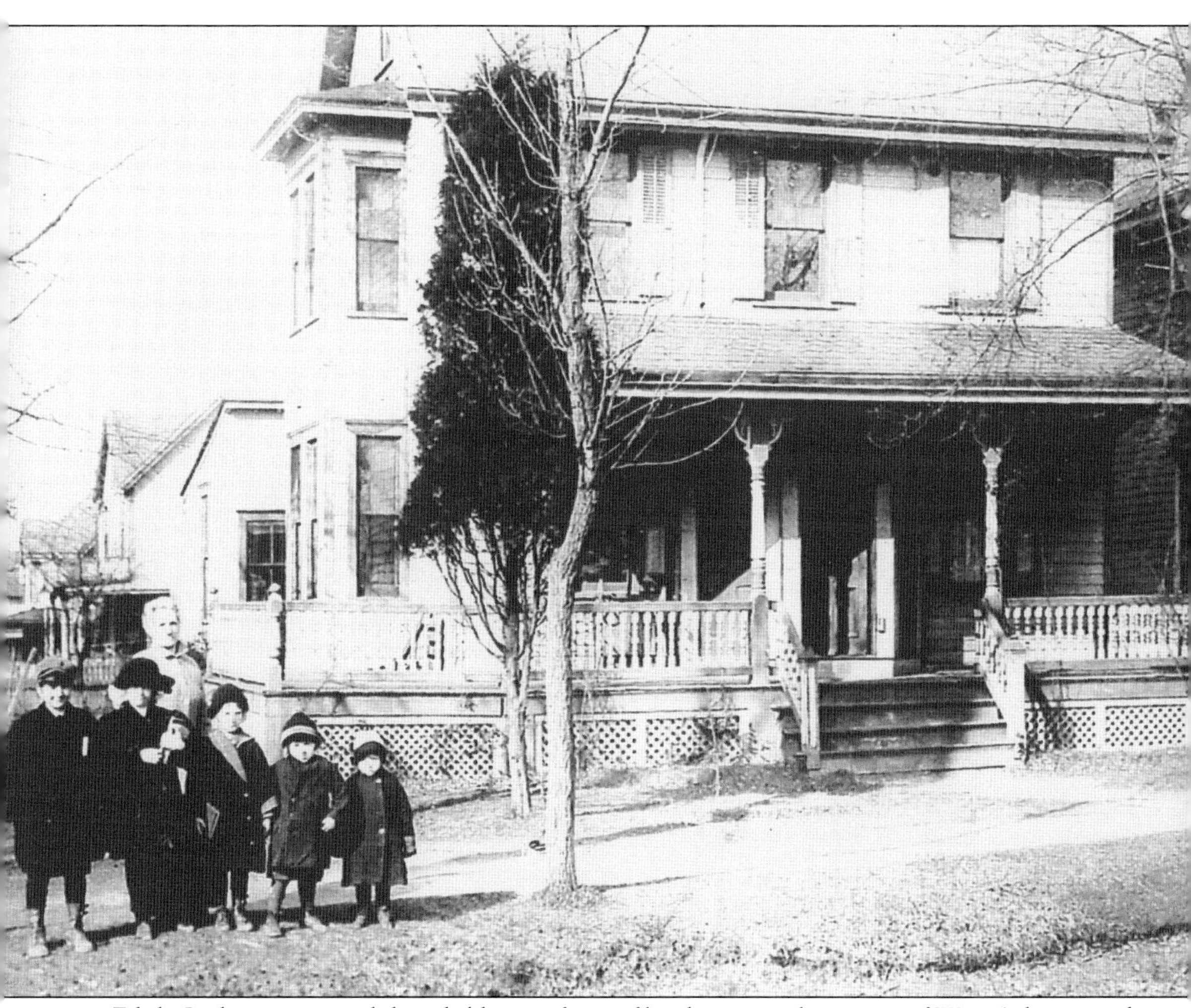

Edith Graham poses with her children in front of her home on the corner of West Atlantic and West Monroe Avenues around 1920. Pictured from left to right are Donald, Marjorie, Hazel, Kathryn, and Malcolm. The Graham family would later add Bill and Albert to their brood. Albert would one day become Magnolia's mayor.

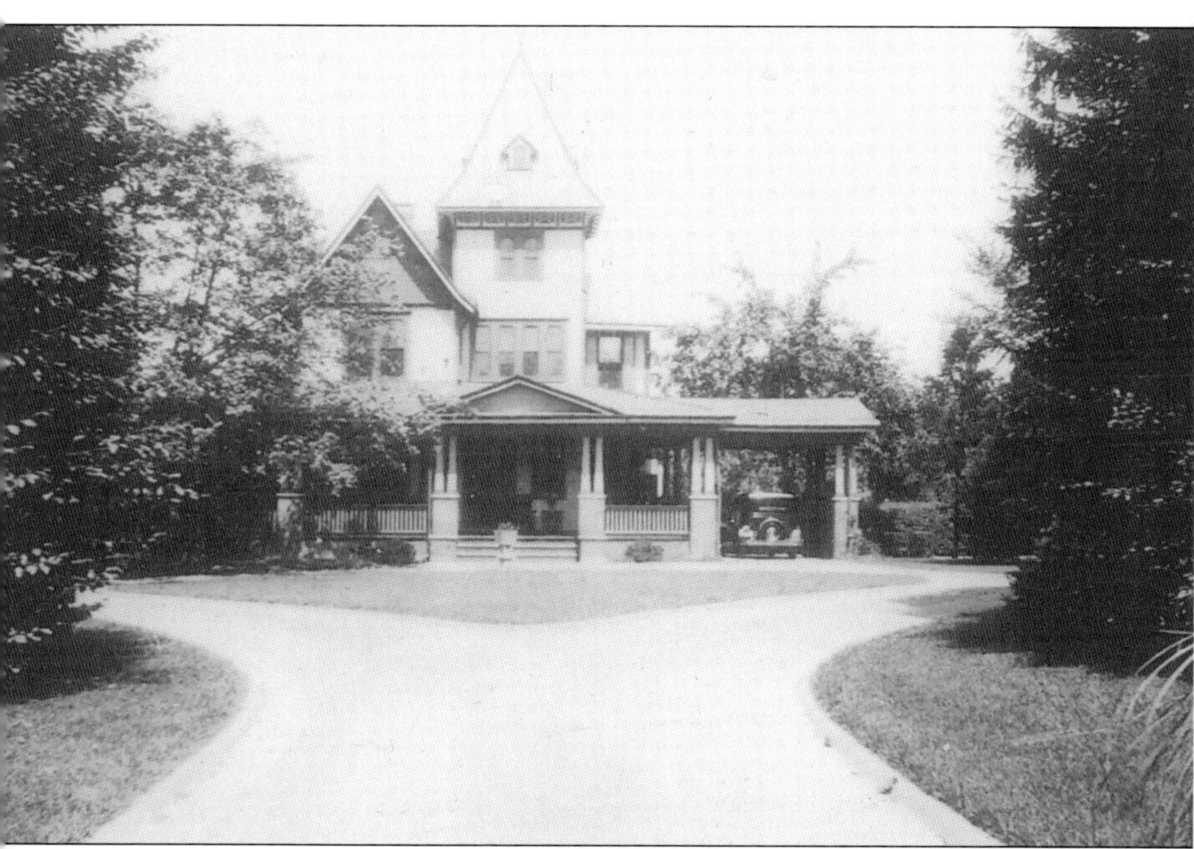

While the farmland around the original Albertson farmhouse was sold and developed in the 1880s, the Evesham Road home remained in the family into the 1970s. This home, owned by John J. Albertson, passed from the family's hands around 1940, and still remains a private residence.

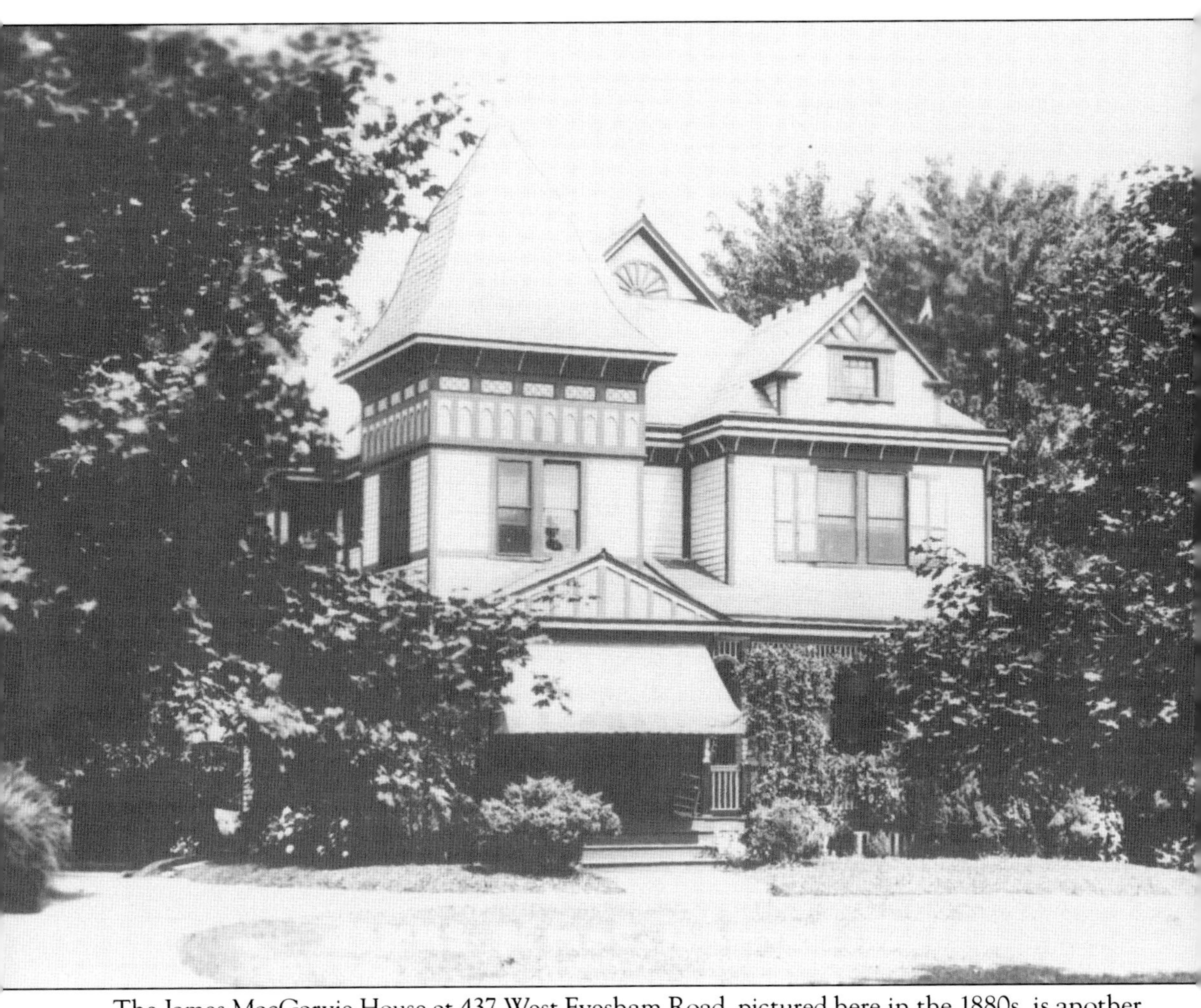

The James MacGarvie House at 437 West Evesham Road, pictured here in the 1880s, is another of Magnolia's magnificent old houses that remains standing. The family also owned a house and farm further down the road, which they sold to developers in the 1880s.

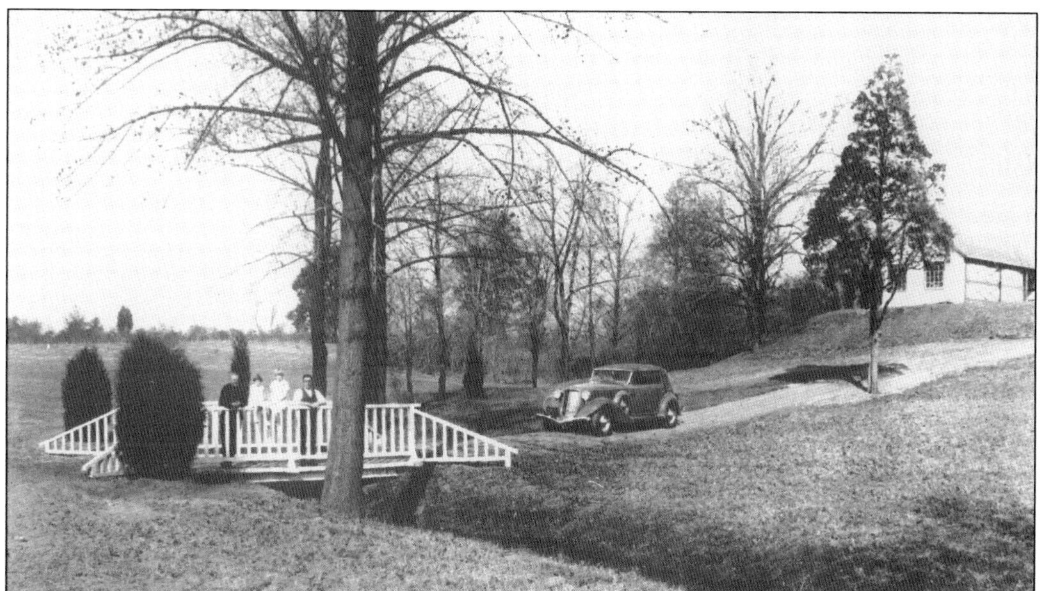

The MacGarvie family owned this sizeable farm on Evesham Road and sold the property in the mid-19th century when the family patriarch decided he should move closer to "town" in his later years. The Otterbranch housing development was built on the old MacGarvie farm. The farmhouse remains a private home today.

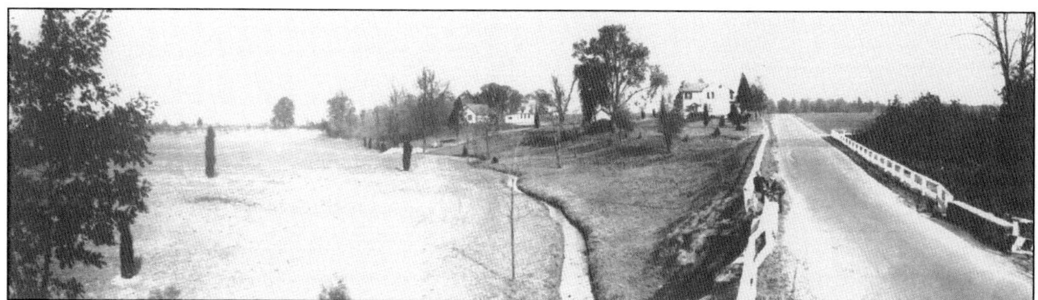

The old stone bridge on Evesham Road, running along the MacGarvie farm, was a favorite place for Magnolia kids to gather. The location of the bridge can be recognized today by a noticeable depression in the road.

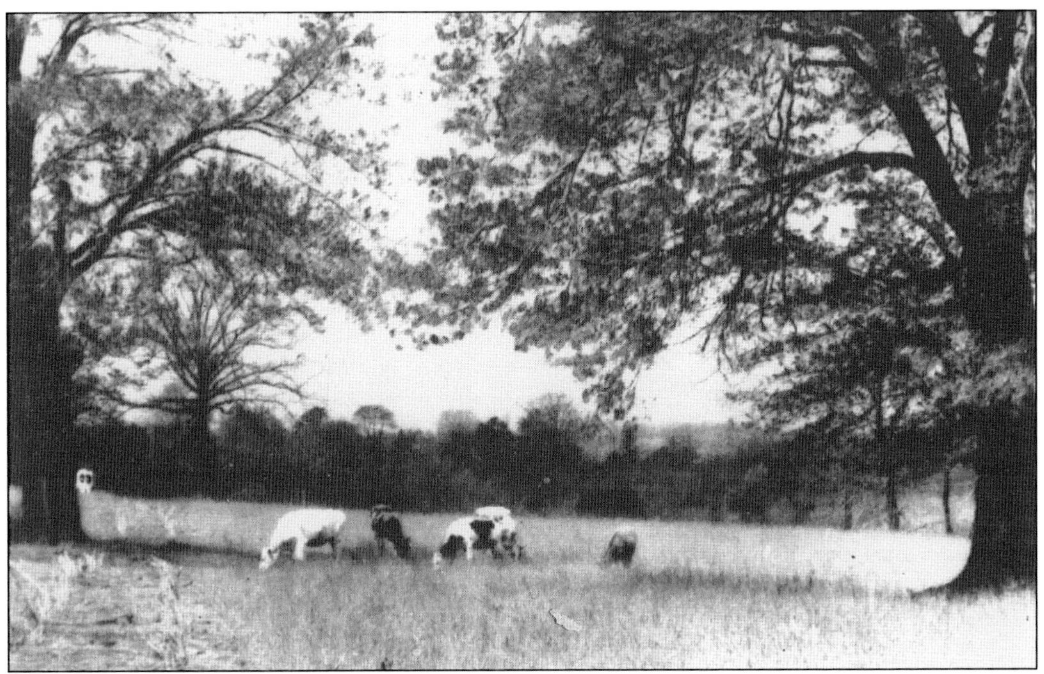

In 1886, the Magnolia Villa Company organized, purchased three of the largest farms in the area, and started building homes. Today most of Magnolia's housing remains single-family homes, although there are three apartment buildings in the borough. The original development sites included 85 acres of the Strang's farm, 50 acres that belonged to the McKittrich brothers and 220 acres representing a portion of the Albertson plantation.

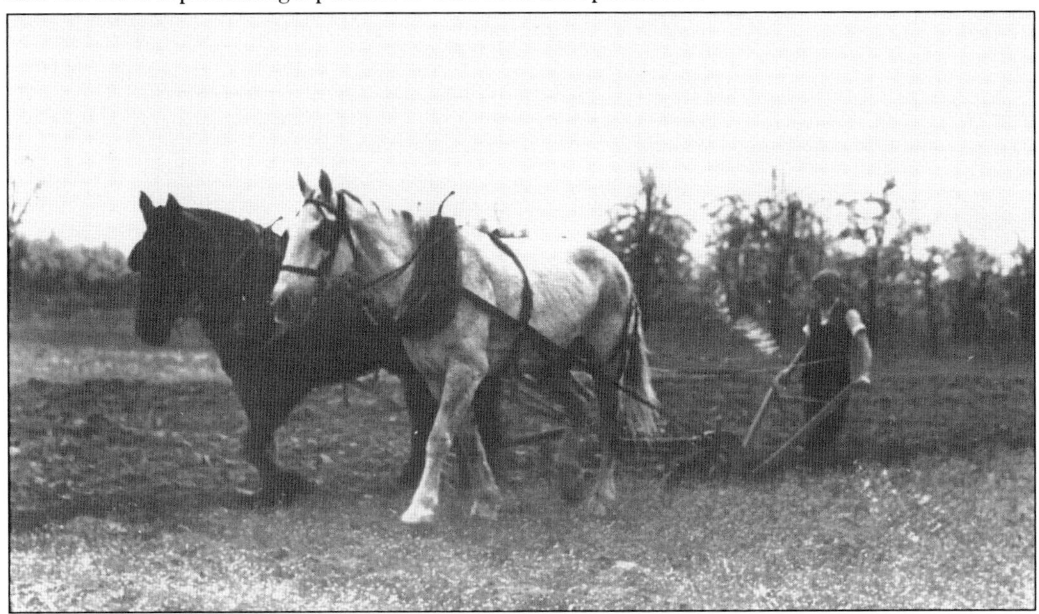

Lew Mitten Sr. plowing the fields with Blackie and Whitey at Miller's Farm was a common sight before the first 18 houses, known as Brooke Gardens, were built behind the school in the 1950s. Mitten and John Paul raised corn, asparagus, and tomatoes and harvested fruit from wild pear trees on the fields along Lincoln and Camden Avenues.

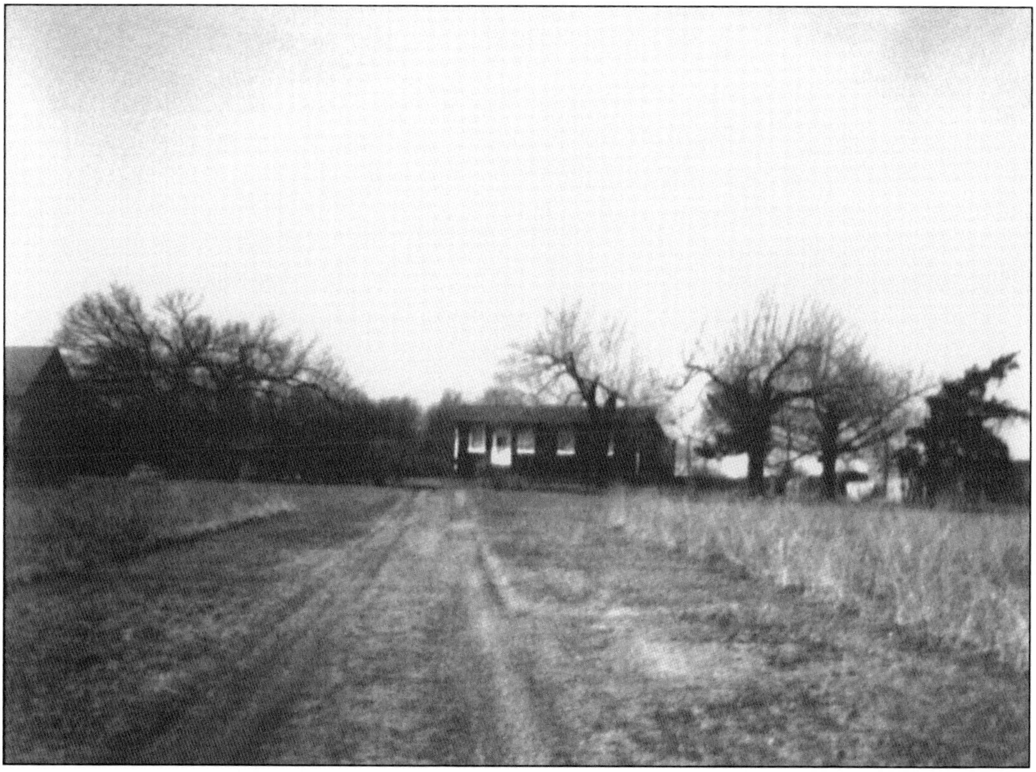

In the 1960s, apartments replaced the Mailes' (later the Whites') farm pictured here. Originally called Brooke Terrace Apartments, they are now known as Coventry Place Apartments.

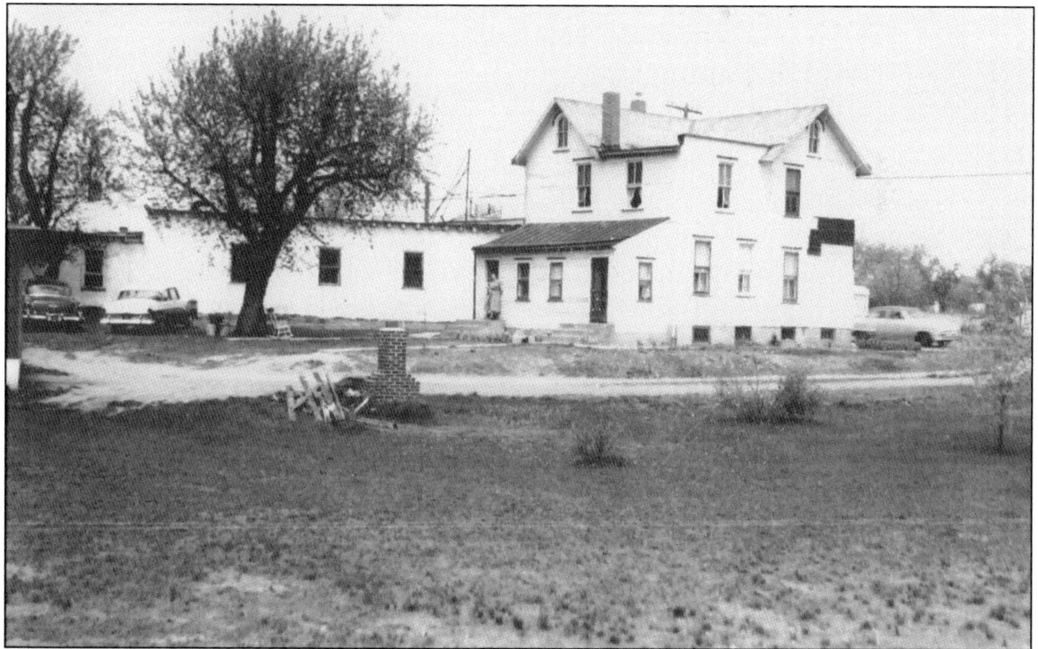

Fred Bruckner's house, seen here in 1958, stood next to the Sunshine Café on the White Horse Pike. The family also owned a hotel across the street.

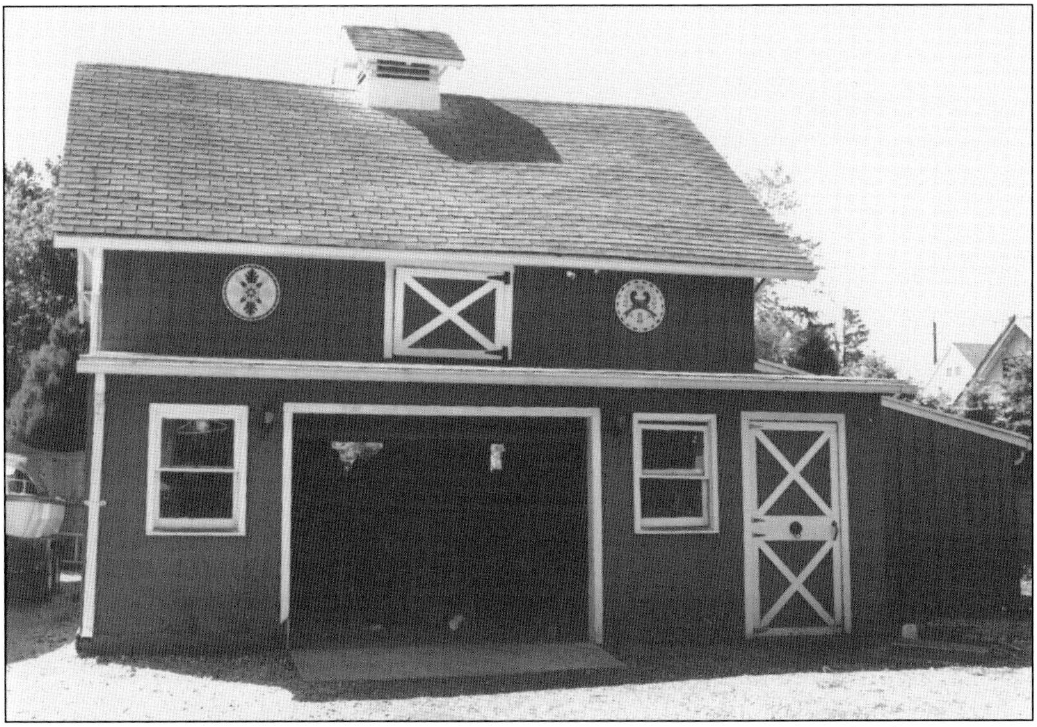

Although a countless number of barns once stood in Magnolia, today only three remain, including this red barn at the Lyon home on Madison Avenue.

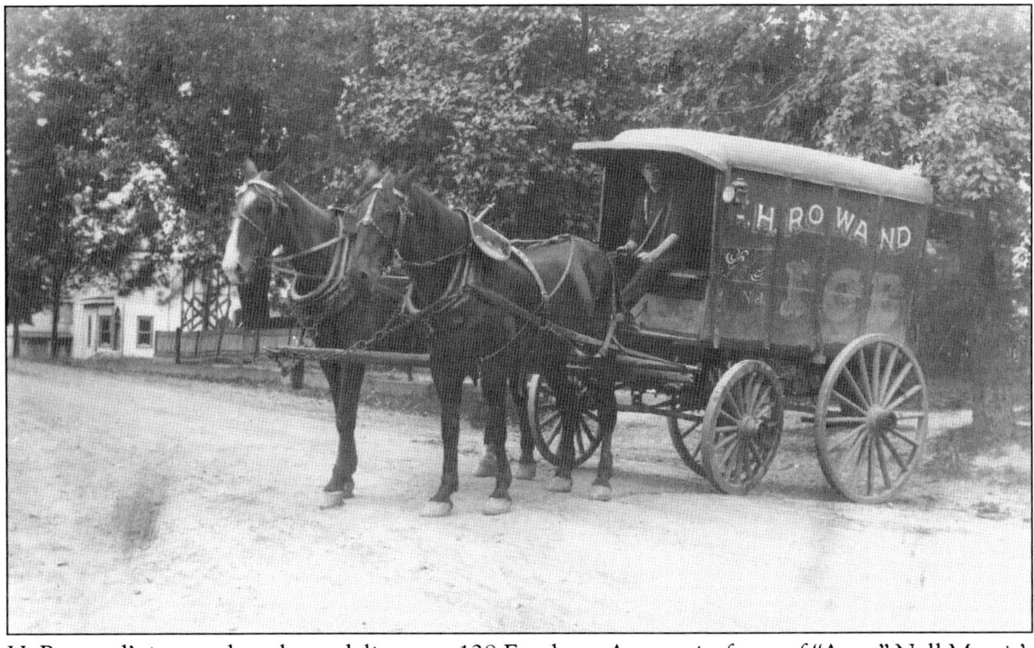

H. Rowand's ice truck makes a delivery at 138 Evesham Avenue in front of "Aunt" Nell Morris's house on Evesham Road around 1920. At one time, more than a dozen delivery trucks made the rounds in the borough, supplying everything from fresh fruit and vegetables to bread and milk. Local milkman Tony Kaiser employed Magnolia's first Dodge van for deliveries.

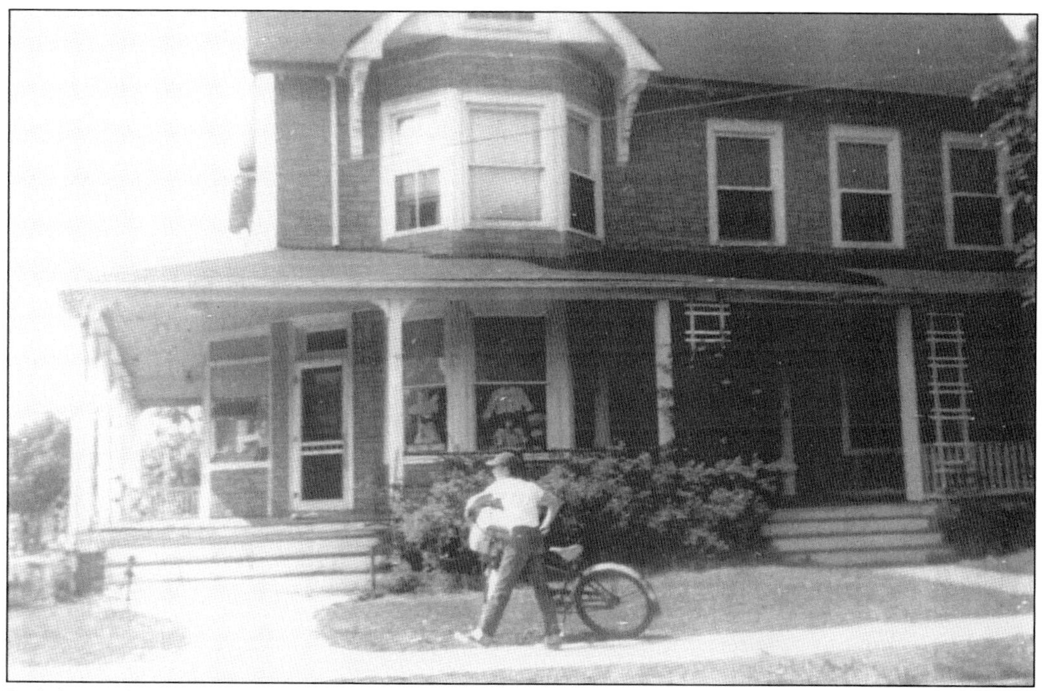

Ralph Deal Jr. completes his morning route, delivering the *Courier Post* to a home at Evesham Road and East Atlantic Avenue in the 1950s.

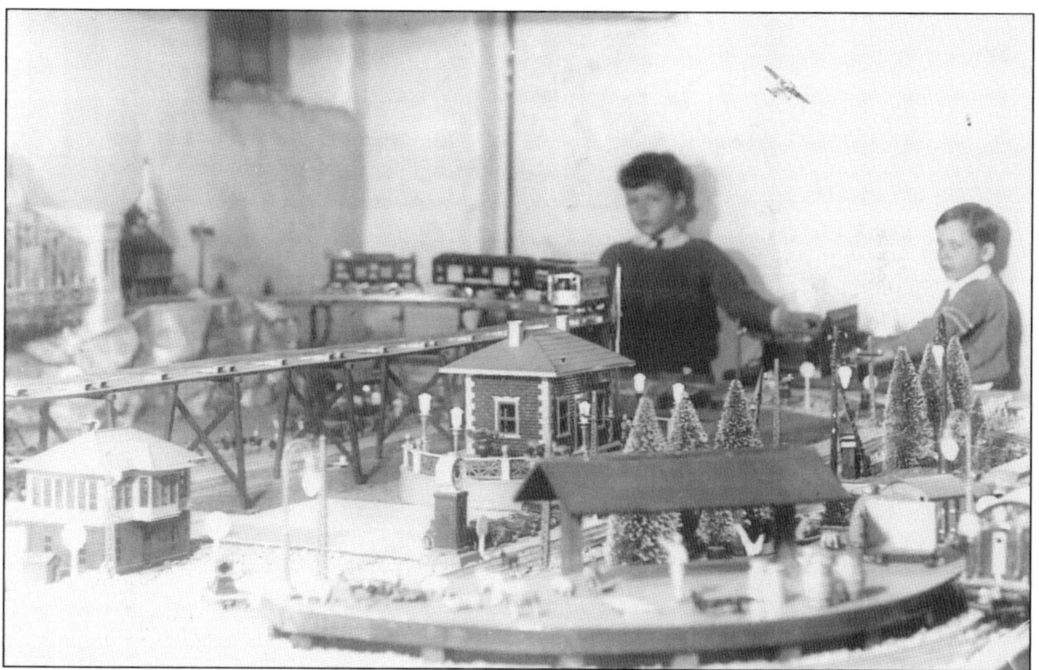

In the Hineline home at 546 West Evesham Avenue, setting up the train display was a Christmas tradition. F. Budd Hineline Jr. (left) and Richard Haines Hineline (who went on to become president of Camden Lime Company and a leader in Camden County historic preservation) are pictured here around 1932 operating the trains.

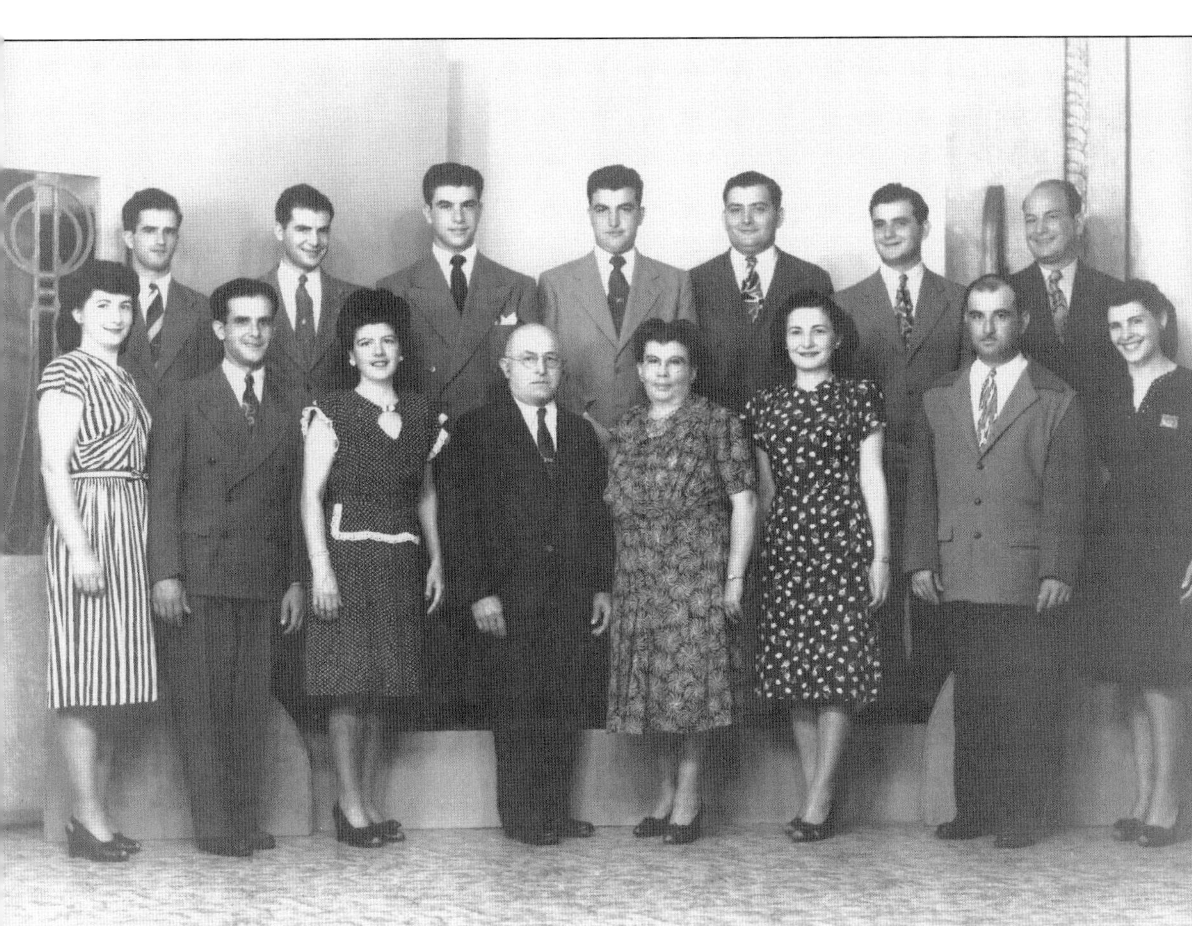

In Magnolia's earlier days, its homes were defined by the people who inhabited them. Many of those families also built their businesses around the needs of their neighbors. The D'Amico family, pictured here, was a perfect example. Pictured are, from left to right, (first row) Mary, Orlando, Rose, Frank, Antonetta, Gertrude, Phillip, and Josephine; (second row) William, Santino, Frank, Peter, Samuel, Anthony, and Harry. The family patriarch, Frank, established a barbershop in town, and was later joined by sons Phil and Pete. Sam became the borough clerk, while Harry opened a liquor store. Although a large family, the D'Amicos lost the title of largest clan to the Renshaw family, which reportedly had 18 children.

Magnolia resident Spencer C. Moore II (pictured at right) was a member of the history-making 92nd Infantry Division, known as the Buffalo Soldiers. Of the 12,846 Buffalo Soldiers who saw action in Italy during Word War II, 2,848 were killed, captured, or wounded. The division captured nearly 24,000 prisoners during the assault. In the photograph below, Moore is greeted by Pres. Bill Clinton at the White House during a Buffalo Soldiers reunion in January 1997. Members of the Moore family have lived in the Magnolia territory for more than 200 years.

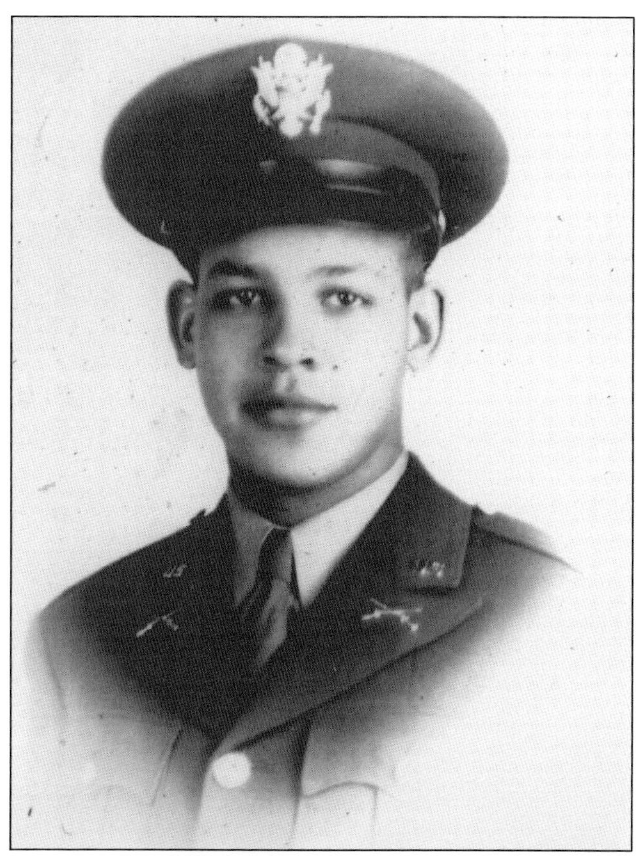

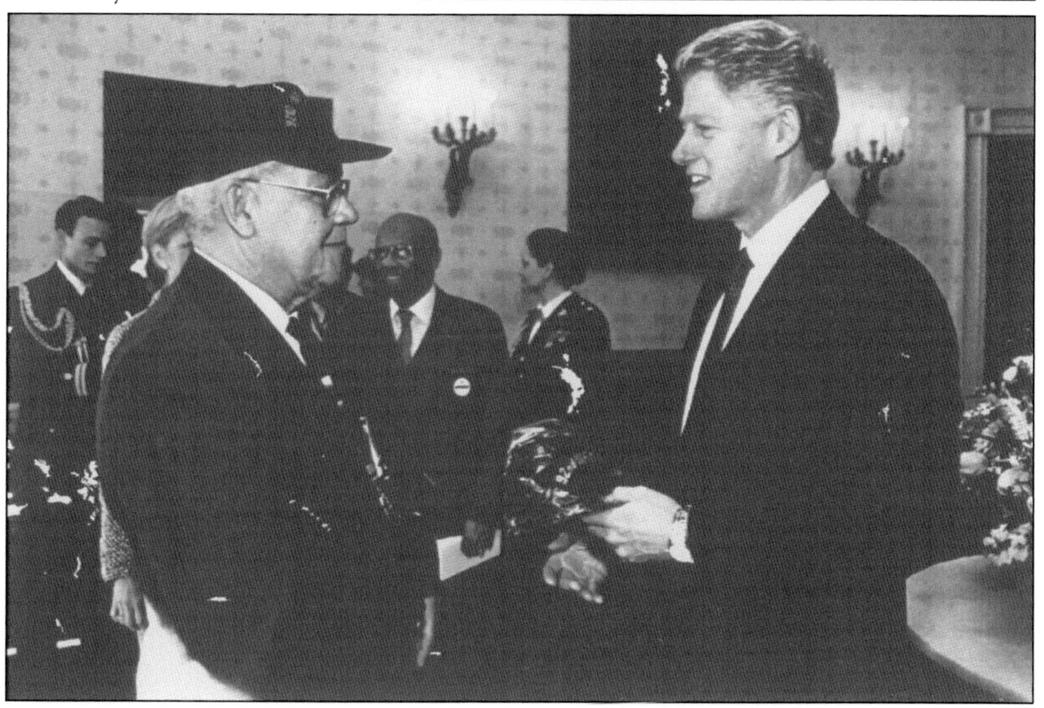

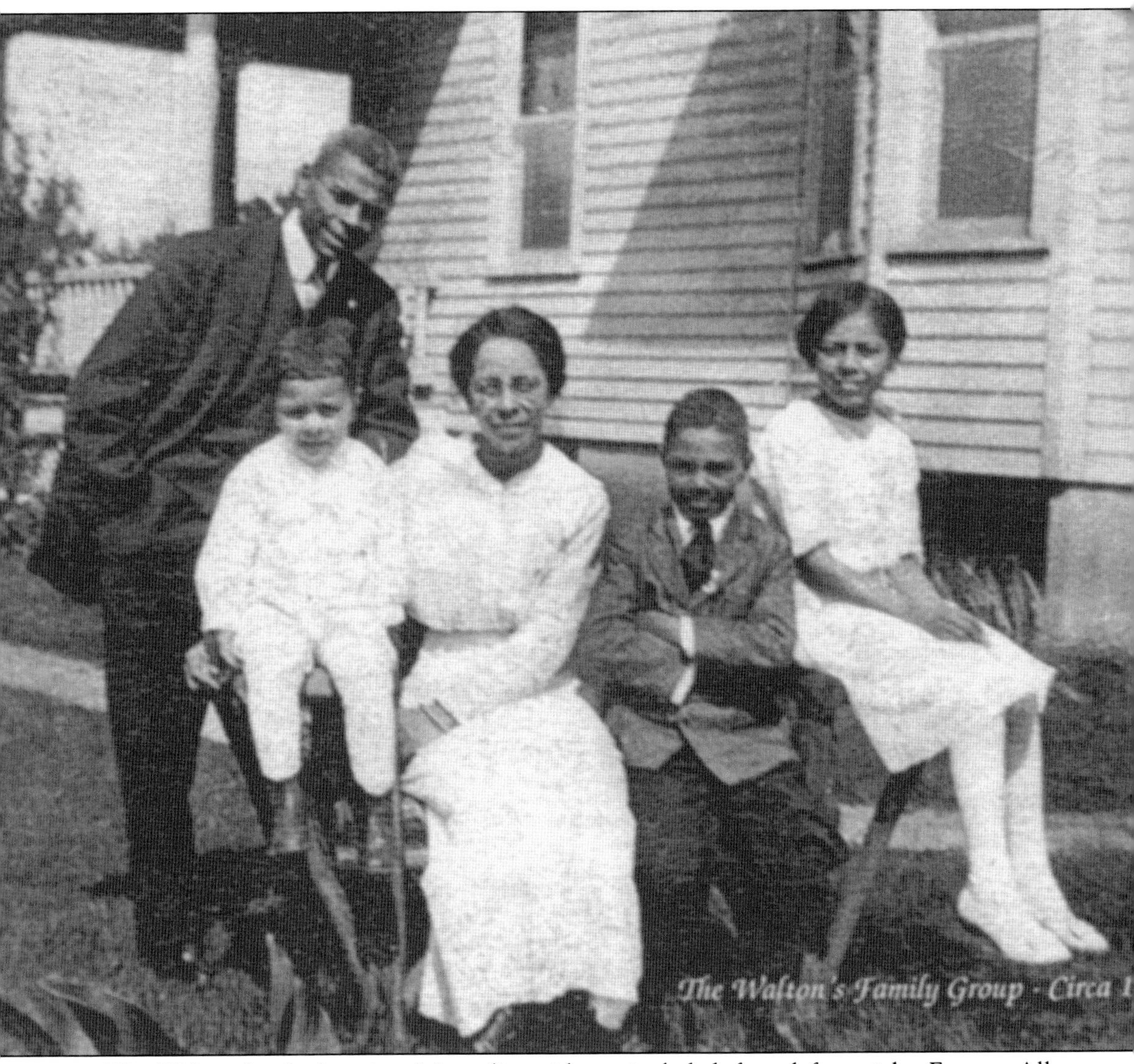

The Walton family, longtime Magnolia residents, included, from left to right, Everett, Allen, Gertrude, George, and Lucille. Musically gifted, they formed the Walton Quartet and performed at the Grace Temple Church in Lawnside. This photograph, taken around 1921, shows the family outside their home in the 100 block of East Adams Avenue.

Three

SERVING THE COMMUNITY

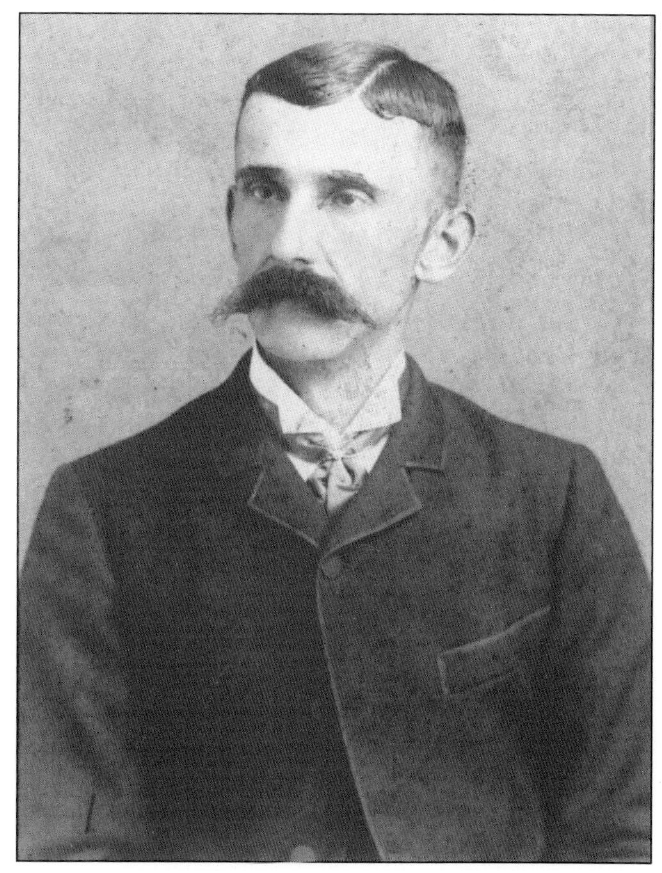

Harry Wolohan was elected Magnolia's first mayor in 1915, a year after the borough incorporated. He won election over Walter Supplee by just 20 votes, paving the way for 51 years of Republican control, and served from 1915 to 1917. Originally borough meetings were held in Wolohan's store and home. Later the borough rented space in area meeting halls before moving to the back of the firehouse on Evesham Road.

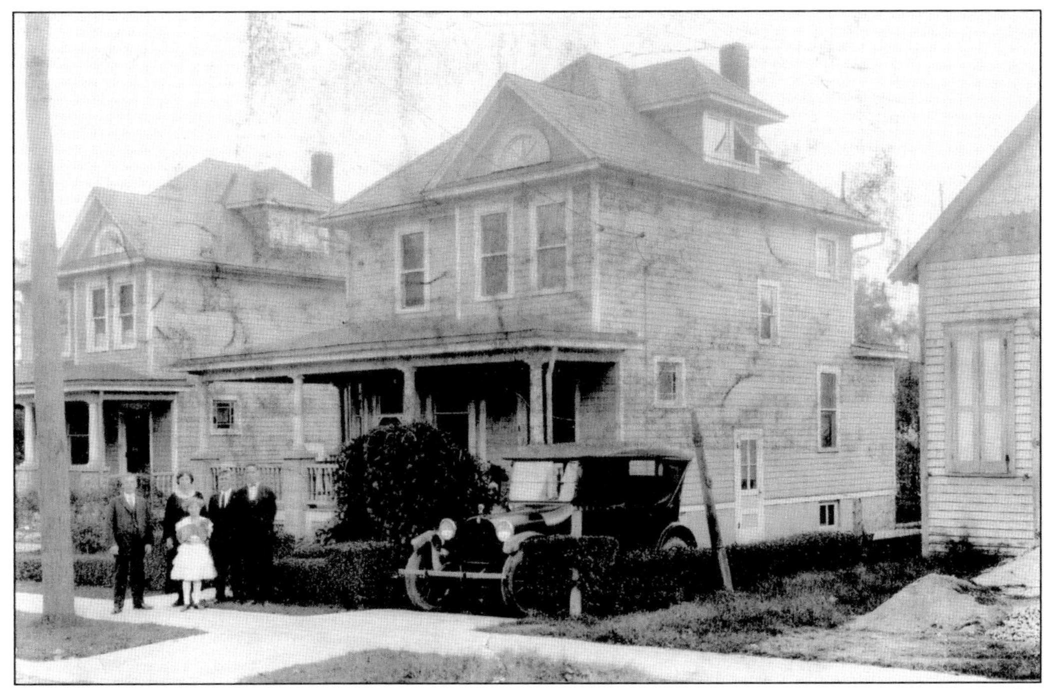

Margaret Hale, an early Democratic committeewoman, poses in front of her home in the 200 block of Jackson Avenue. Among the family members in this 1930s photograph is her son Joe Donovan, a painter in the borough. On the left is the Banse family home.

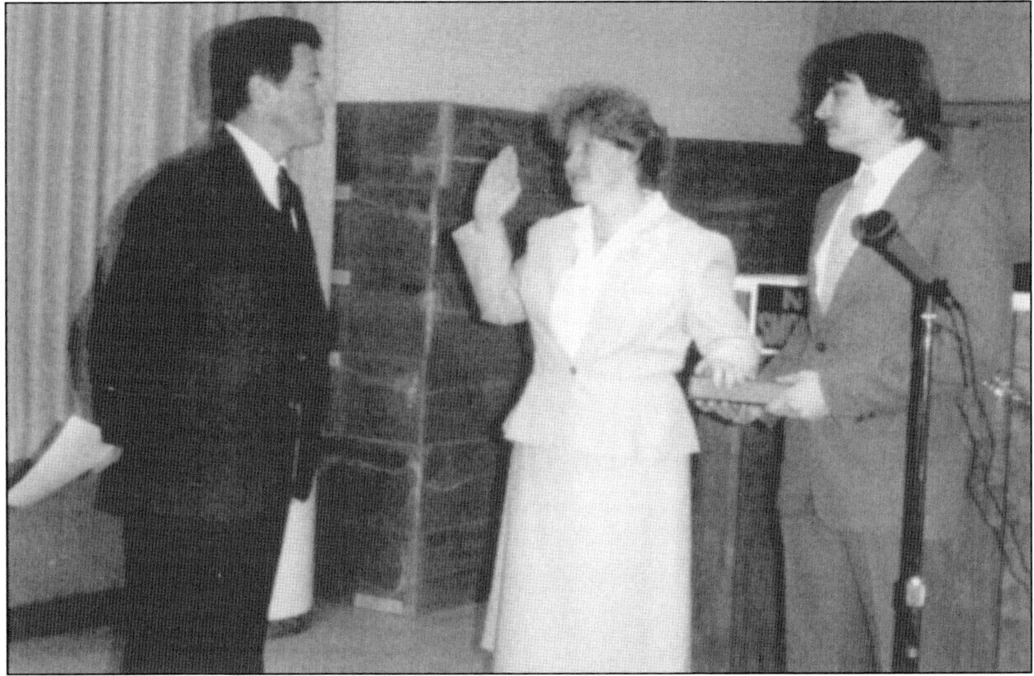

Then-congressman James Florio (left) swears in Betty Ann Cowling-Carson, Magnolia's second female mayor in 1992, as her husband, Brian Carson, looks on. In her 15th year in office, she is the borough's longest serving mayor.

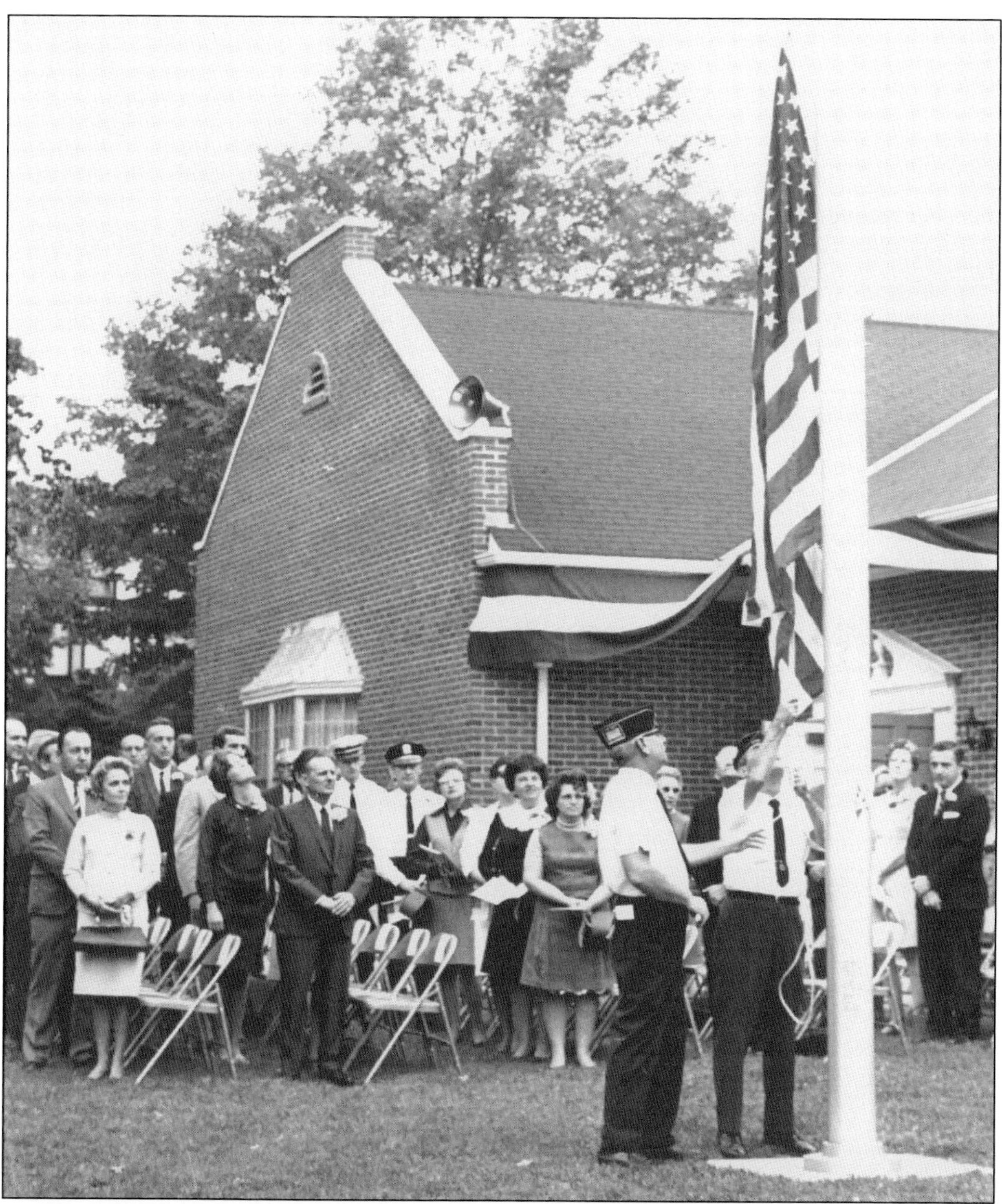

Magnolia's first freestanding borough hall was dedicated on October 12, 1968. Constructed on land purchased from the Haeffner family on Evesham Road, the building cost taxpayers $180,000, including furnishings, and became a necessity following a 1964 fire that heavily damaged a portion of the firehouse that housed the municipal offices. While the building was under construction, the borough was offered space at the American Legion Hall and Vaughan Heating and Air Conditioning. The flagpole seen here was presented to the borough by Mayor John Reid and his family in memory of their son Michael, who was a casualty of the Vietnam War.

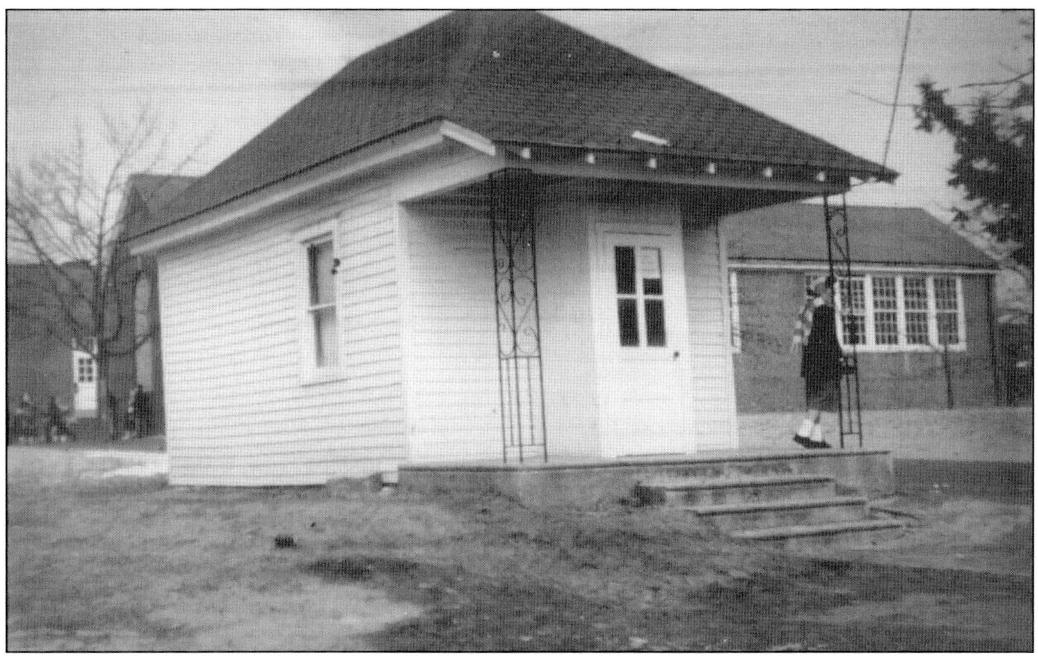

The Magnolia Library began on Rae Lynch's front porch on Warwick Road. It later was established in this tiny building, which previously served as the borough's post office and was moved from its original Evesham Road location to the Lincoln Avenue School grounds. In its early days, the library was run by Emily Davis and Margaret Smith.

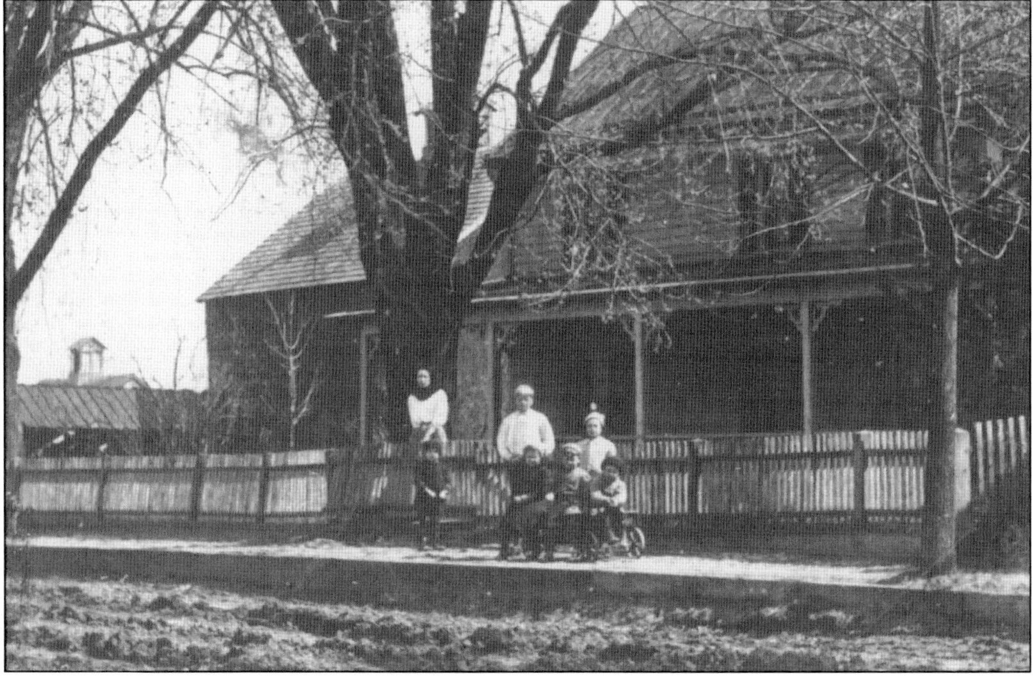

Countless residents worked to make Magnolia a community, including "Aunt" Nell Morris, a nursing-trained borough resident who regularly tended to the sick and those in need until shortly before her death in 1972. Her Evesham Road home is pictured here in 1930.

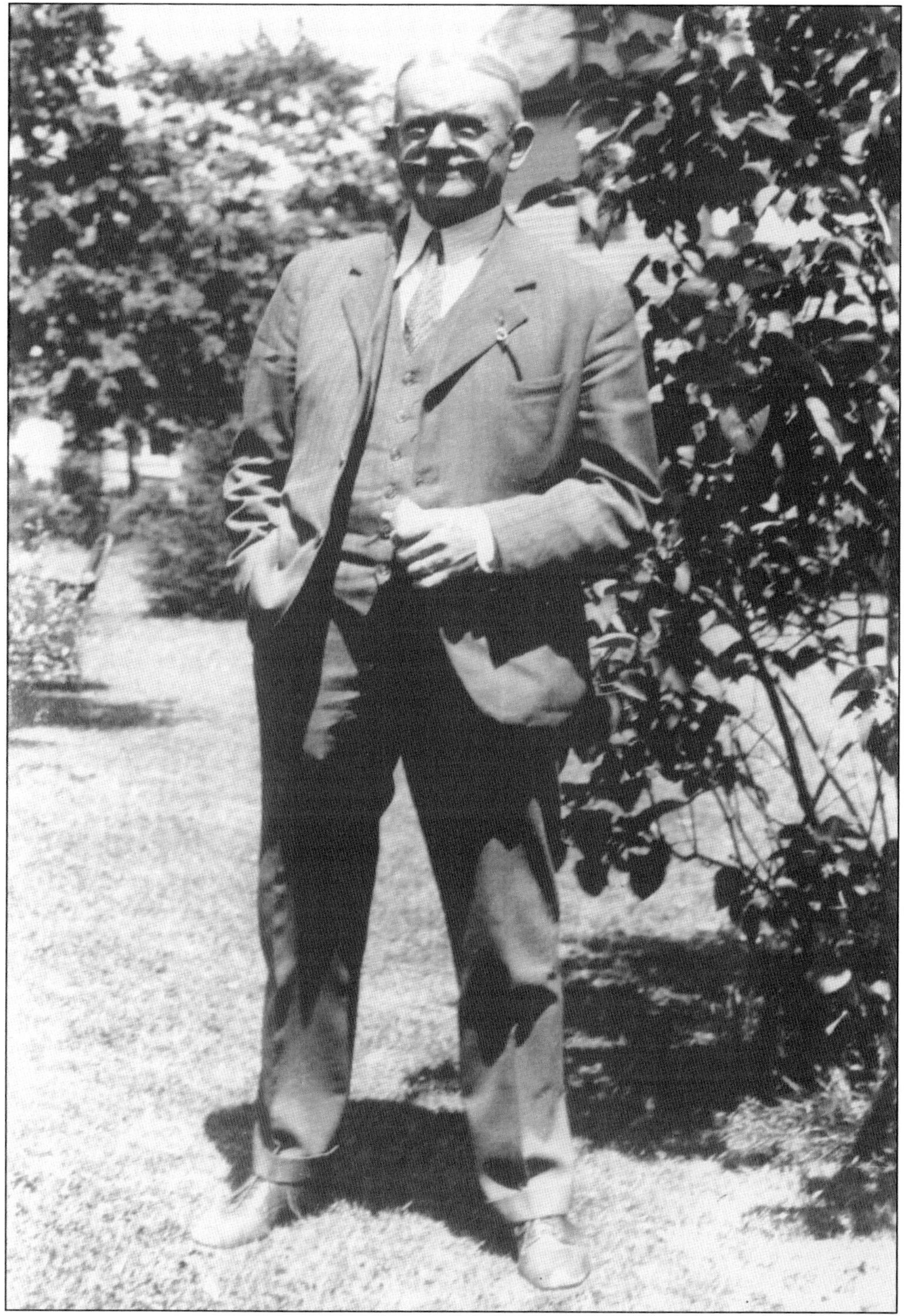

Dr. Leslie C. Lyon was one of three early physicians in Magnolia. Pictured here in 1936, he delivered most of the borough's babies during the Depression, often accepting chickens and other items as payment. Lyon came to Magnolia in 1899 as a general practitioner and served as the school physician in nearby Barrington in the 1920s.

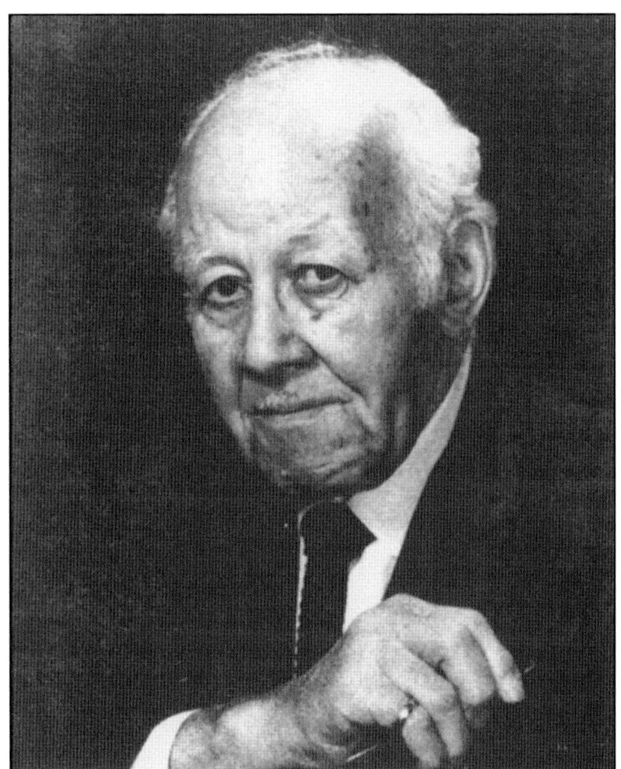

Dr. Roscoe Moore, pictured here in 1911, made his home visits to patients via horse and buggy. Born in Magnolia in 1888, the son of Spencer Clayton Moore and Laura Reeves, he attended Greenland School until the age of 10, then moved to Camden, returning to the borough after college. In addition to treating the sick and delivering babies in Magnolia, Moore was the Lawnside school physician for 53 years.

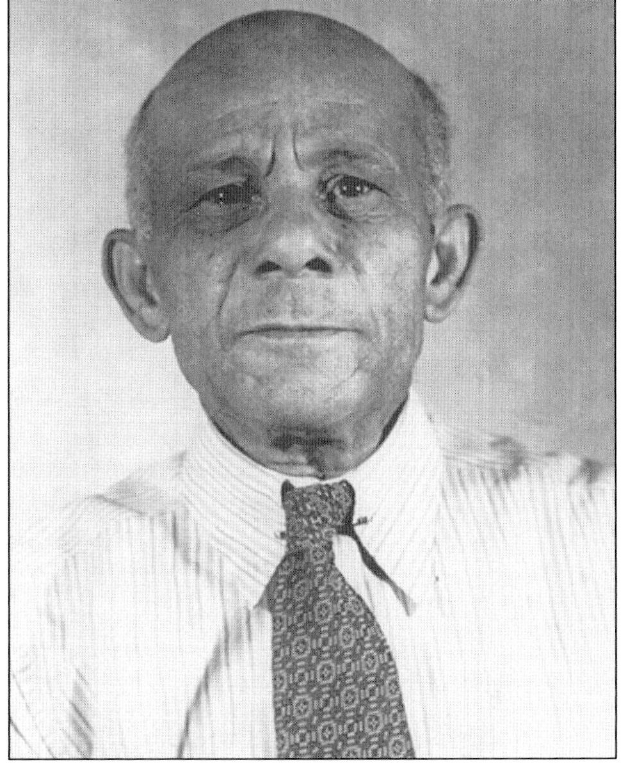

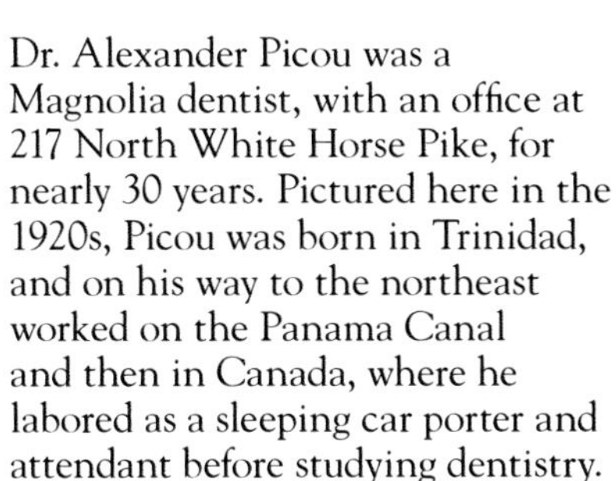

Dr. Alexander Picou was a Magnolia dentist, with an office at 217 North White Horse Pike, for nearly 30 years. Pictured here in the 1920s, Picou was born in Trinidad, and on his way to the northeast worked on the Panama Canal and then in Canada, where he labored as a sleeping car porter and attendant before studying dentistry.

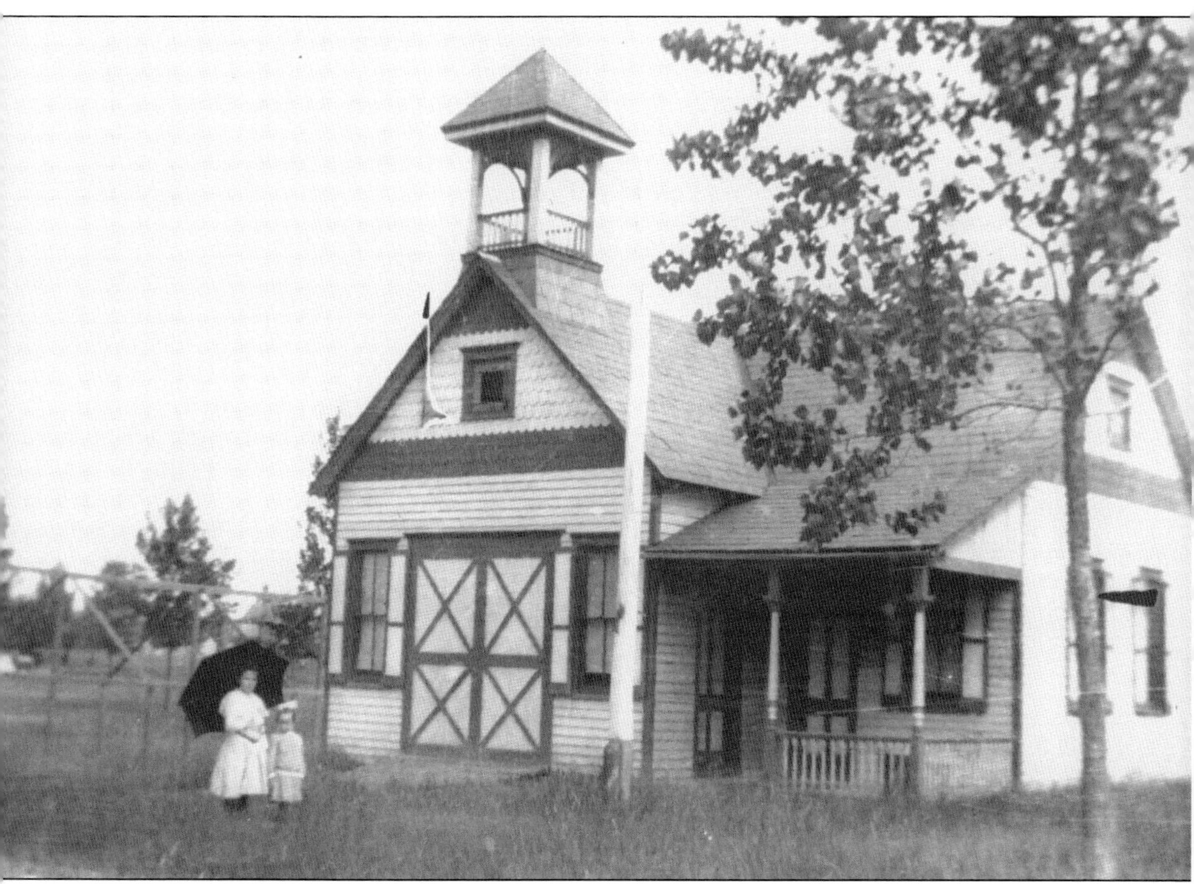

The Magnolia Fire Department was incorporated in 1893 and members held their early meetings in the homes of the founders. In 1899, George Brookes donated land at 208 Jackson Avenue to erect this firehouse, which cost $852.50 to construct. One of the young girls posing in front of the building in this undated photograph is Marian Galloway Garman. Magnolia's original fire alarm was a steel locomotive wheel rim donated by the Atlantic City Railroad. One clang meant a fire was underway in the northern part of the borough, two rings sent firemen to the eastern section, three rings summoned help to the southern section, and four rings denoted a blaze in the western section.

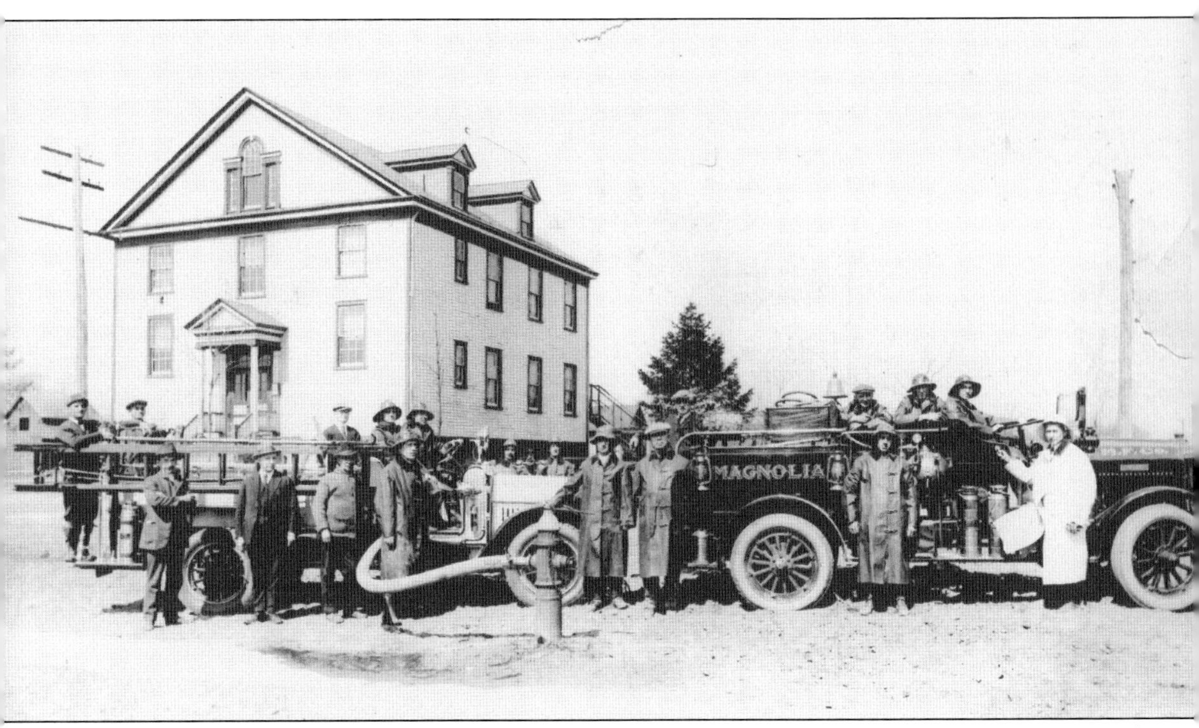

In 1914, Magnolia's fire company became one of the first communities in the region to use motorized equipment. In this undated photograph, fire department members practice using their 1919 Vim chemical wagon and 1925 Reo pumper at a fire hydrant in front of the Lincoln Avenue School.

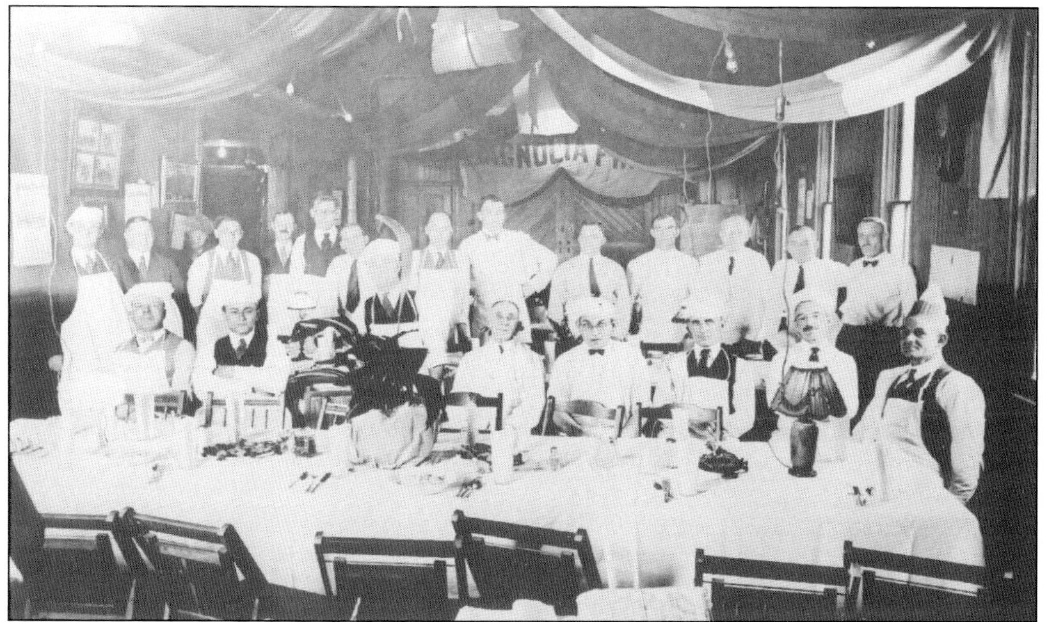

Fire department members prepare food for an installation dinner at the fire hall on March 21, 1925. Pictured are, from left to right, (first row) Robert Bowdoin, Walter Allen, three unidentified, Sam Rodman, Fred Lynch Sr., and Robert Schmitz; (second row) Fred Baker, Henry Abbott, Billy Lomeier, unidentified, Walter Weigert, Guy Bergstrom, Ben Acosta, George Dorsham, Walter Unterbrink, Fred Lynch Jr., Walter Smith, Andrew Cramp, and two unidentified.

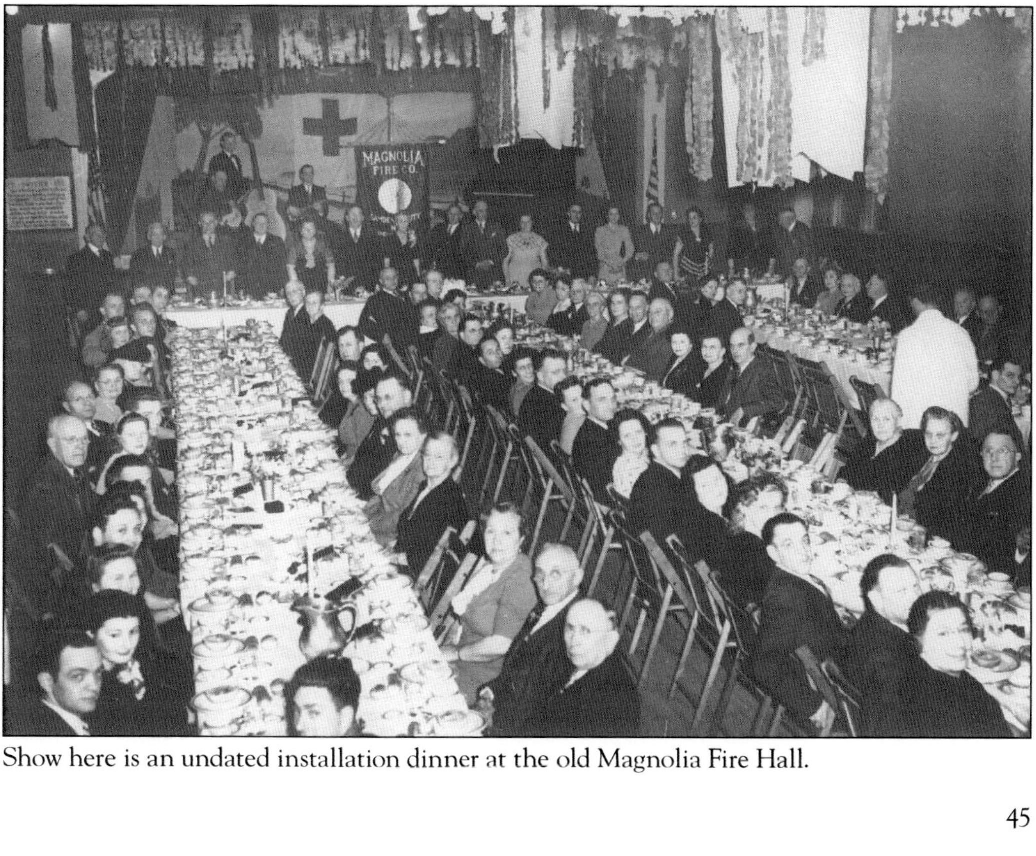

Show here is an undated installation dinner at the old Magnolia Fire Hall.

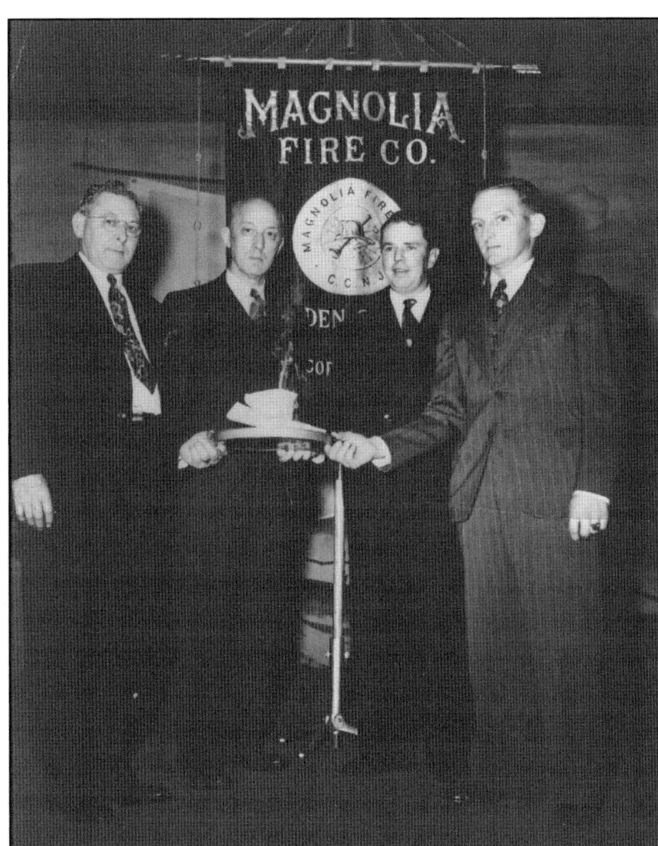

Fire department officers, seen here from left to right, Walter Allen, George Dorsham, Clifford Supplee, and Lew Mitten Jr. are installed at the start of a new year.

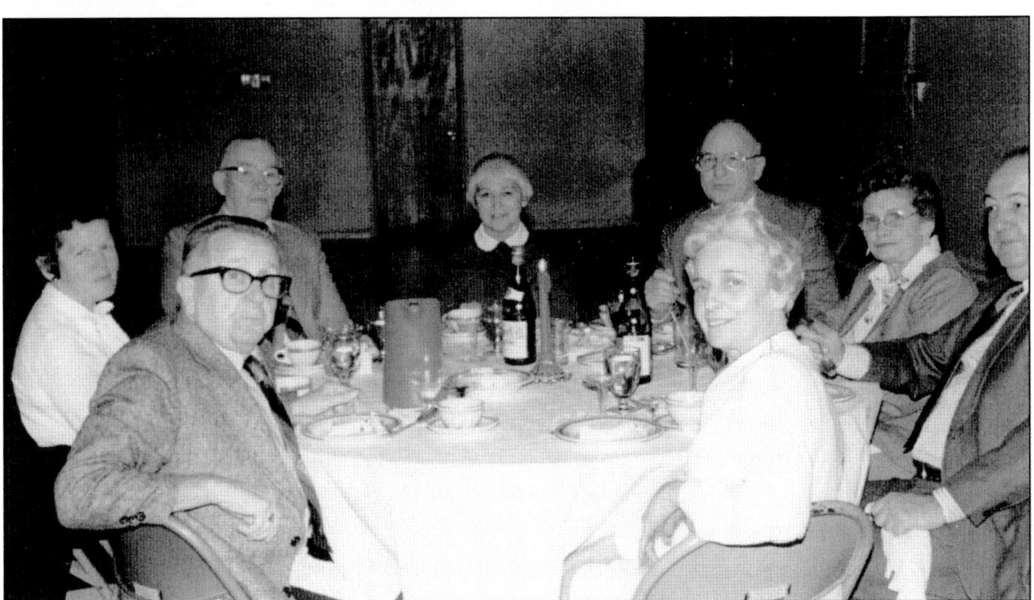

Seen clockwise from bottom left, Magnolia residents Charles and Edna Frake, Al and Gladys Graham, Harry and Vivien Turner, and Jack and Sheila Reid enjoy themselves at a fire department installation dinner in this undated photograph.

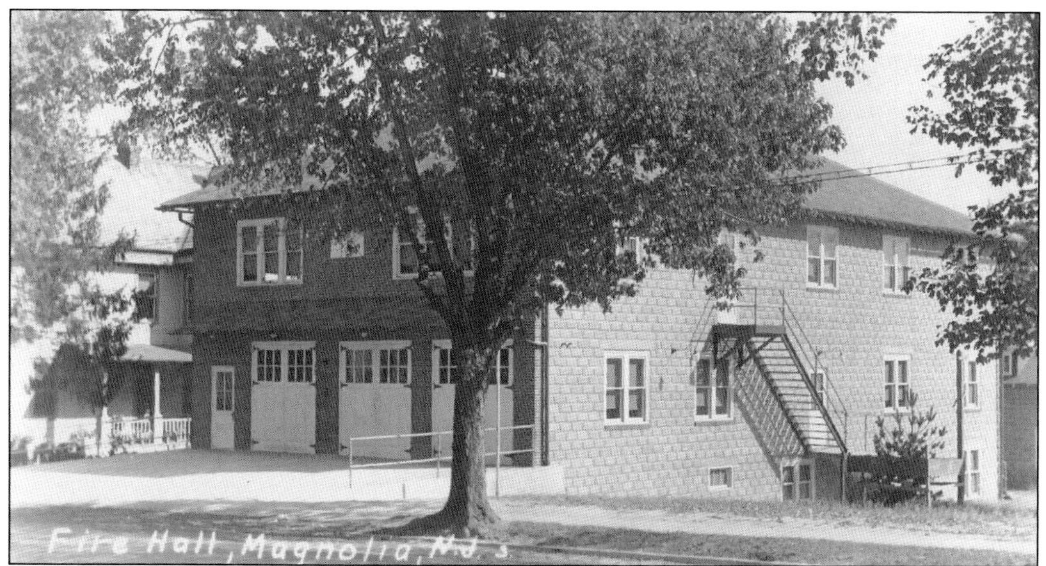

This new, modern firehouse was built on Evesham Road in 1929 and served as the municipal offices as well. To reach the borough clerk and other borough officials' offices, residents entered the building through one of the garage doors and proceeded to the back of the building. The fire escape was installed as a precaution for those using the second-floor banquet hall.

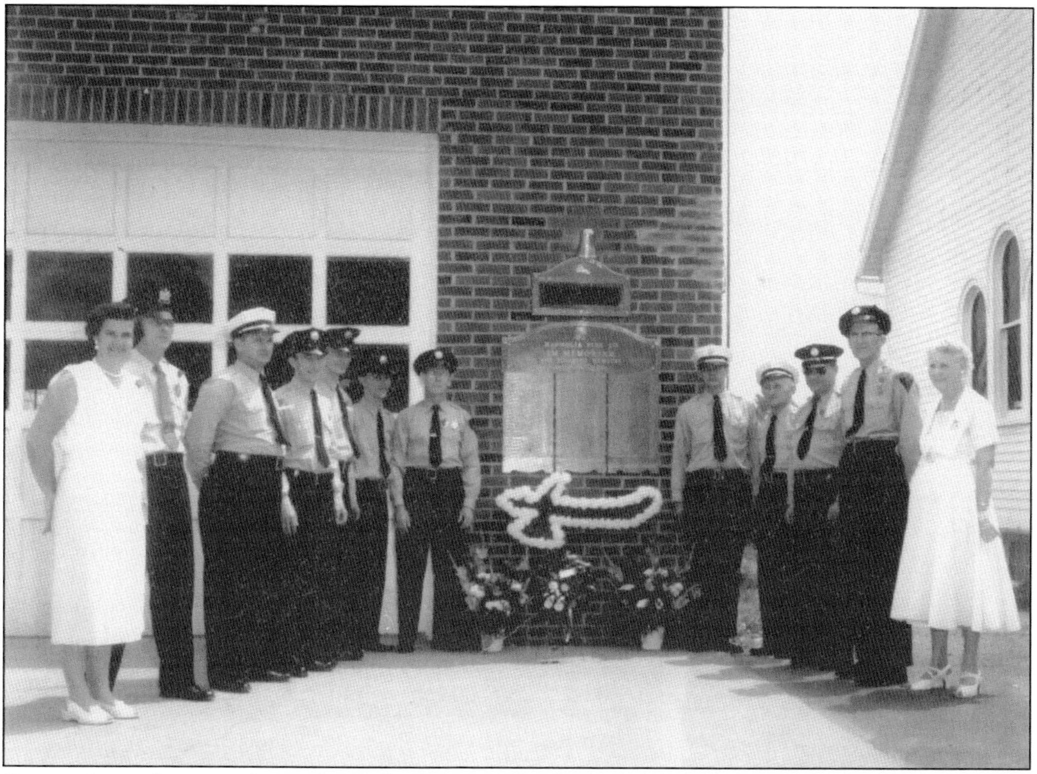

Posing for a photograph at the dedication of the firehouse monument are, from left to right, Flossie Oliver, Charles Oliver, Harold Harley, Tom Euler, Bobby Arnold, unidentified, Bill Johnston, Al Wiedemann, Lew Mitten Sr., Gil Hymerling, Fred Shields, and Lottic Allen.

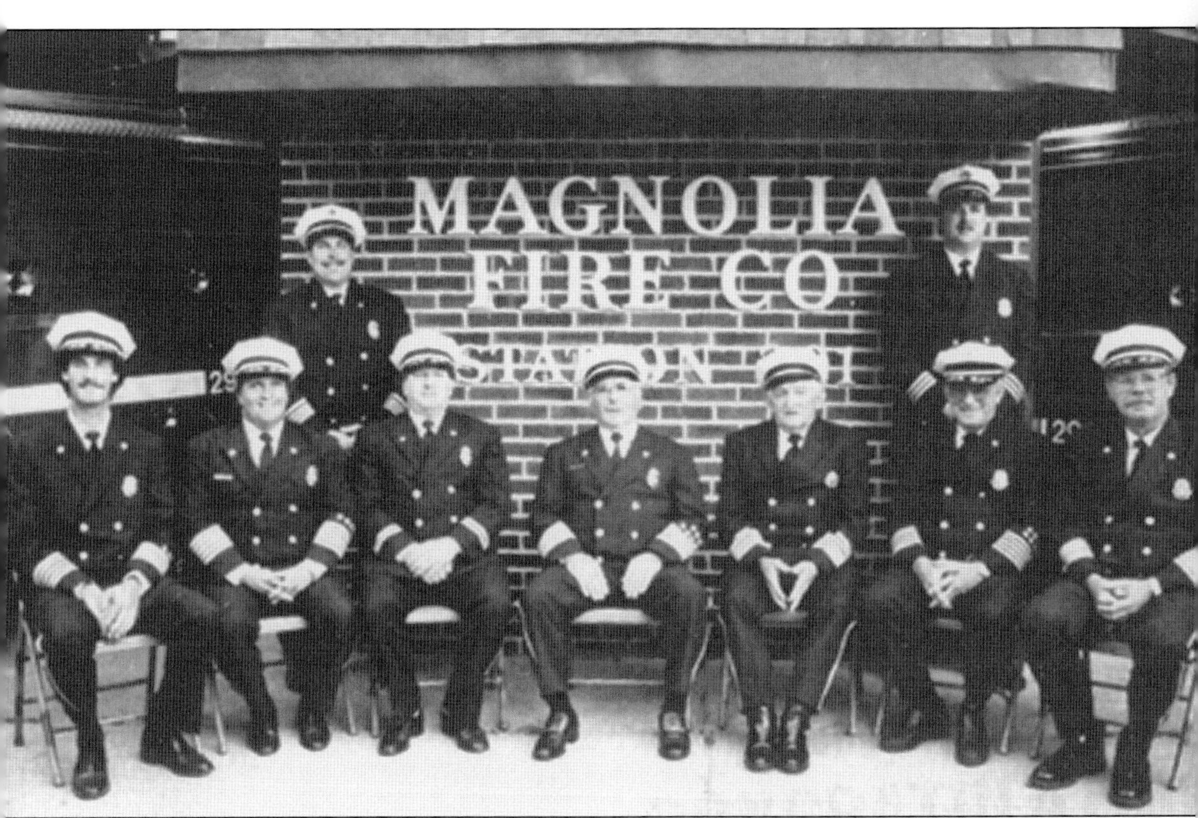

Several local residents who had held the position of fire chief attended the 100th anniversary of the fire department, including, from left to right, (first row) Michael Wolf, Donald Ebersole, Emil Altman, Walter Riebel Sr., Lew Mitten Sr., Tom Euler, and Gordon Jeffries; (second row) first assistant Gary Riebel and second assistant John Wolf Jr.

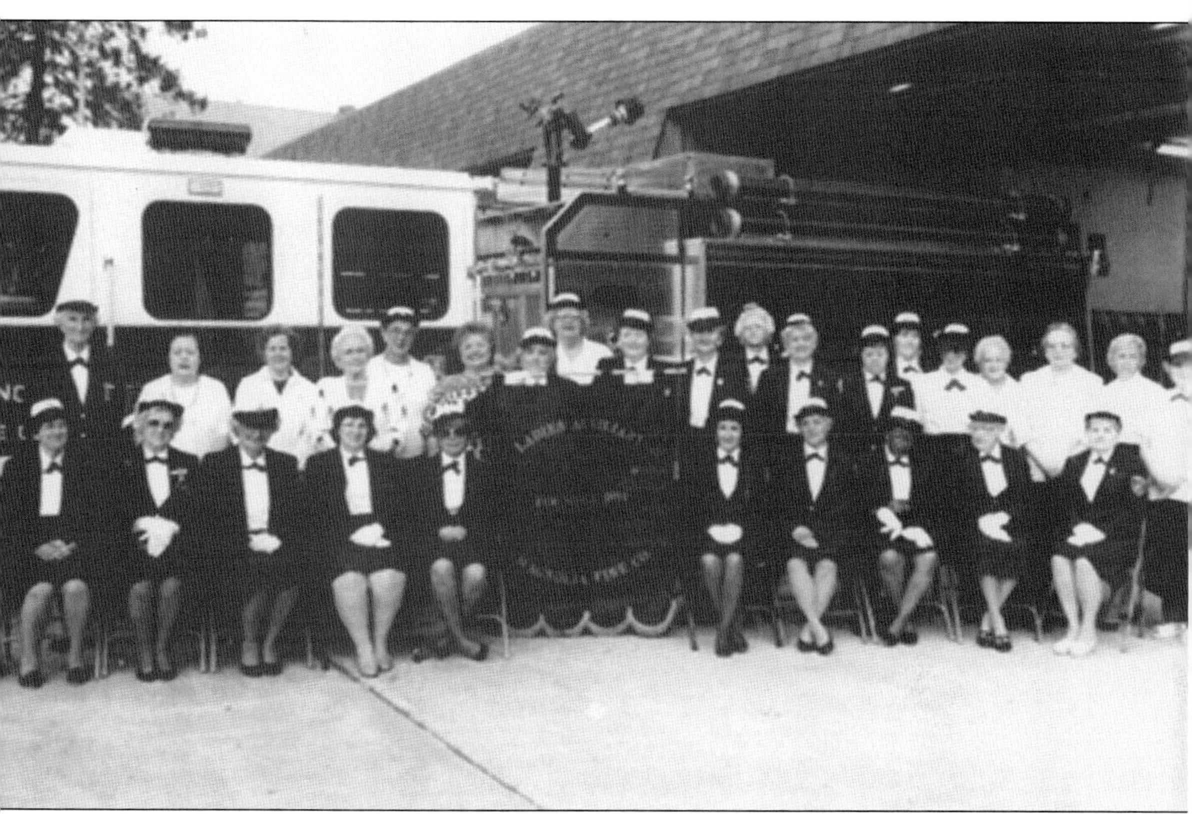

A few dedicated women founded the Magnolia Fire Department's Ladies Auxiliary in 1895, just two years after the fire department began operations. Nearly 100 years later, in 1993, the auxiliary had grown considerably and included, from left to right, (first row) Sue Grubbs, Florence Oliver, Irmagard Lank, Helen Bradley, Dorothy Kube, Mary Martz, Dorothy Dean, Lillian Golden, Mae McKenna, and Marie Bracken; (second row) Roberta Adams, Ronnie Rainey, Edna Frake, Sheila Reid, Charlotte Wilson, Gisella Arnold, Esther Kube, Pat Cromer, Joyce Smith, Jane McKenna, Helen Gallagher, Helen Calhoun, Ann Harris, Tish Cowling, Mary Harris, Ruth Beebe, Lydia Jones, Florence Bahm, and Vivien Turner.

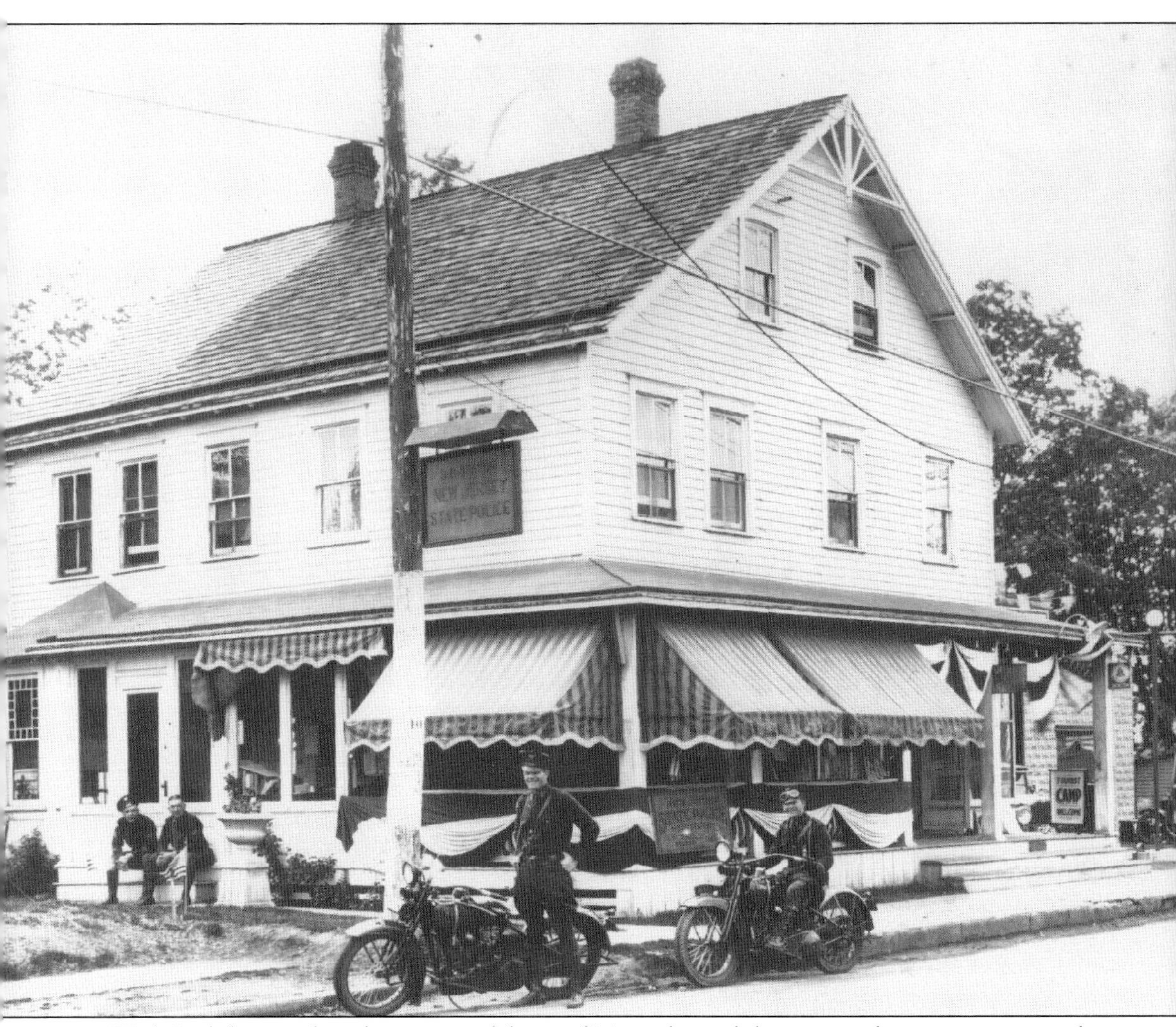

With Prohibition, the relative peacefulness of Magnolia and the surrounding communities along the White Horse Pike was shattered by a growing wave of violent crime. Vigilante groups were formed in the borough, as well as in Barrington and Haddon Heights, in an effort to help IRS agents assigned to the area contain the alcohol sales-driven crime wave. Ultimately the state police were forced to set up a substation in Magnolia on the White Horse Pike to control the gangland killings and machine gun battles along the county roadway. The state police unit, pictured here in front of the substation, was assisted by local special officers including ? Headley, Bill Frass, ? Brown, Charles Charman, Walter Hunt, Claude Maxwell, ? Bryant, and Eugene Landin.

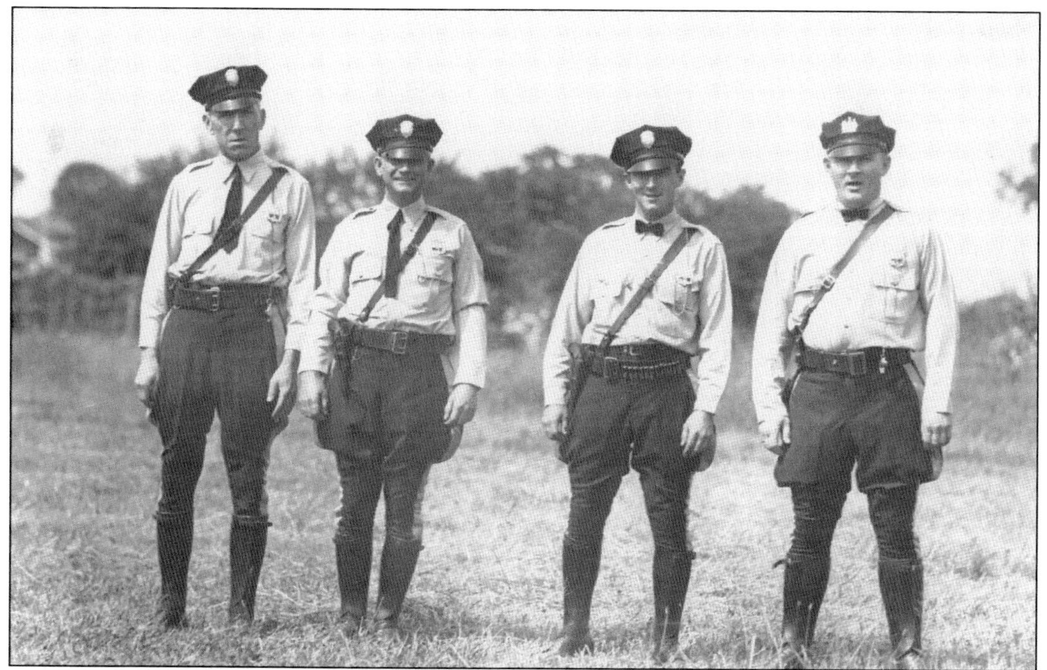

Until 1958, Magnolia's police force was composed entirely of local special officers, who were paid 50¢ per hour for part-time work and used their own cars when responding to calls. In 1929, the borough's special officers were, from left to right, Walter Shoemaker, Walter Hunt, Bill Spiegle, and Charlie Knecht. Claude Maxwell served as chief of the unit.

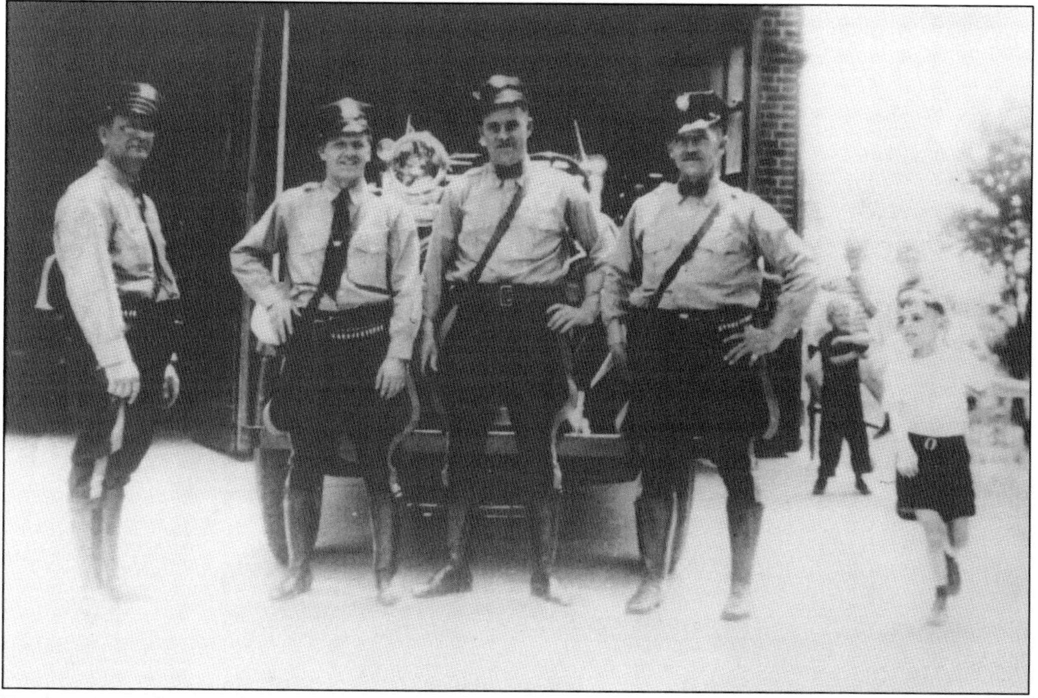

By the 1940s, Dave Adams (far left) had assumed the position of chief of the special unit, which included, from left to right, Len Sawyer, Andrew Wesley James Sr., and Claude Maxwell.

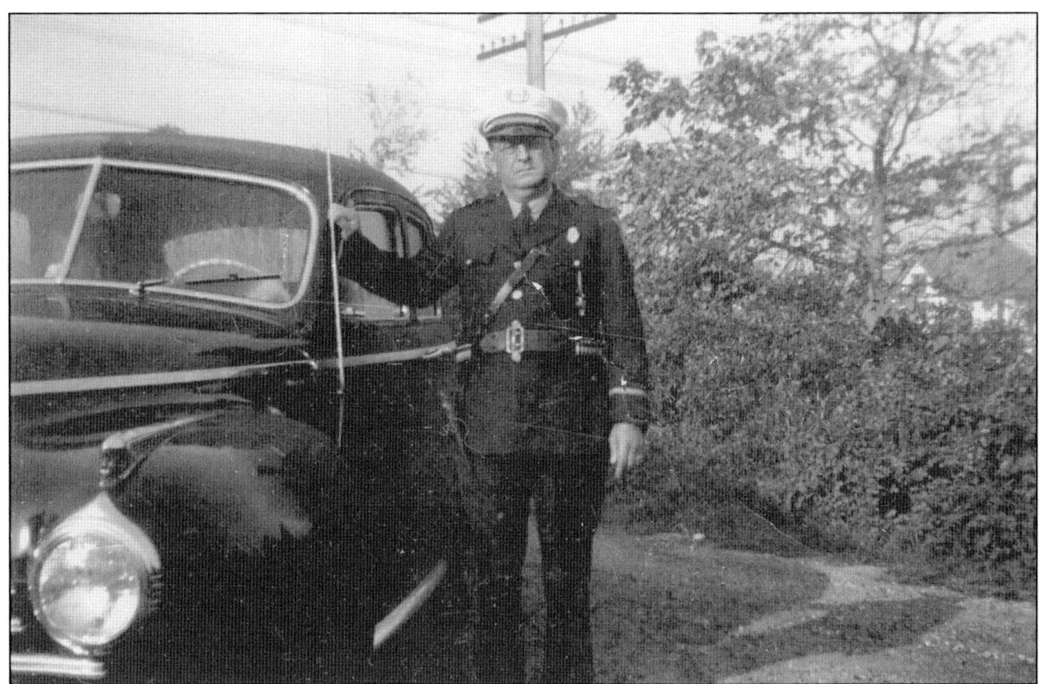

Dave Adams was appointed the first full-time police chief when the borough established a regular police department in 1958. Two full-time officers, Charles Oliver and Paul Jones Sr., also were hired at that time.

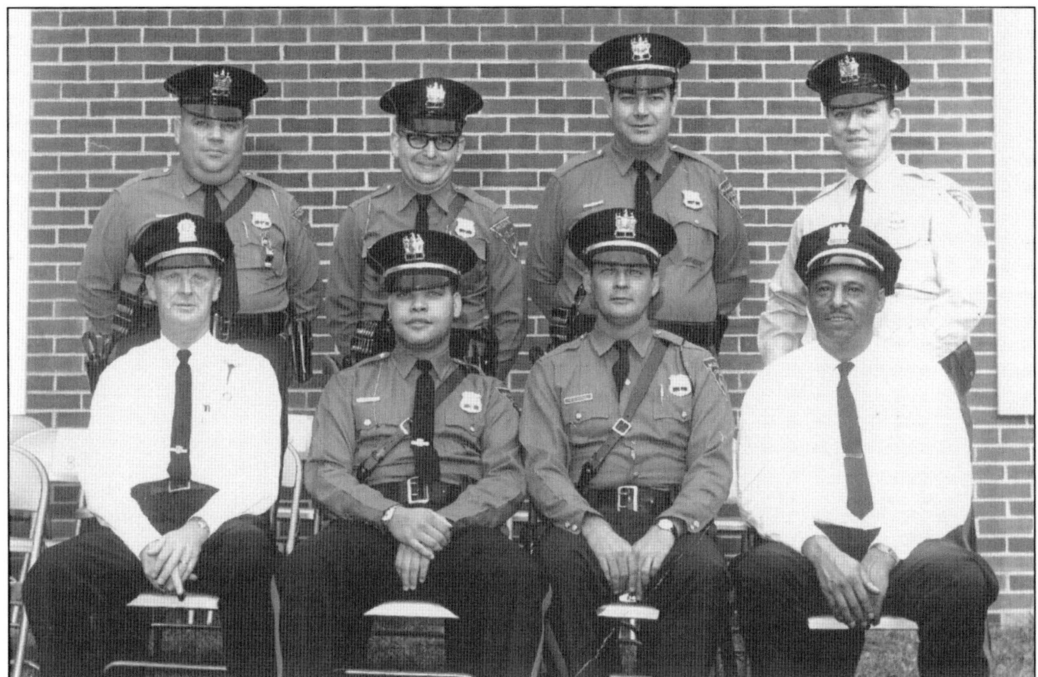

As the borough grew, so did its police force. In the late 1960s, Chief Charles Oliver supervised the force. Seen here from left to right are (first row) Oliver, Michael Moore, William Little, and Sgt. Paul Jones; (second row) Joe Leitenberger, Lew Mitten Jr., John Hunt, and Jack Kendall.

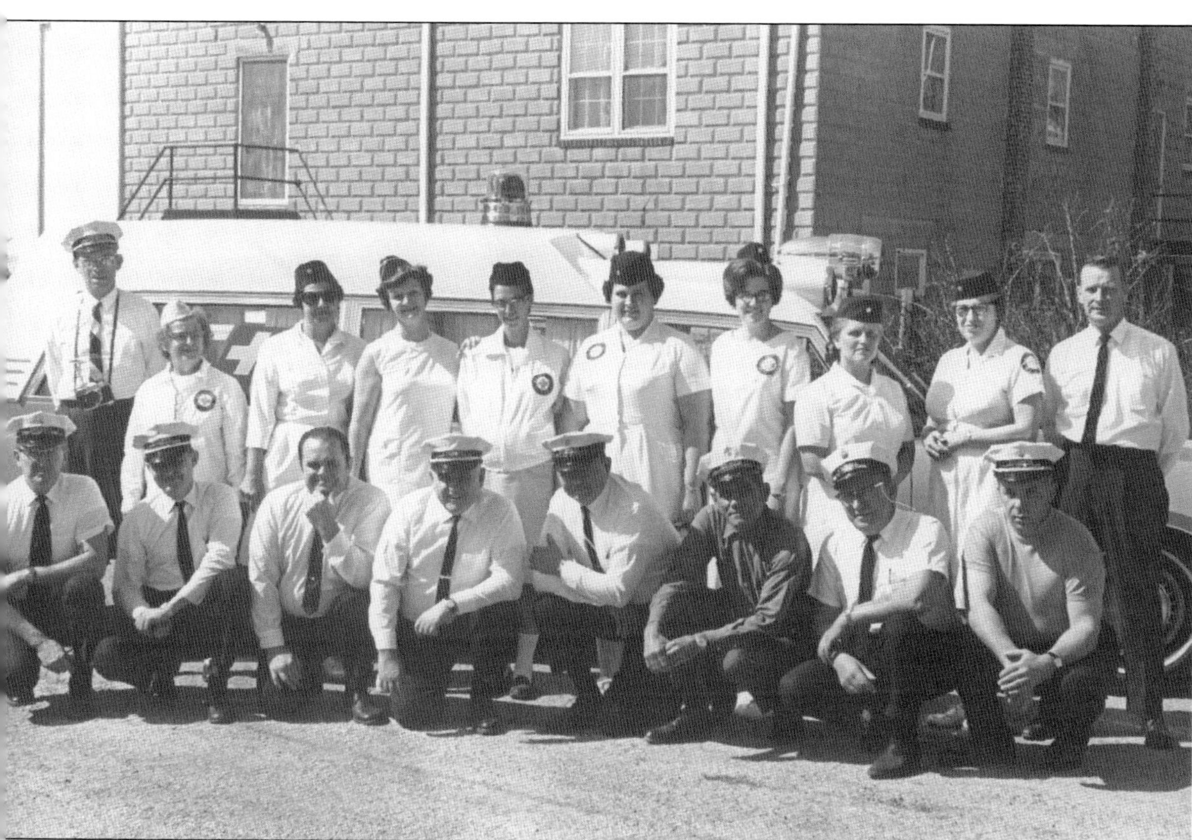

In 1952, the Edwin I. Johnson American Legion Post 370 sponsored the establishment of a local volunteer ambulance squad servicing Magnolia and Somerdale and collected newspapers to raise money to purchase a used ambulance the following year. The first president of the squad was Edward Cox. Pictured here in this undated photograph are, from left to right, (front row) members Carl Thrower, Bob Gouck, unidentified, George Bakley, unidentified, Matt Thistlewood, Fred Warner, and Bill Scott; (second row) George Belzer, Betty Nelson, Mary Vadurro, Marge Vaughan, Beverly Ford, Elaine Belzer, unidentified, Susan Buckley, Mae McKenna, and Charles Oliver.

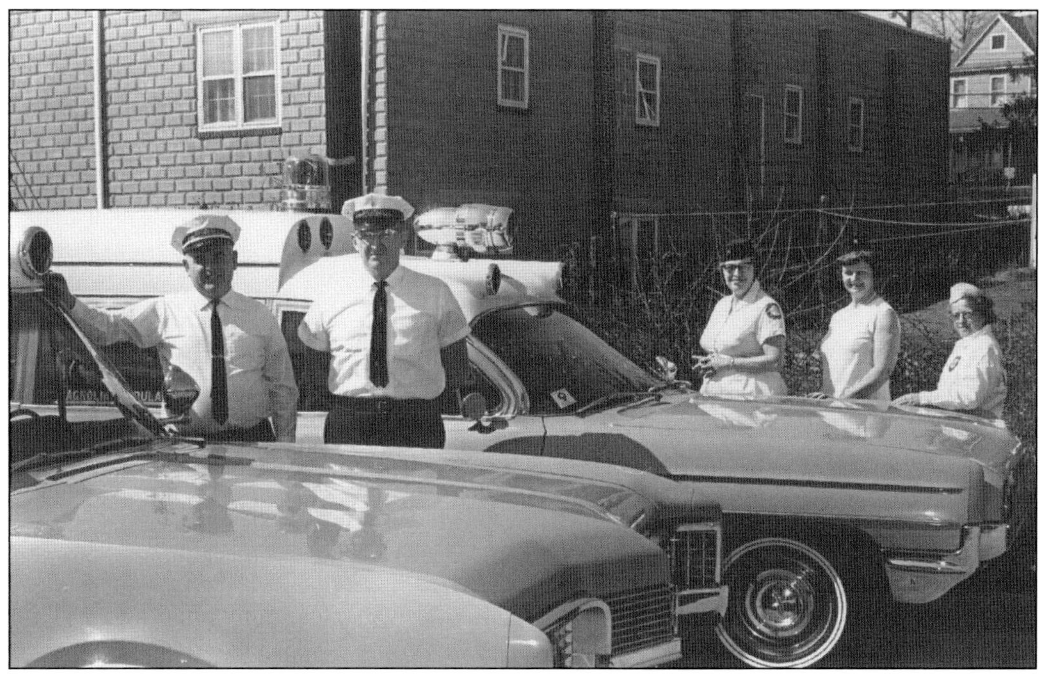

The squad's equipment was housed in the firehouse until 1962, when the borough authorized them to use an available building behind the firehouse, where the ambulance squad remains today. Squad members George Bakely, Carl Thrower, Mae McKenna, Marge Vaughan, and Betty Nelson inspect Magnolia's ambulances as they are relocated into their new home, which was deeded to the squad in 1975.

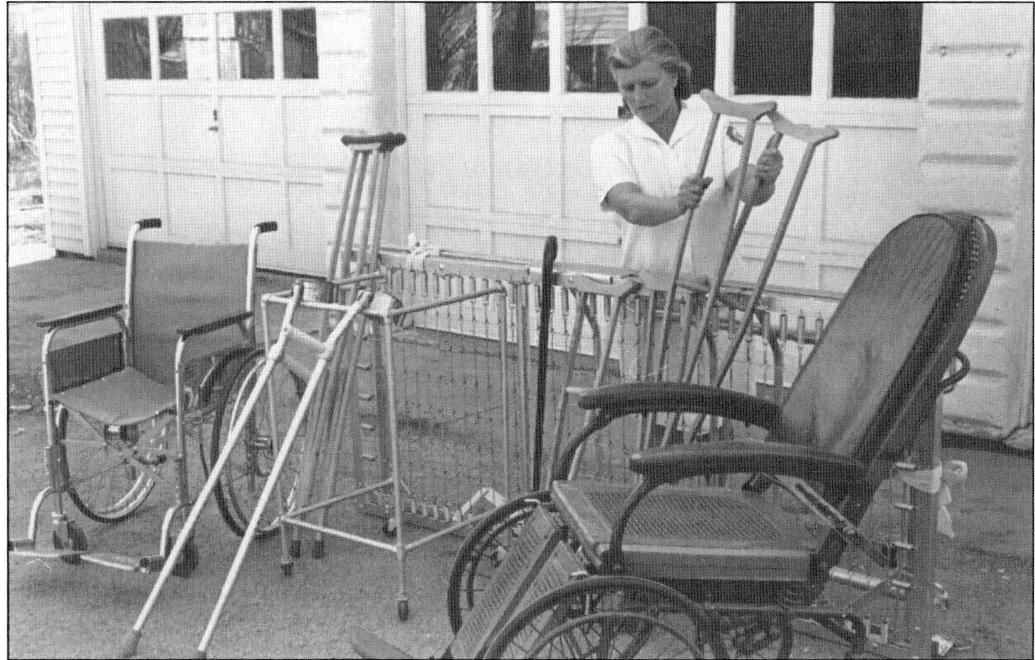

Sue Buckley inspects some of the squad's other equipment, including wheelchairs, walkers, and crutches, before they are relocated.

Four

GETTING DOWN TO BUSINESS

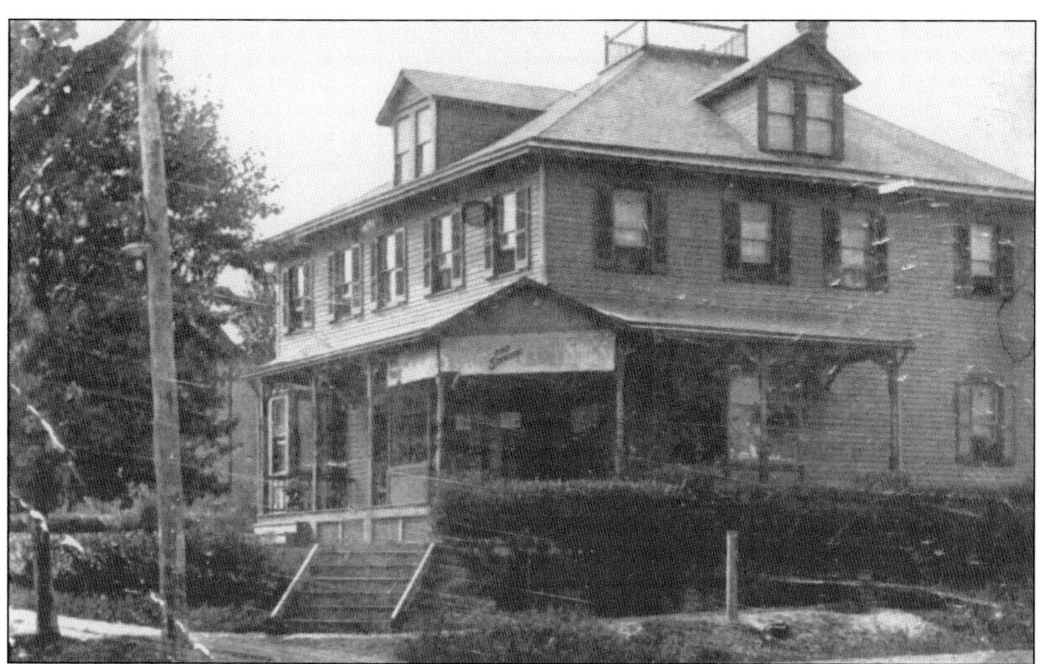

Harry Wolohan, Magnolia's first mayor, owned and operated this store on the corner of Evesham and Warwick Roads. The store stocked a wide variety of dry goods and was a popular place for local children to purchase penny candy. The building also served as Wolohan's home. It remains a private residence today.

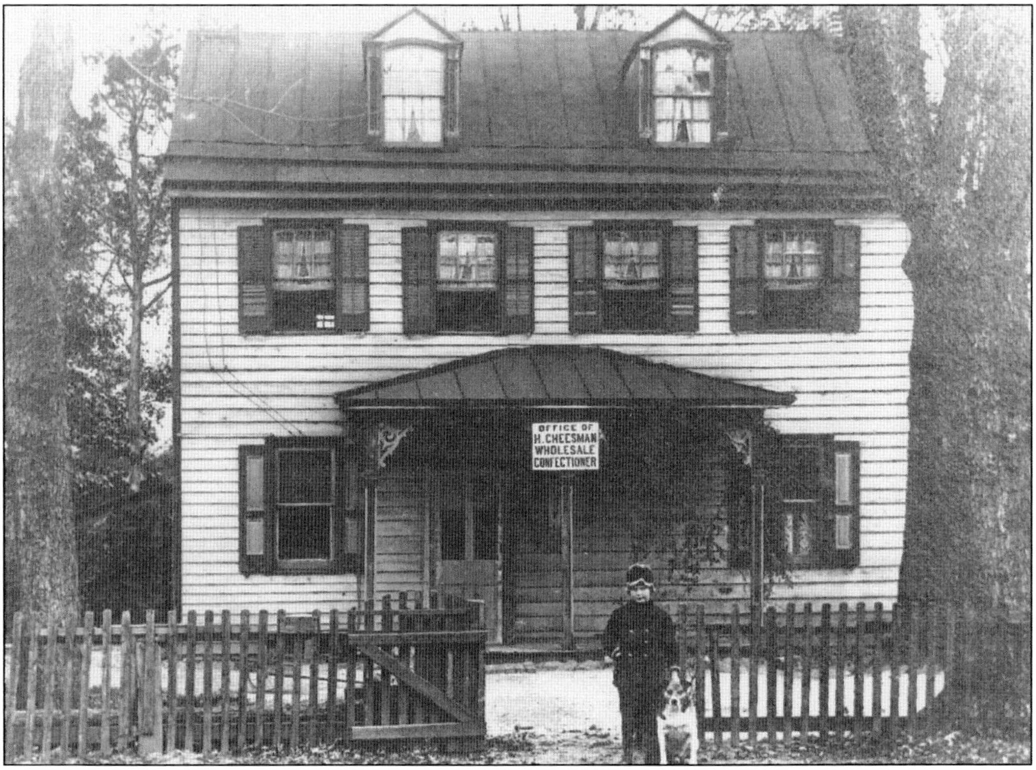

Joseph Cheesman stands in front of his family's home and wholesale confectioner office on Evesham Road and the White Horse Pike in 1916.

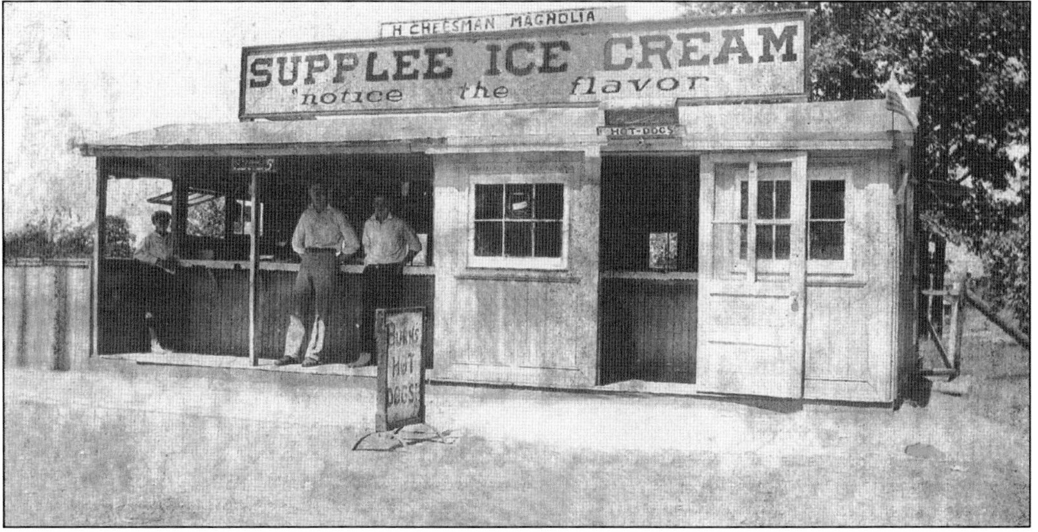

This ice cream stand was added onto the Cheesman's house on the White Horse Pike side to sell Supplee ice cream in the 1930s. The ice cream stand was popular among motorists traveling to and from the Jersey Shore.

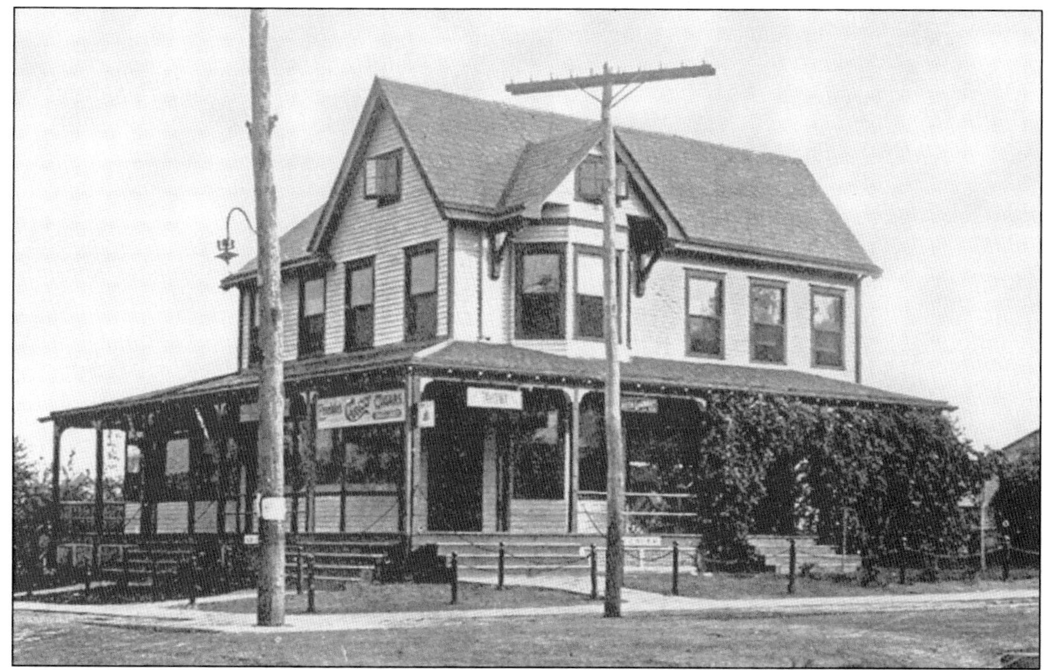

Earlier ice cream made Magnolia a regular stop on the train route for some travelers, who looked forward to visiting Ed Graeff's store on Evesham Road and Atlantic Avenue, alongside the railroad tracks. His supply of Crane's ice cream, which was well-known for its great taste, regularly arrived by train from Philadelphia.

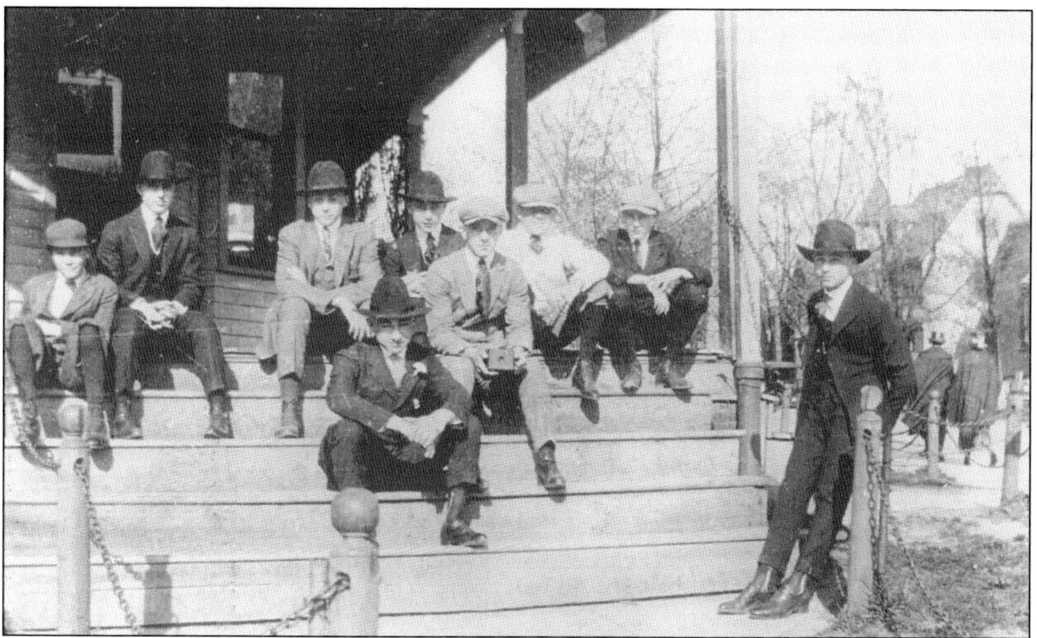

Graeff's store also boasted a wide selection of candy and patent medicines, two barber chairs, and a poolroom, making it a natural hangout for local kids. Congregating on the steps in April 1918 are, from left to right, unidentified, Ronald Halderman, Thomas Mezger, Earl Lynch, Edward Duffield, unidentified, Leslie Lyon Jr., George McGur, and John Graham.

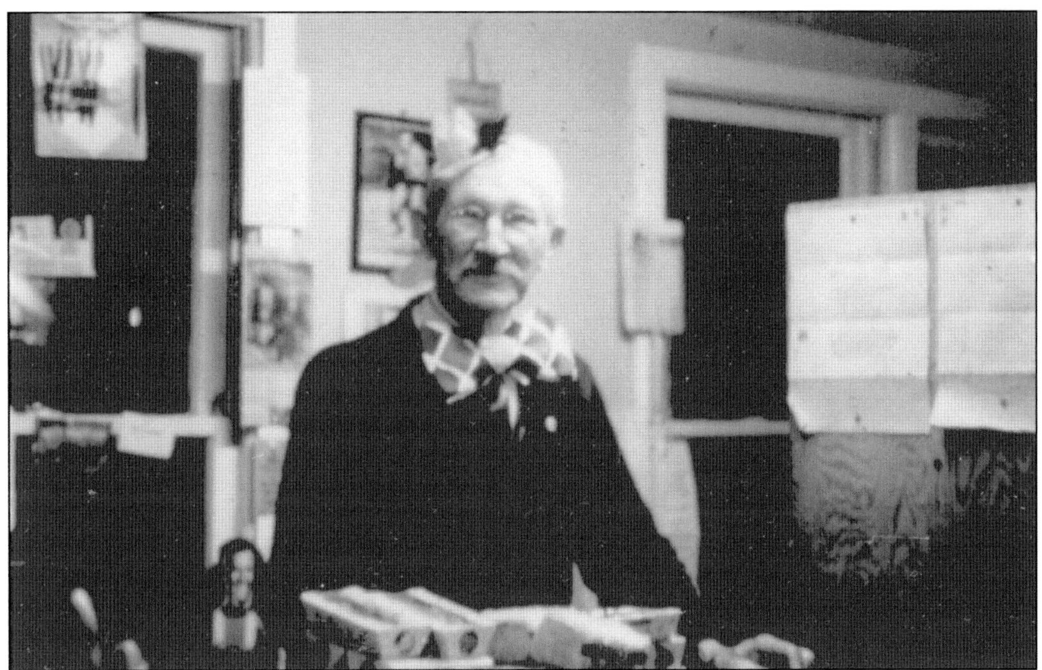

In the 1930s and 1940s, Frank Clapp, owner of Clapp's Ice Cream Store, made his own frozen treats, flavoring his ice cream with fruit grown behind his White Horse Pike shop. Longtime locals remember his fresh strawberry ice cream as the best around.

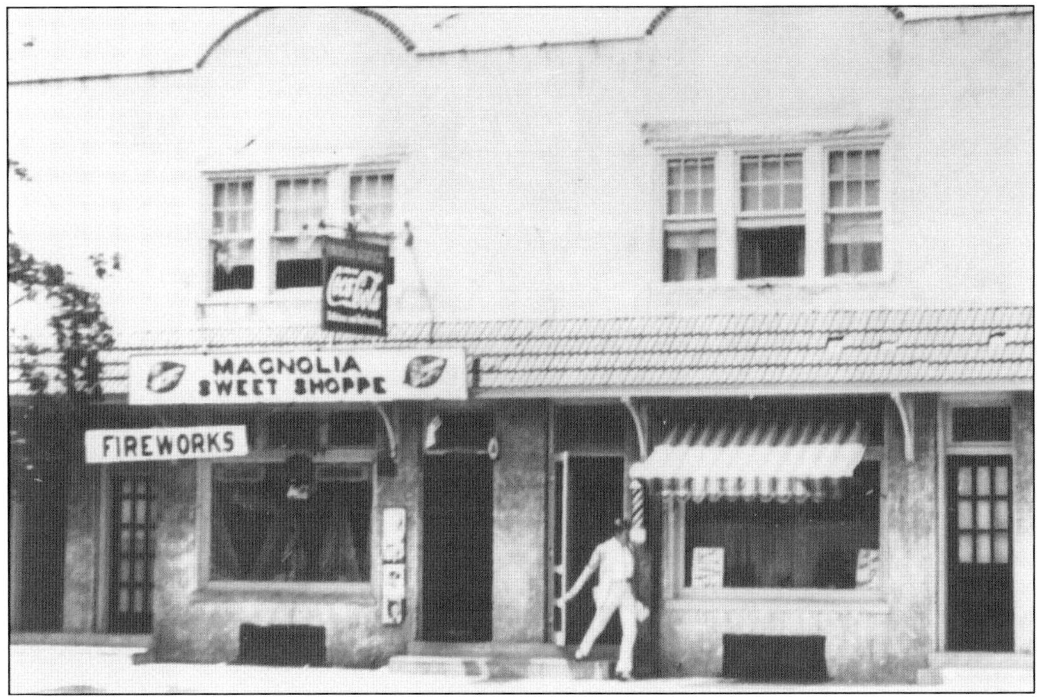

The Euler's Magnolia Sweet Shop was the place to buy candy, Breyer's ice cream, and more in the 1930s. The store was located in the 300 block of Evesham Road, next to Bruce Abbott's Barber Shop.

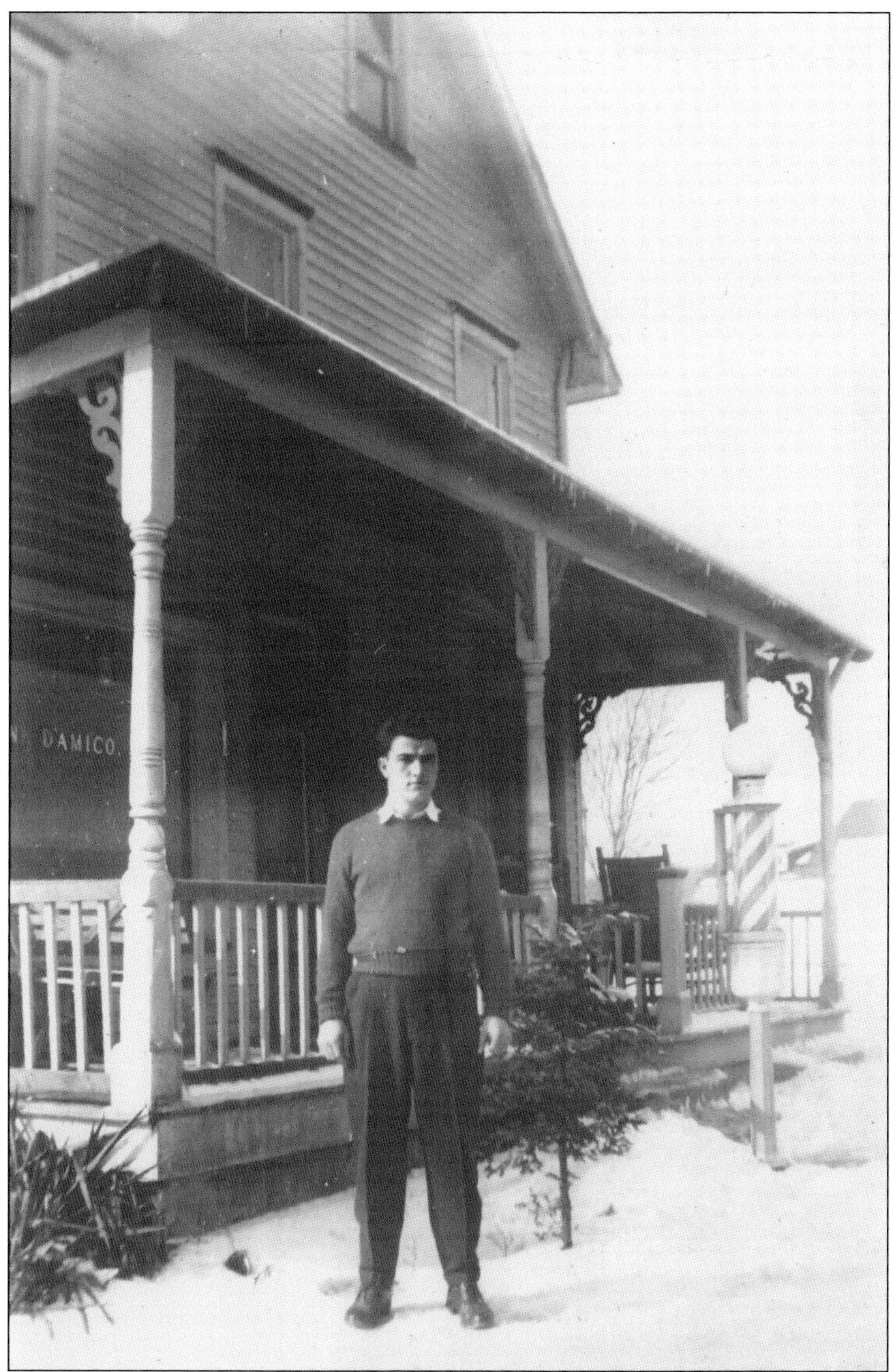

The D'Amico family operated the Frank D'Amico and Sons Barber Shop on the White Horse Pike for years. In this 1930 photograph, Pete D'Amico poses in front of the shop, which was torn down to make way for a planned McDonalds, near Jefferson Avenue.

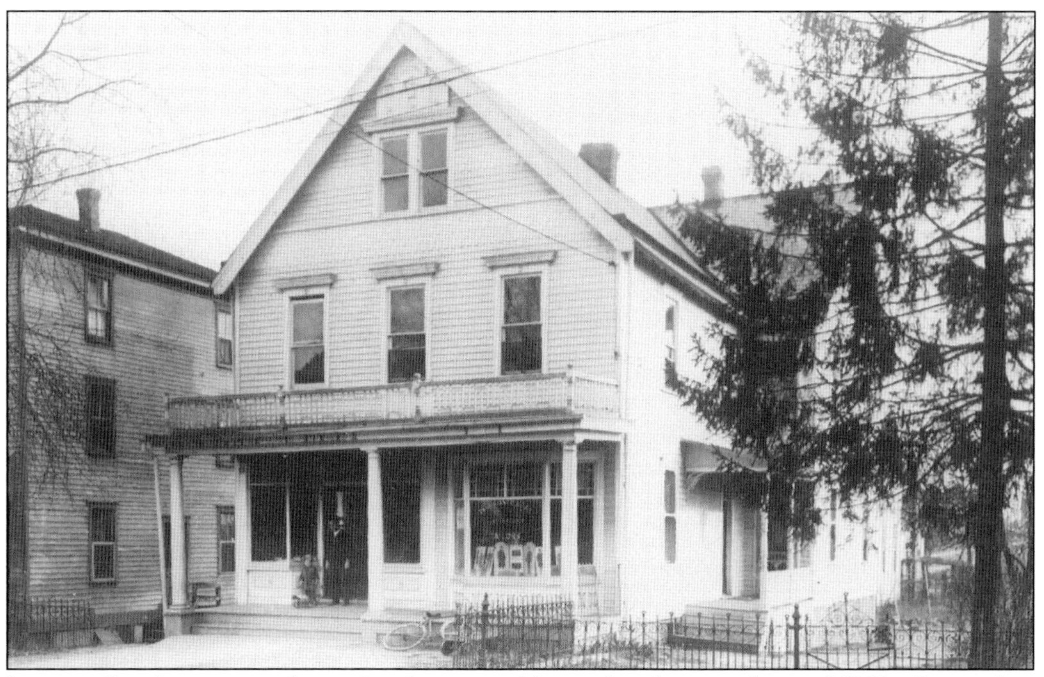

Letterio Panebianco stands in the doorway of his tailor shop in the mid-1920s. Located at 108 West Evesham Road, it stood next to Foster's Hardware Store, which is partially visible on the left.

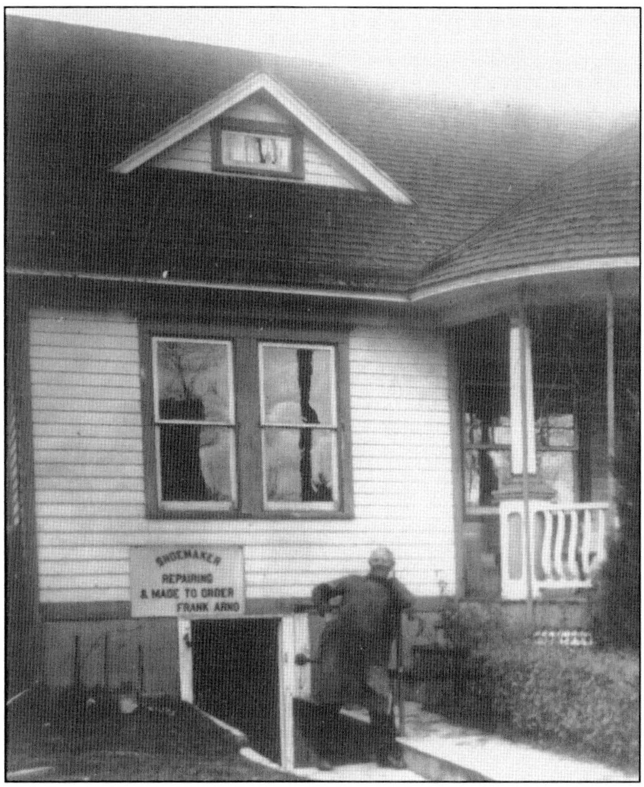

Frank Arno poses outside of his shoemaker shop, which he operated in the basement of his West Evesham Road home, offering repair services and shoes made to order. He later moved the operation next door as his business grew.

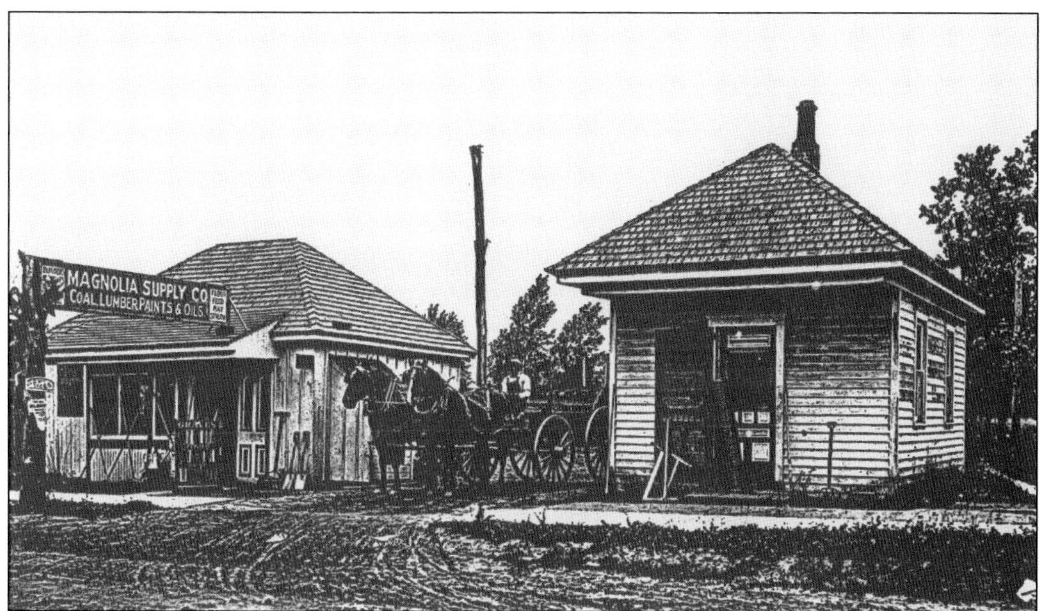

A delivery wagon prepares to leave the Magnolia Supply Company in 1910. Stocking lumber, coal, oils, and paints, the business was located at Atlantic and Madison Avenues.

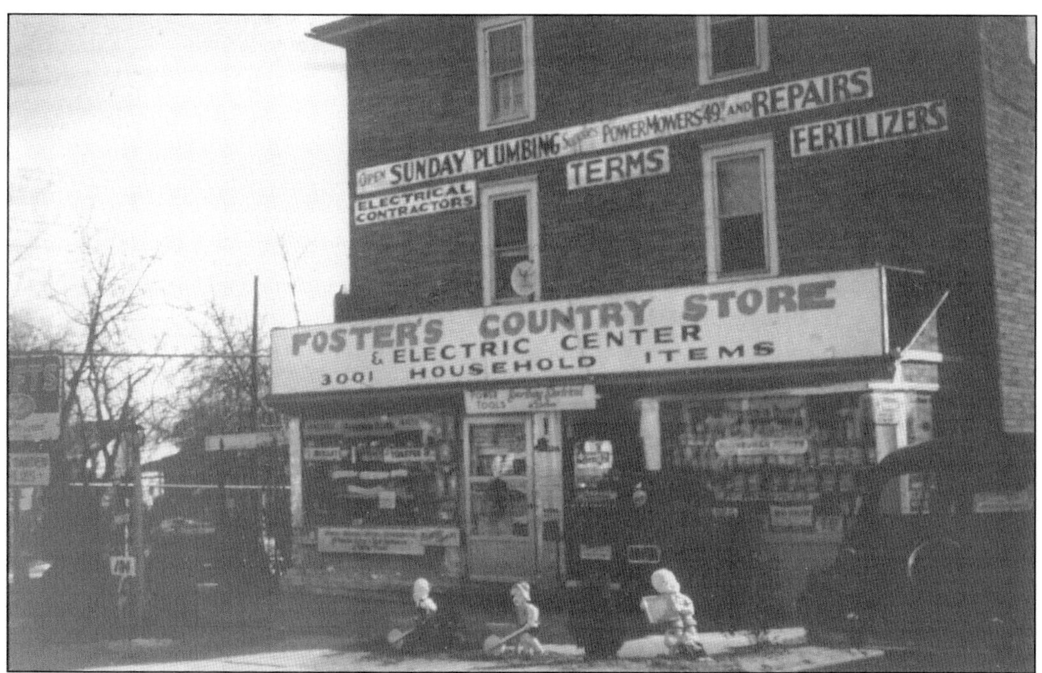

Foster's Country Store and Electric Center, in the 100 block of West Evesham and Warwick Roads, claimed to stock over 3,000 household items and also provided electronic repair services. Owned by electrician Joe Foster, who was known for his avid support of local athletics programs, the business held the distinction of being one of the few open on Sundays.

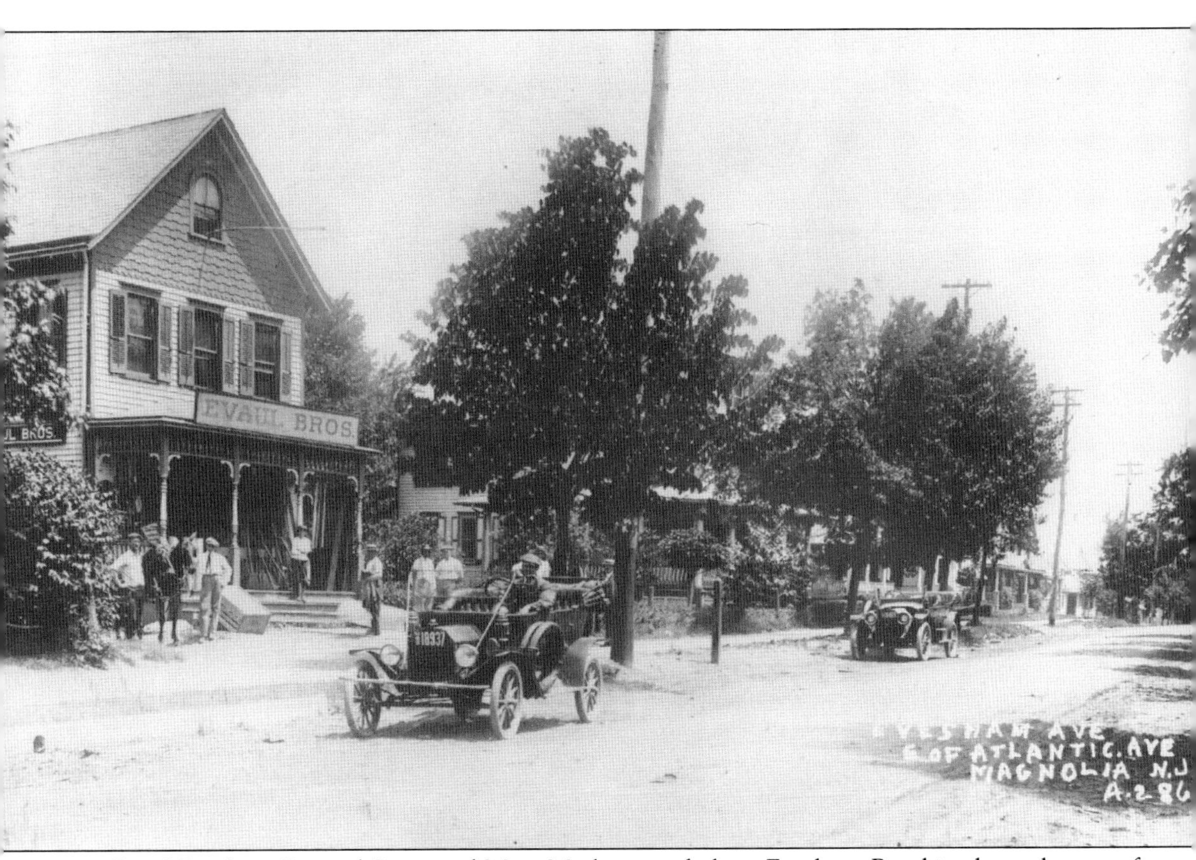

Evaul Brothers General Store and Meat Market stood along Evesham Road in the early part of the 20th century. Pictured here in 1915, it was one of two stores operated by the family. The second was located in Haddon Heights.

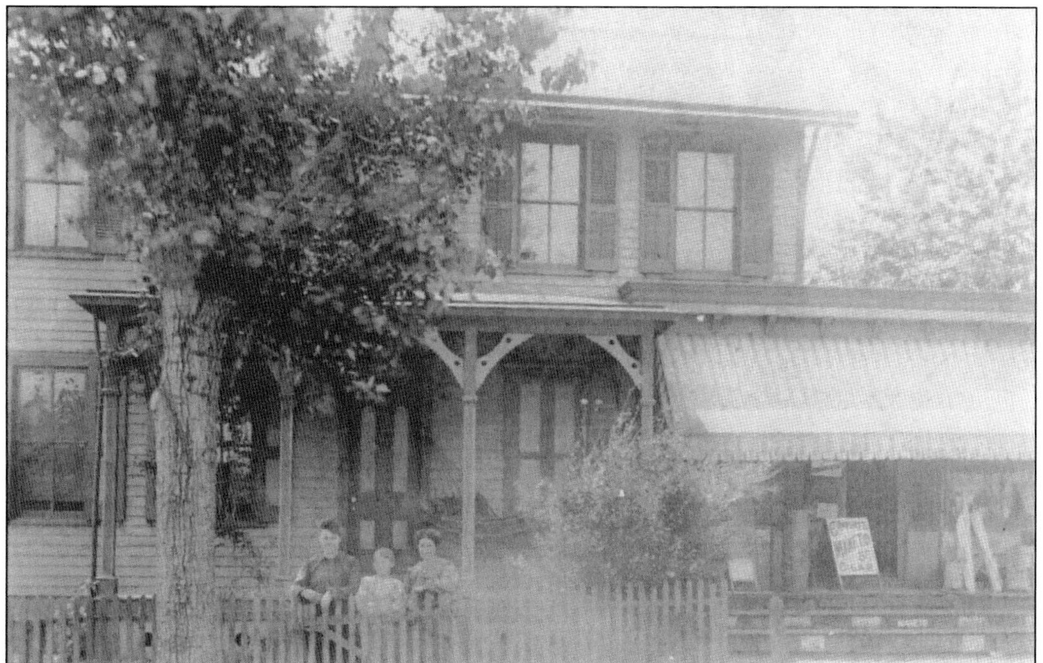

Miller's Store once stood on the White Horse Pike and, like many shops of the day, was attached to the family home.

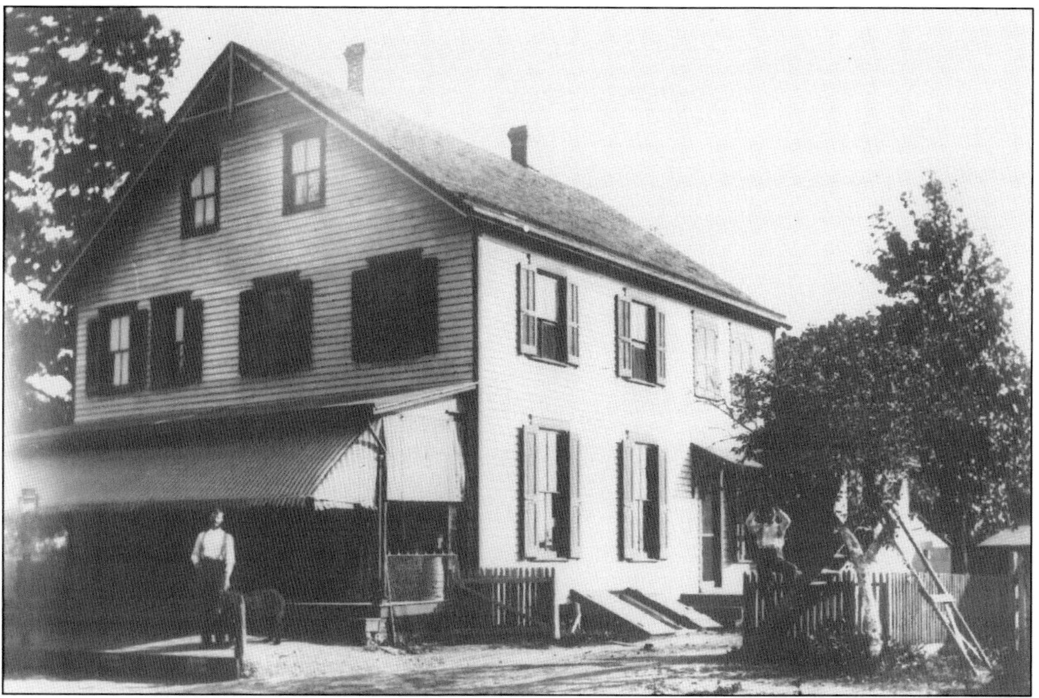

Tom Barrett opened his store at 208 North White Horse Pike after the state police stopped using the building as their substation. The shop, with Barrett standing in the foreground, is seen here in the 1920s. His family provided a portion of their land for the construction of the Magnolia Methodist Church in the early 1800s.

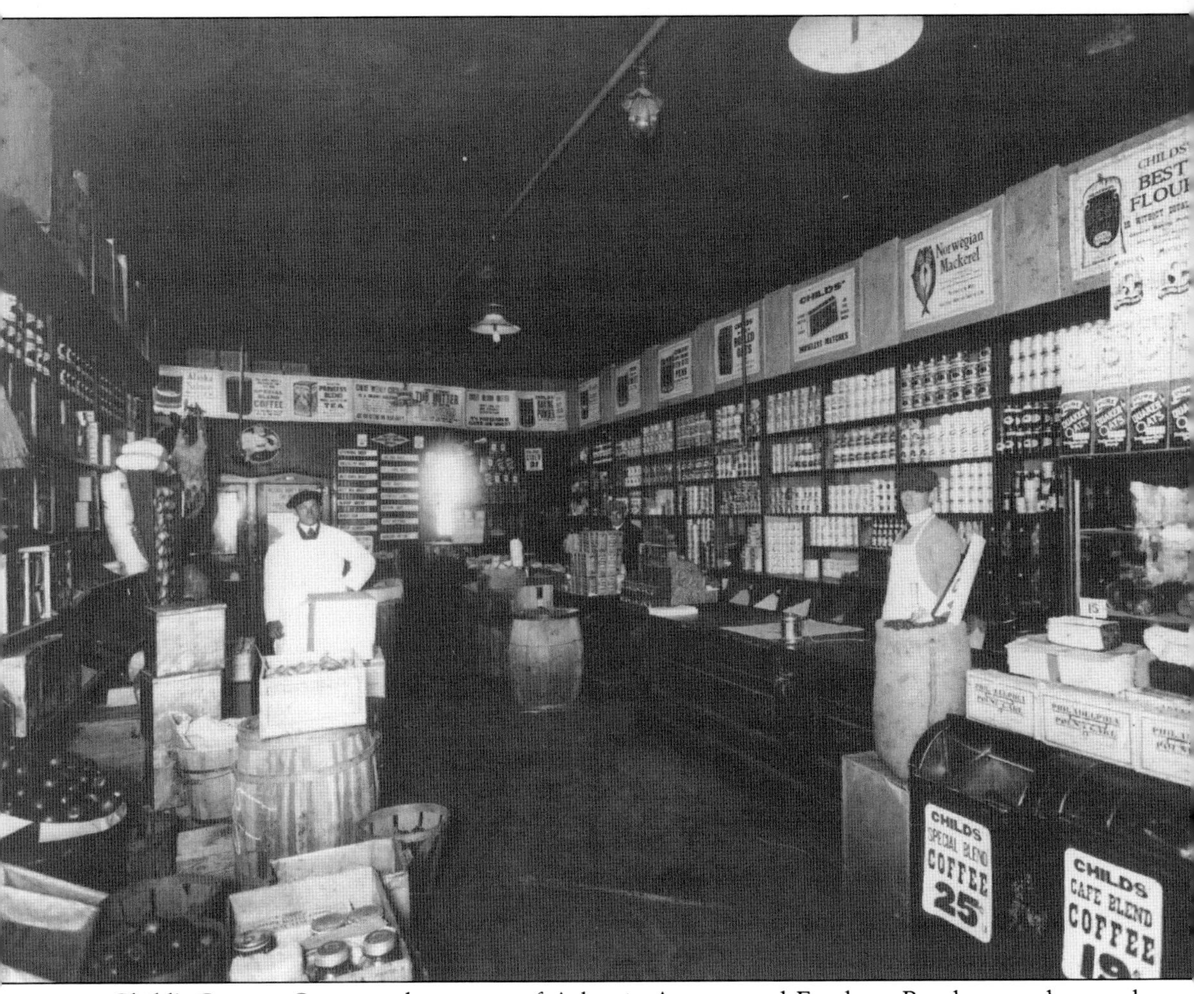

Child's Grocery Store, at the corner of Atlantic Avenue and Evesham Road, opened around 1875 as part of a chain of stores founded in Pennsylvania. In 1917, the chain merged with the Acme Tea Company and became the American Stores, operating under the Acme name.

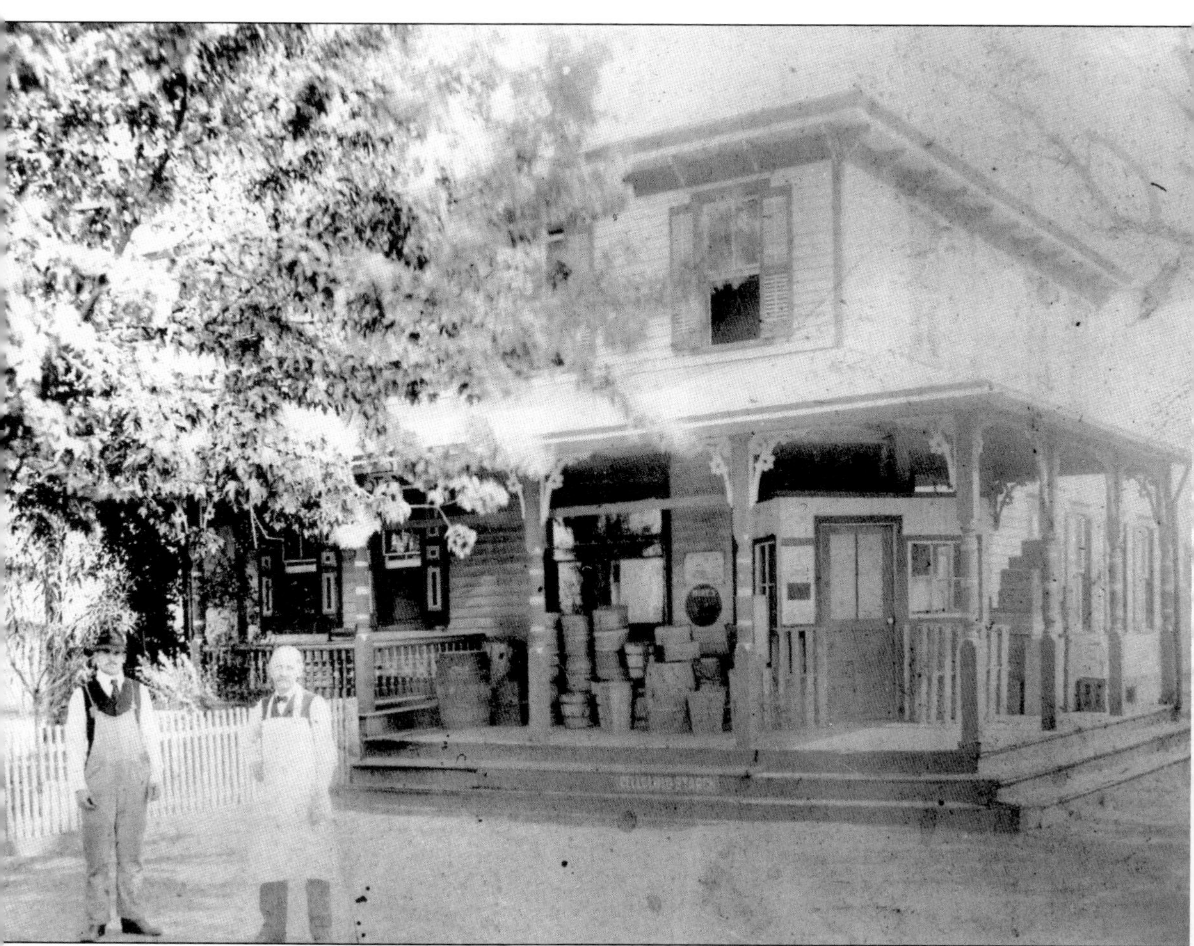

Before Child's Grocery Store donned the Acme name, William Morris, one of the borough's first council members, owned and operated one of the local American Stores' main competitors—the Morris Grocery Store—at the corner of Warwick and Evesham Roads, where the WaWa now stands. Morris, seen here with his son William Morris Jr. in the 1920s, later closed his business, and his son served as manager of the American Stores in Magnolia.

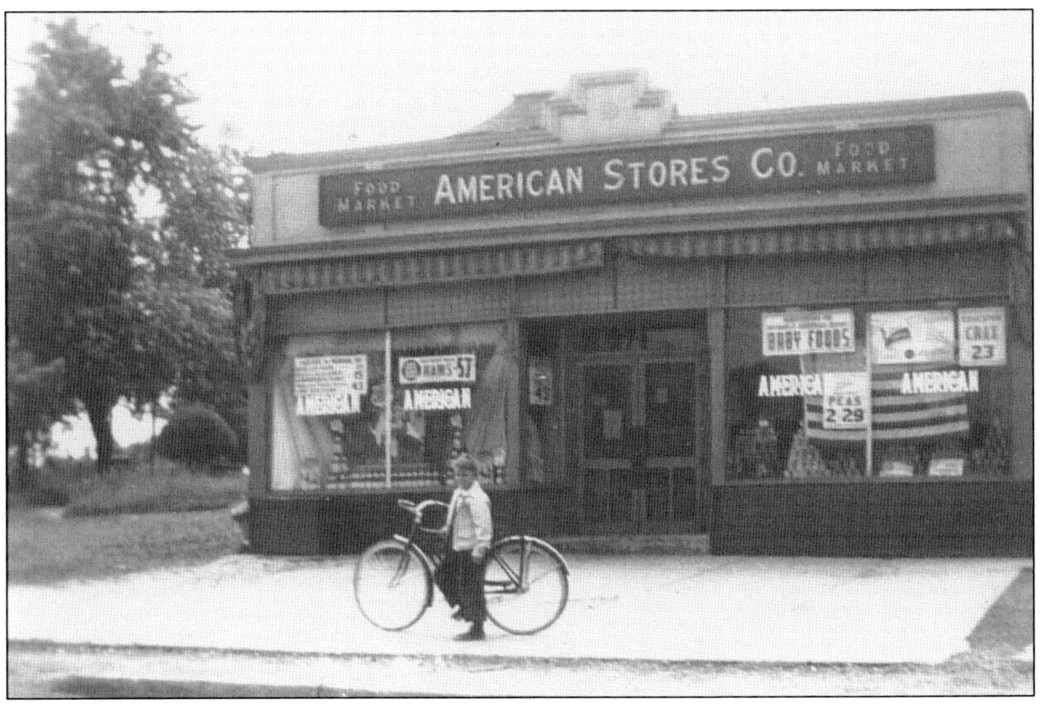

The American Stores stood where the Water Ice Factory now stands. In this photograph taken around 1950, Charles Fairbanks prepares to head into the store to pick up a few things.

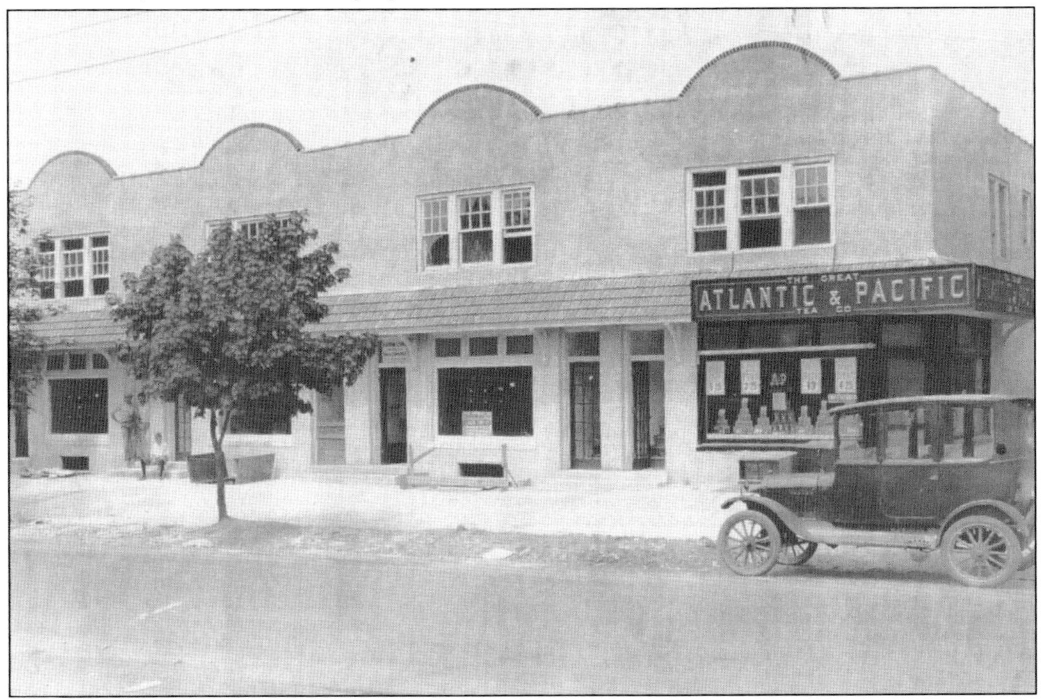

Later competition came in the form of the Great Atlantic and Pacific Tea Company (A&P), which moved in as the anchor store when Magnolia resident David Garton constructed an early group of strip stores in the 300 block of Evesham Road and West Atlantic Avenue.

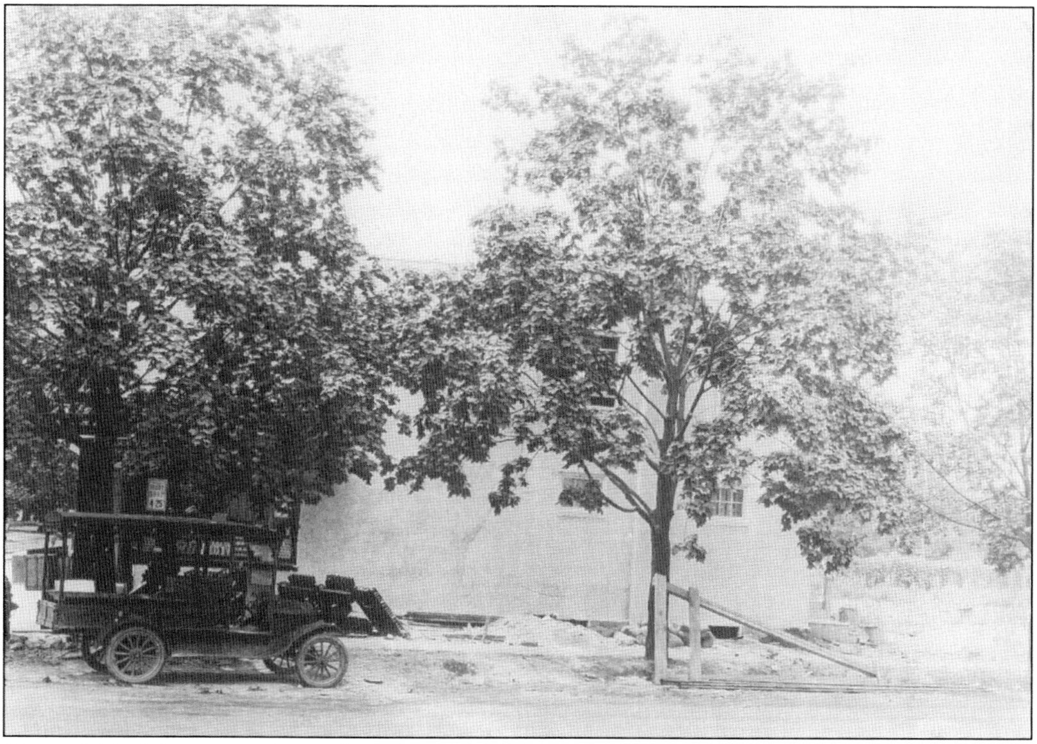

The A&P's delivery truck can be seen parked along West Atlantic Avenue in this photograph dated around 1925.

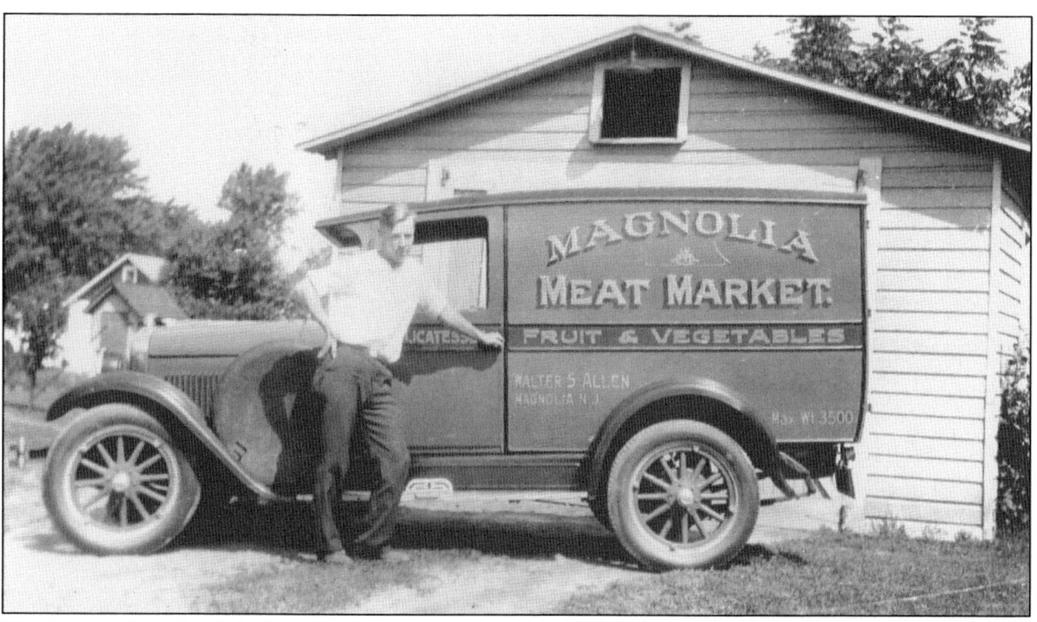

The Magnolia Meat Market, located at East Atlantic Avenue and Evesham Road, made deliveries in this 1925 truck. The market was owned by William Allen Jr.

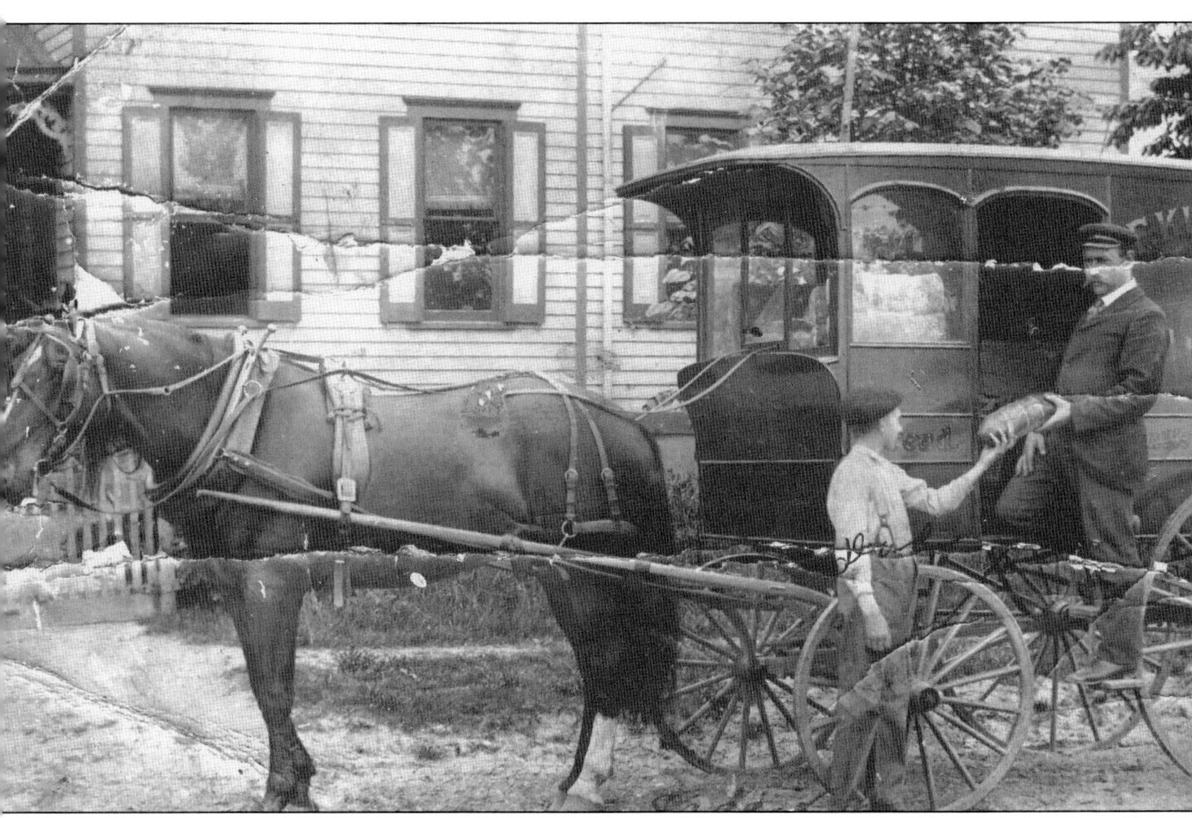

An F. Klein Bakery delivery truck driver makes a delivery to Curt Arnold Sr. at the Arnold family home on Lafayette and Gloucester Avenues.

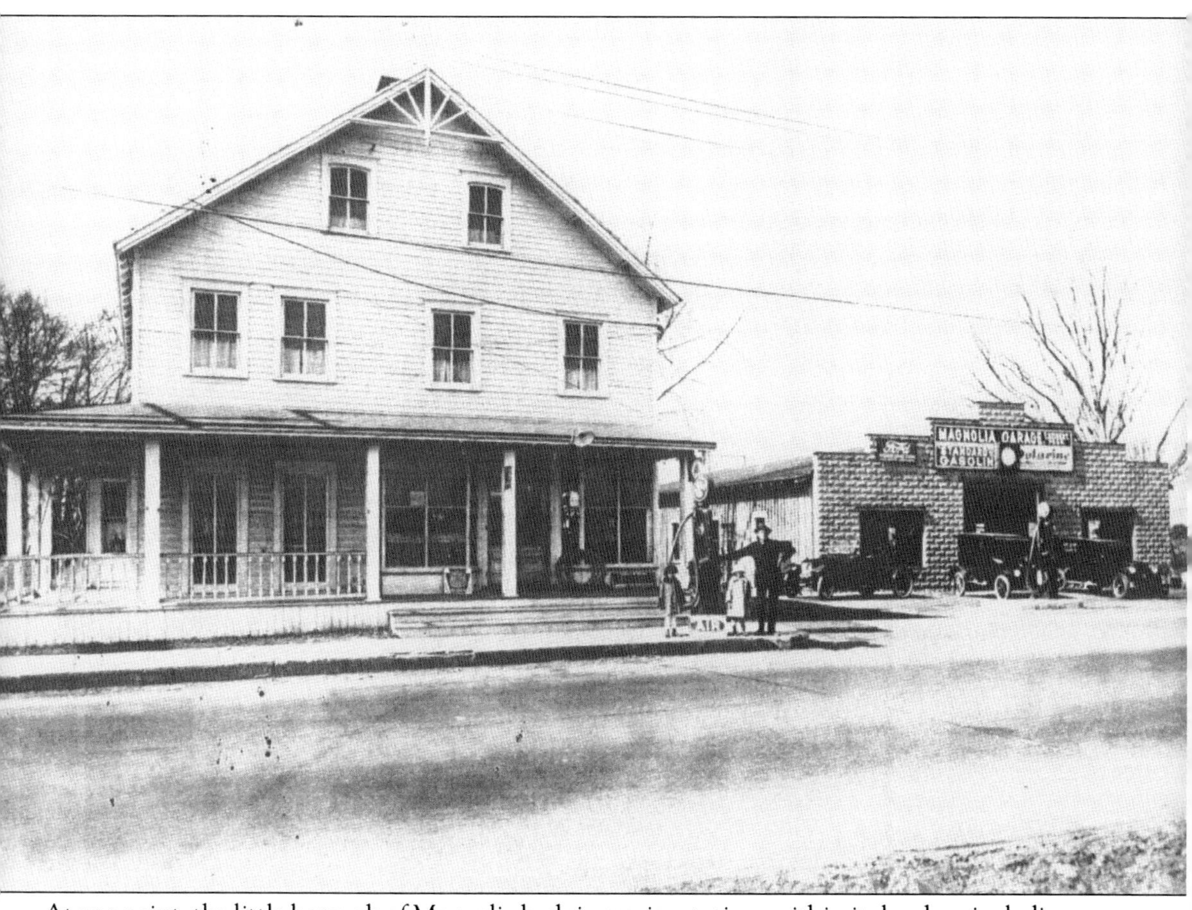

At one point, the little borough of Magnolia had six service stations within its borders, including Reinert's Garage and Store, located on the White Horse Pike, where the police substation and Barrett's store once stood.

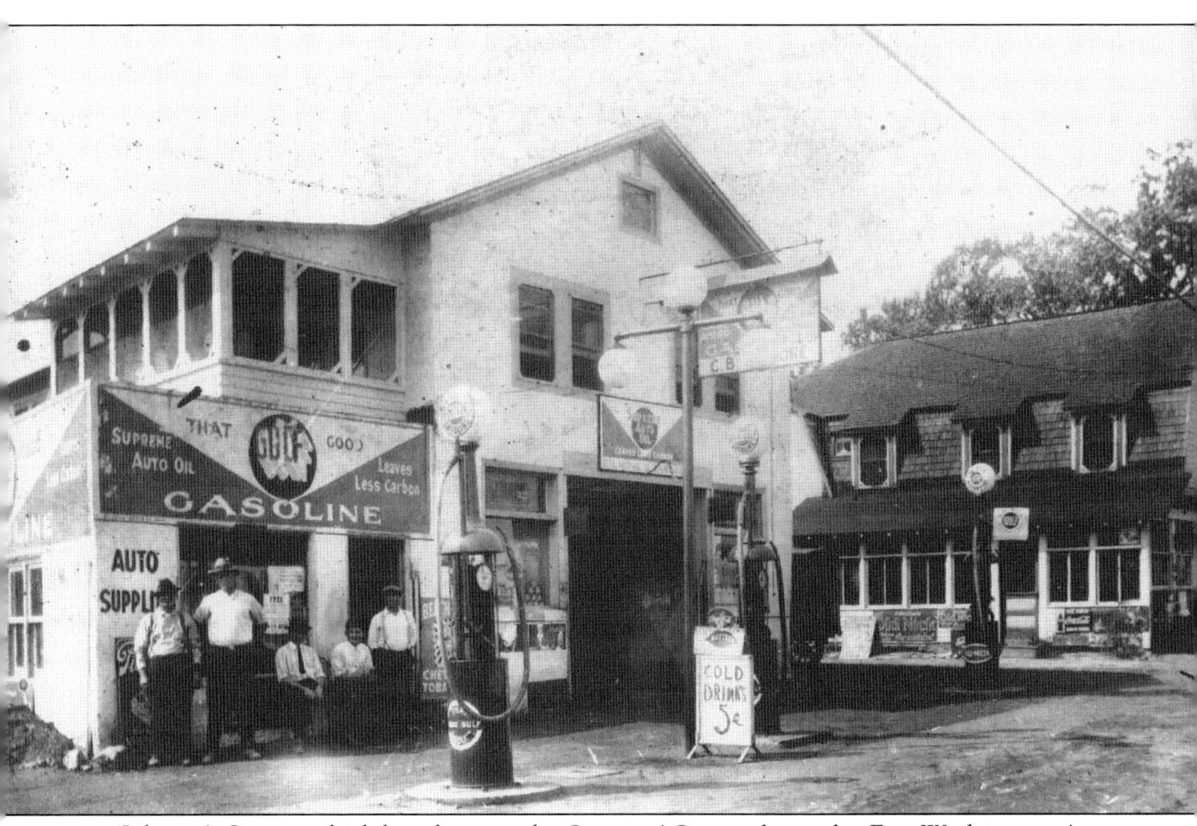

Gilmore's Garage, which later became the Grease n' Go, was located at East Washington Avenue and the White Horse Pike.

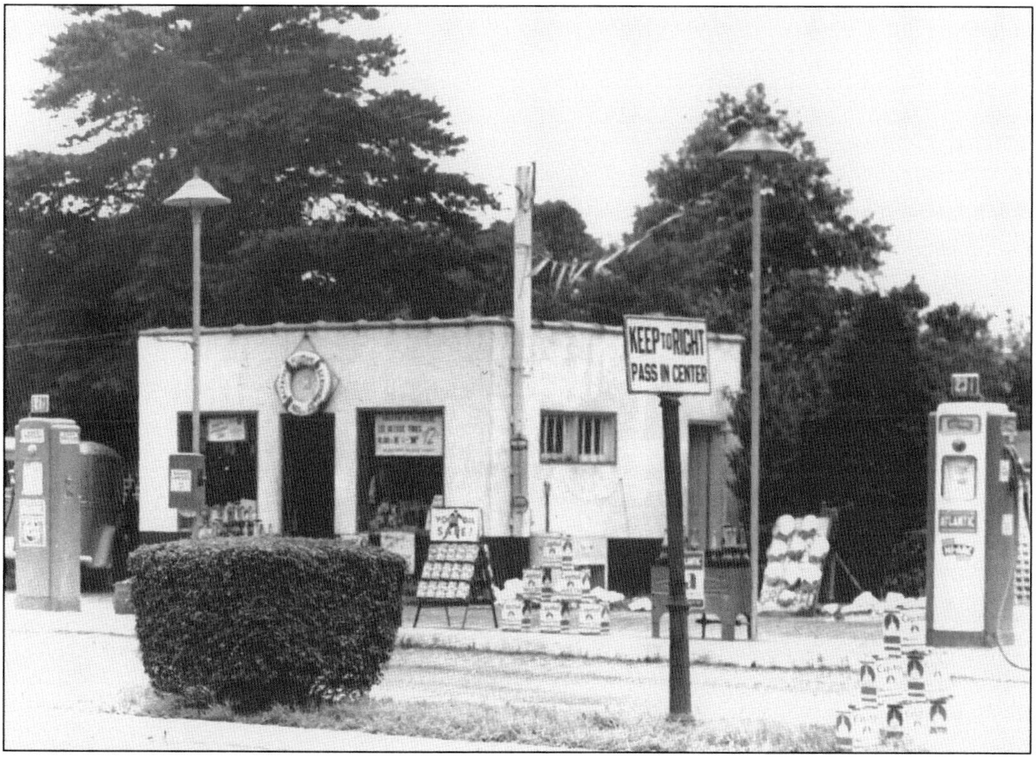

Paulson's Garage, boasting gas at 23¢ per gallon in this 1949 photograph, was located at the White Horse Pike and Monroe Avenue, where the post office now stands.

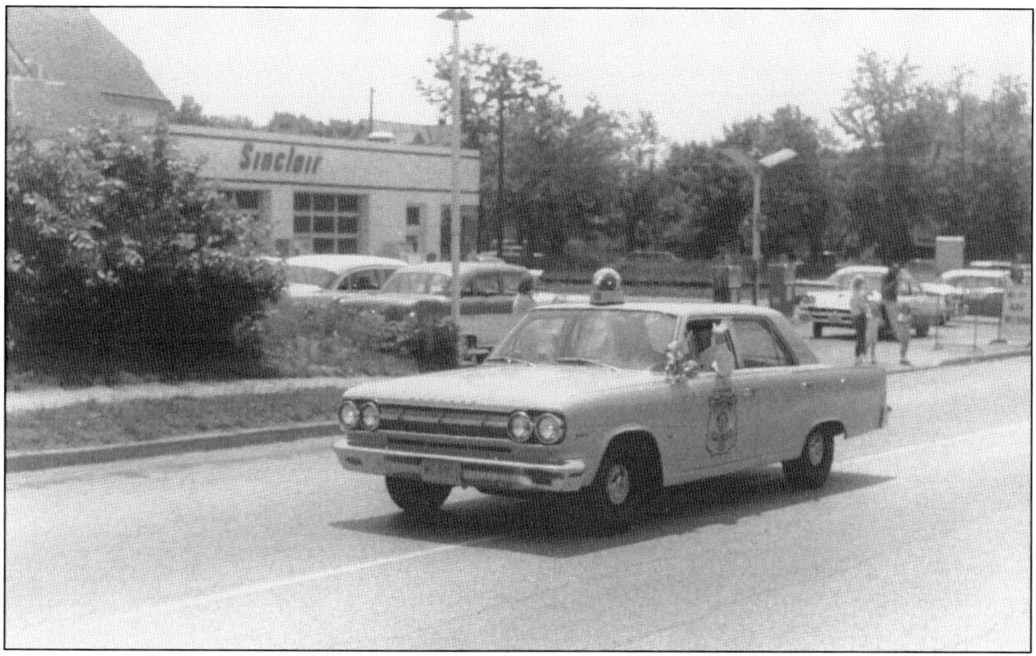

The Sinclair Station was located at Evesham Road and Atlantic Avenue, where Julianno's is presently located.

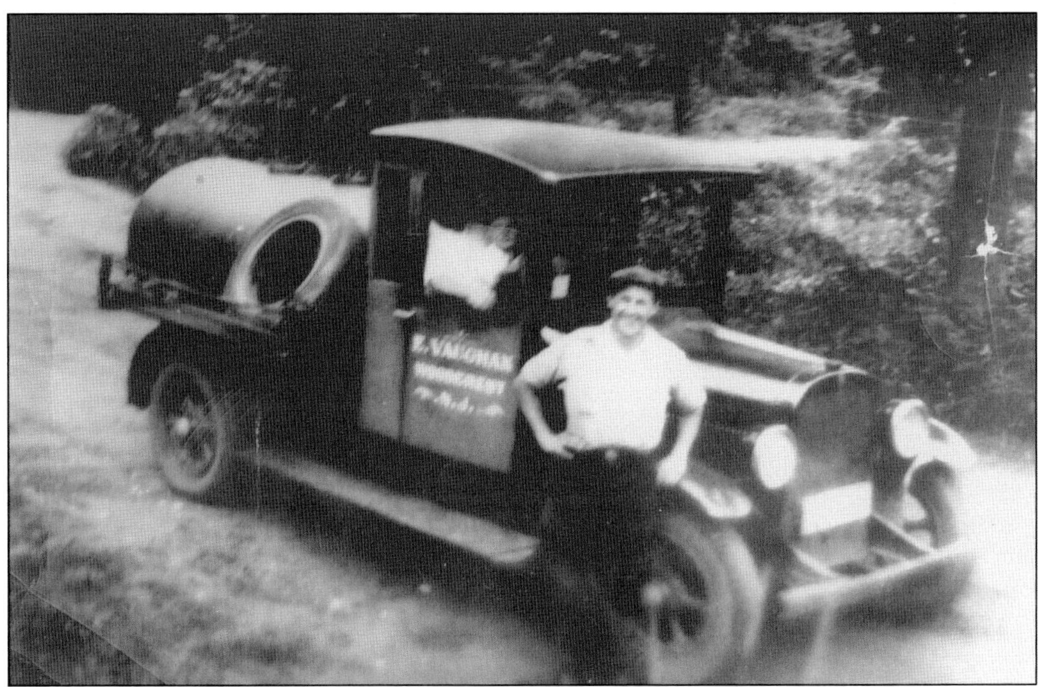

Vaughan Heating and Air Conditioning was founded in 1937 by Elwood Vaughan, who began distributing kerosene to rural South Jersey customers in a used truck and grew the business to include a fleet of service vehicles. The company continues to thrive today, and is Magnolia's longest operating business. Vaughan can be seen in the above, undated photograph with an early company truck. Below a fleet of trucks stands ready for dispatch in front of the company's Barrett Avenue garage.

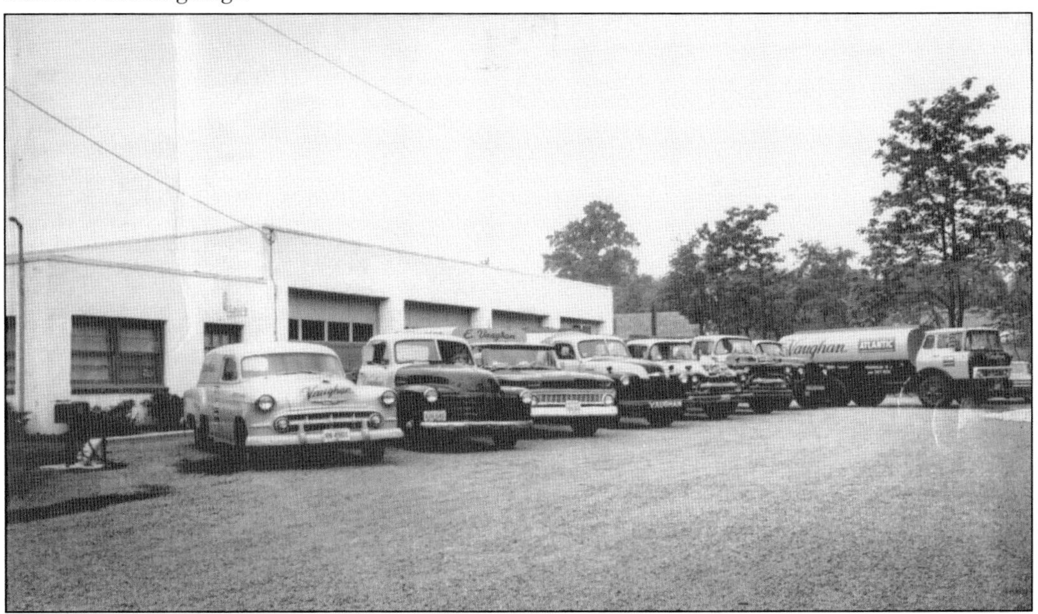

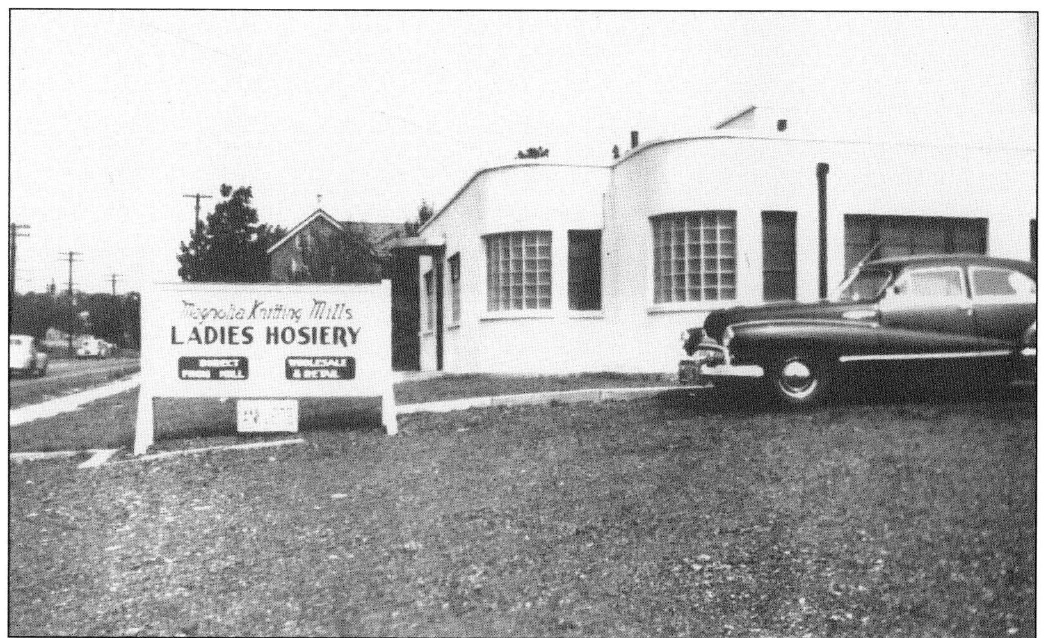

Among the shops that called Magnolia home was the Magnolia Knitting Mills, which originally sold ladies hosiery direct from the mill and then expanded to ladies clothing. Pictured here around 1947, the store was located on the White Horse Pike.

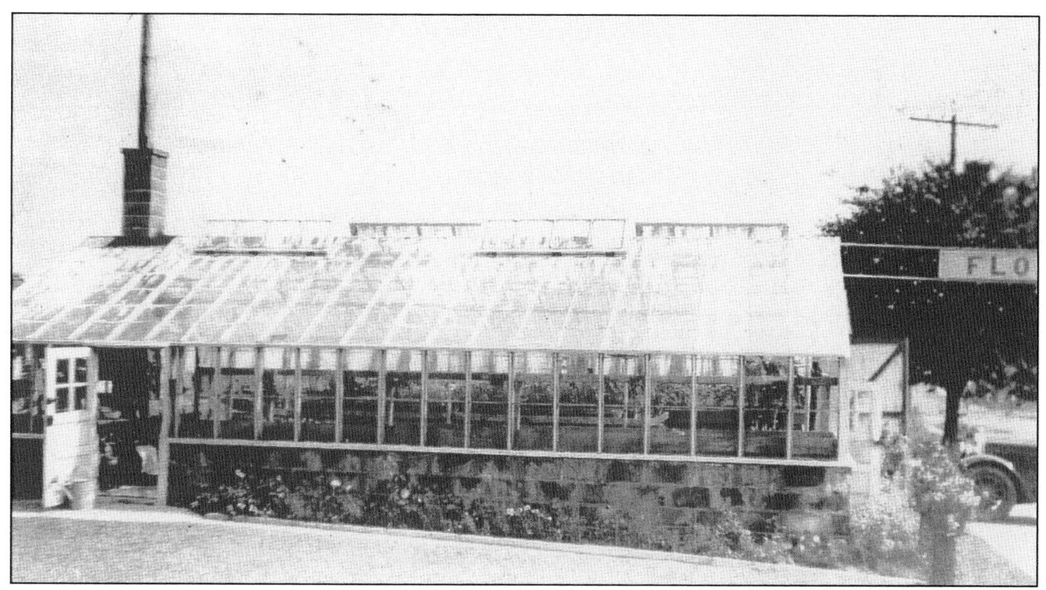

The Fairbanks' greenhouse, pictured here, was located at 336 West Monroe Avenue in 1926.

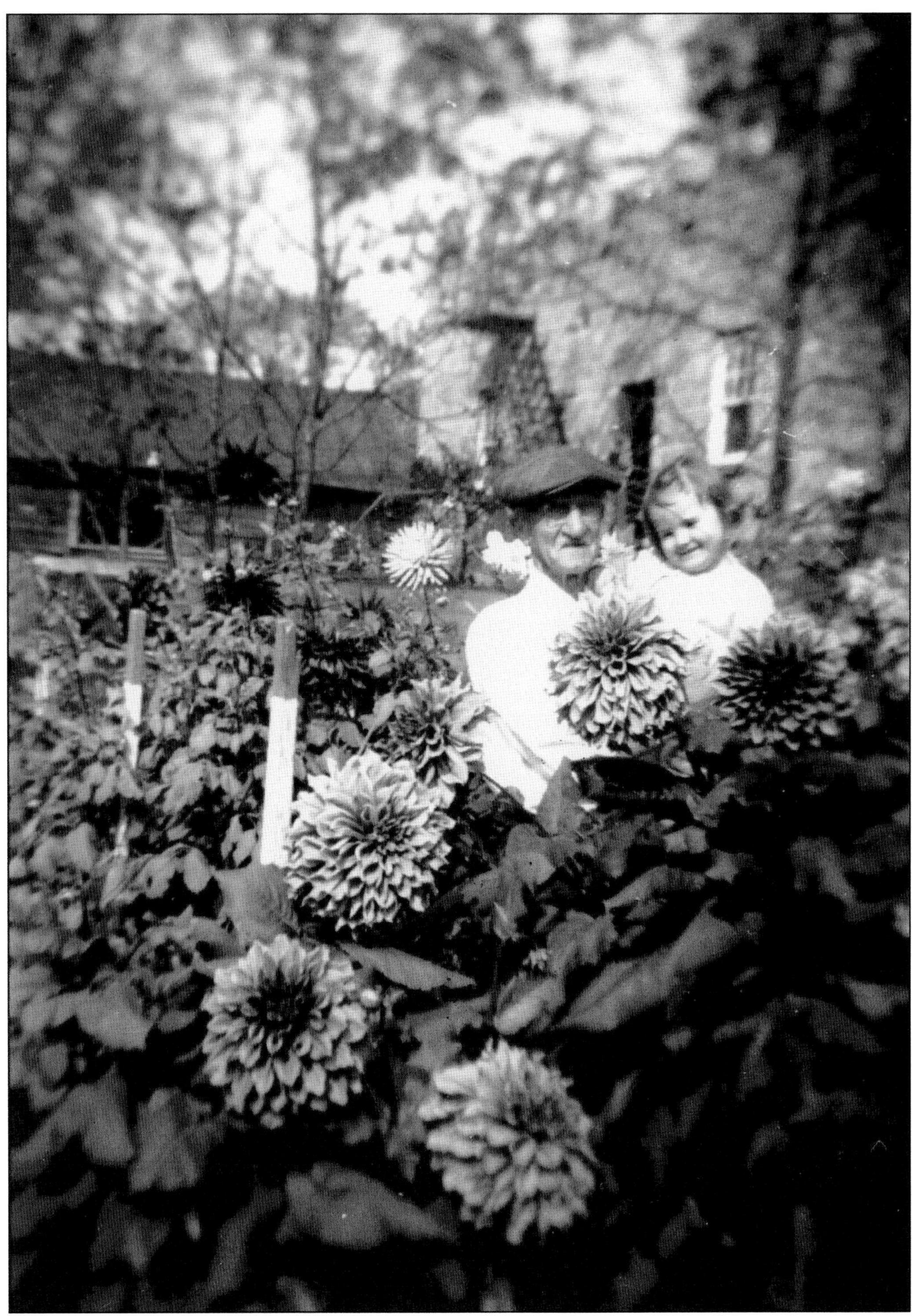

At one time, two nurseries operated in Magnolia. Charles Charmin poses with Frances "Bootsy" Abbott among the flowers at his Evesham Road nursery around 1948.

Five

Sundays and School Days

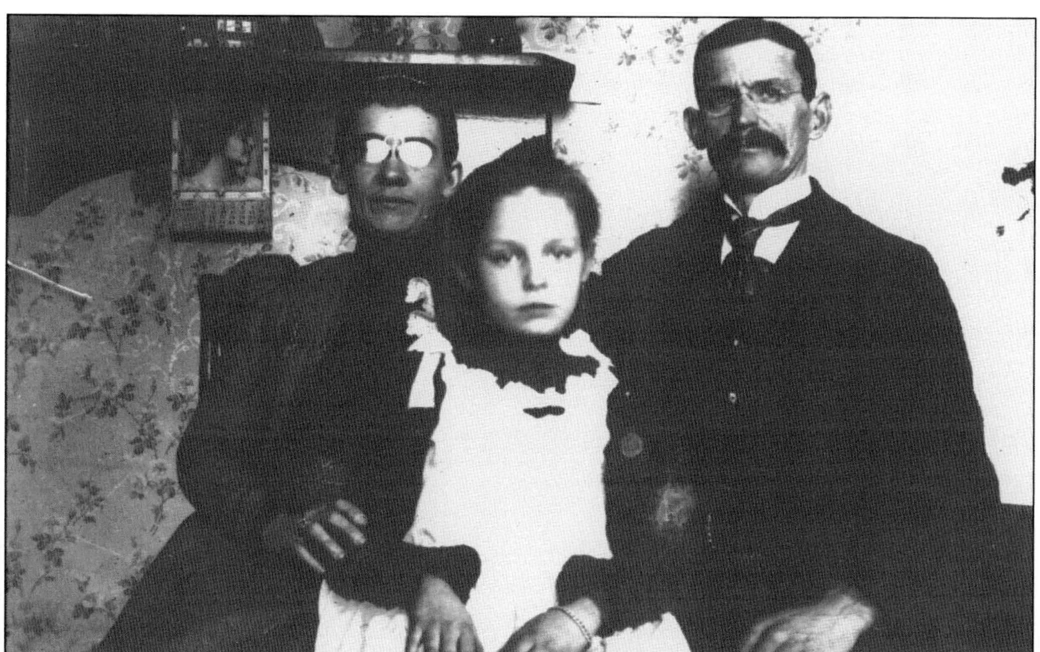

The Thomas Barrett family, pictured here, sold a plot of land for $10 in 1815 for the construction of the Magnolia Methodist Church at Evesham Road and Barrett Avenue. Originally called the Christian Covenant Church of Greenland, the church was founded by seven local residents: Frederick Hines, Jacob Harley, William Jones, Jesse Price, James Chester, Samuel Barrett, and Joseph Webb.

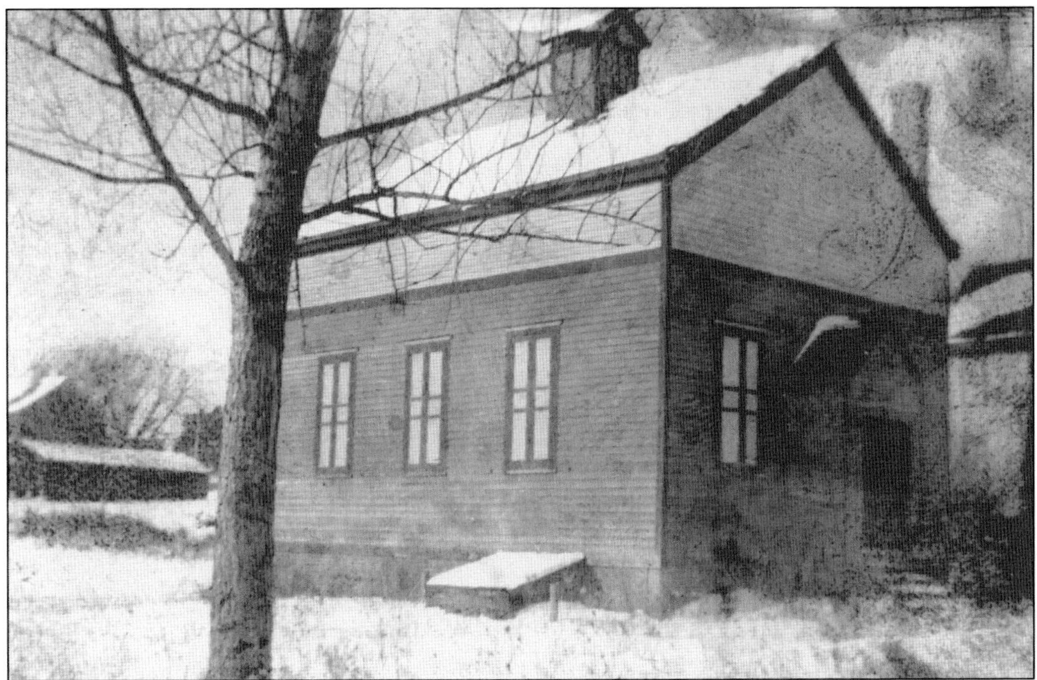

The original Christian Covenant Church of Greenland building was replaced in 1859. Pictured above in the winter of 1895, the church grounds originally included several horse sheds where parishioners parked their horses and wagons during Sunday services. Shown in a more recent photograph, the church holds the distinction of having the only cemetery in the borough and includes the graves of two Civil War veterans.

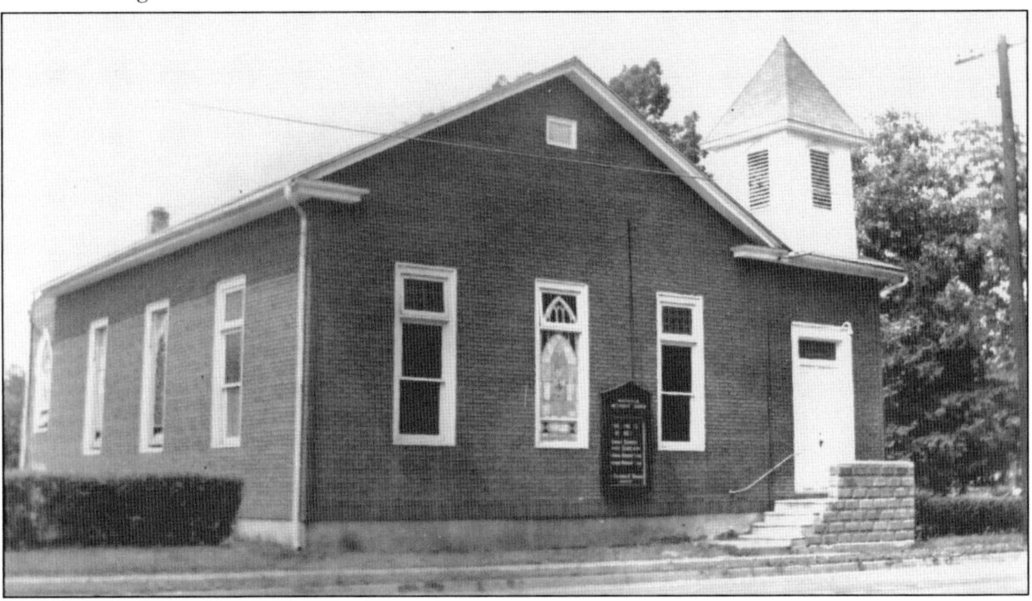

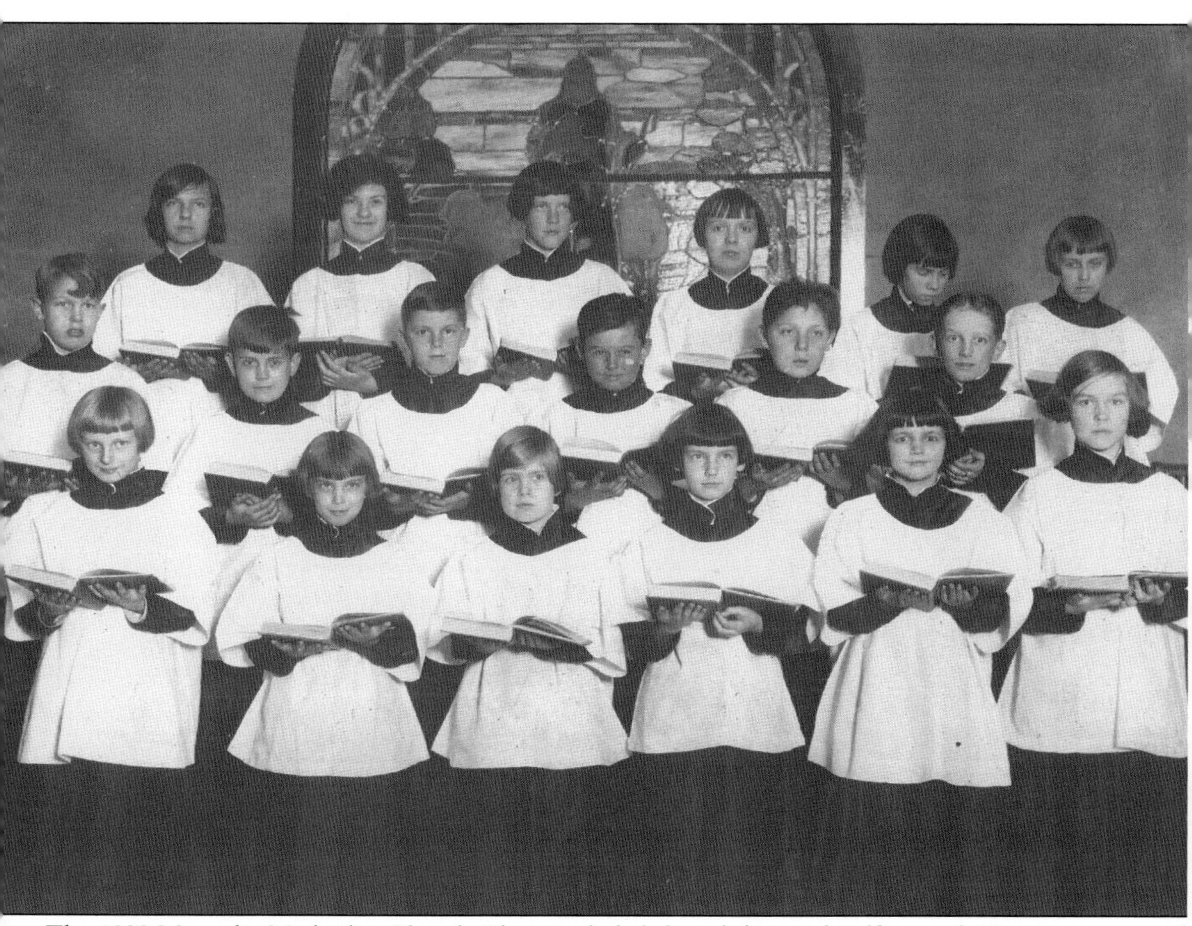

The 1928 Magnolia Methodist Church Choir included, from left to right, (first row) Margaret Cheesman, Dorothy Dean, Mildred Keilley, Nellie Stites, June Lynch, and Marian Hoe; (second row) Billy Price, Billy Rodman, Robert Wilson, Archer Myers, Billy Capie, and Harold Mitten; (third row) Edna Mitter, Carolyn Stites, Marian Morris, Marion Dean, Dorothy Carton, and Mable Lathrope.

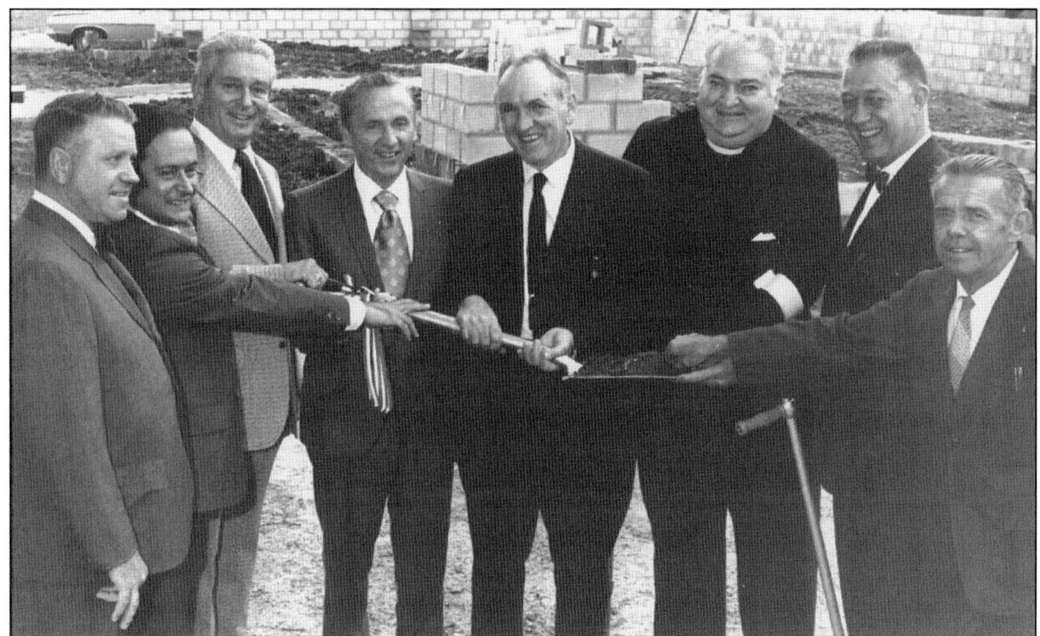

Groundbreaking for the Magnolia Methodist Church Fellowship Hall, on Evesham Road across from the church, took place in 1972. Participating in the ceremony are, from left to right, two unidentified, Mayor Joseph Adolf, congressman John E. Hunt, Charles Wilson, Rev. Sheppard Joslin, congressman Edwin Forsythe, and builder Fred Durst. The hall is used for Sunday school and social events.

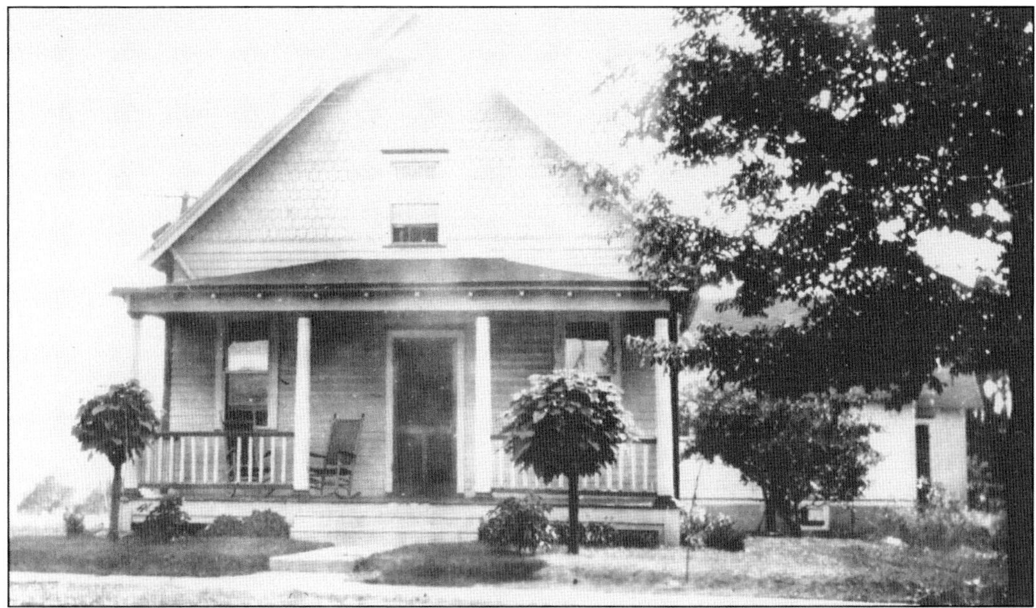

The Holy Trinity Lutheran Church was established in 1893. Members originally met in local homes until this church was constructed at Warwick Road and Washington Avenue in 1894. As the congregation grew, the church relocated. The original building, pictured here, was converted into a private home and was torn down in 2006 to make way for a parking lot for the South Jersey Christian Church.

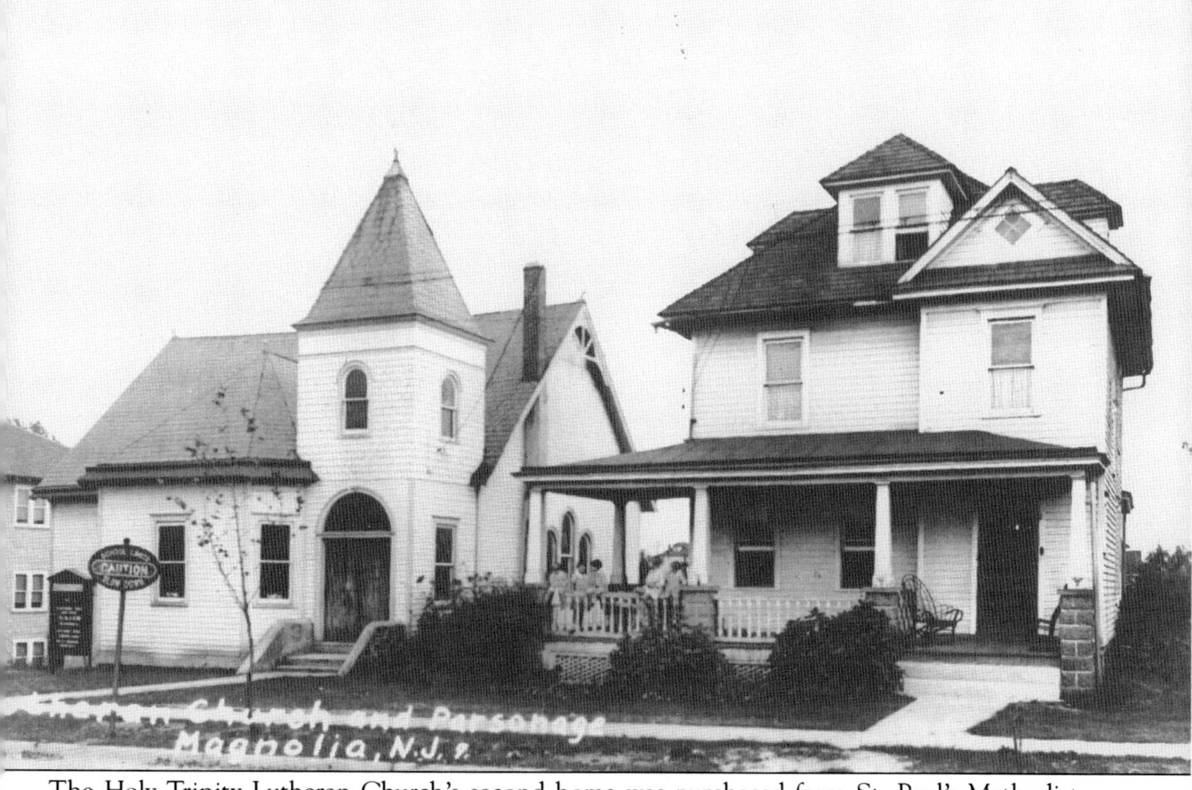

The Holy Trinity Lutheran Church's second home was purchased from St. Paul's Methodist Protestant Congregation in 1915, and the house next door was purchased the following year as the parsonage. In 1943, the church, which stood where a portion of the firehouse now stands, was renamed Holy Trinity Evangelical Lutheran Church. Later it was sold to Community Gospel Church, and in the 1960s burned to the ground following a lightning strike. The parsonage remains a private home.

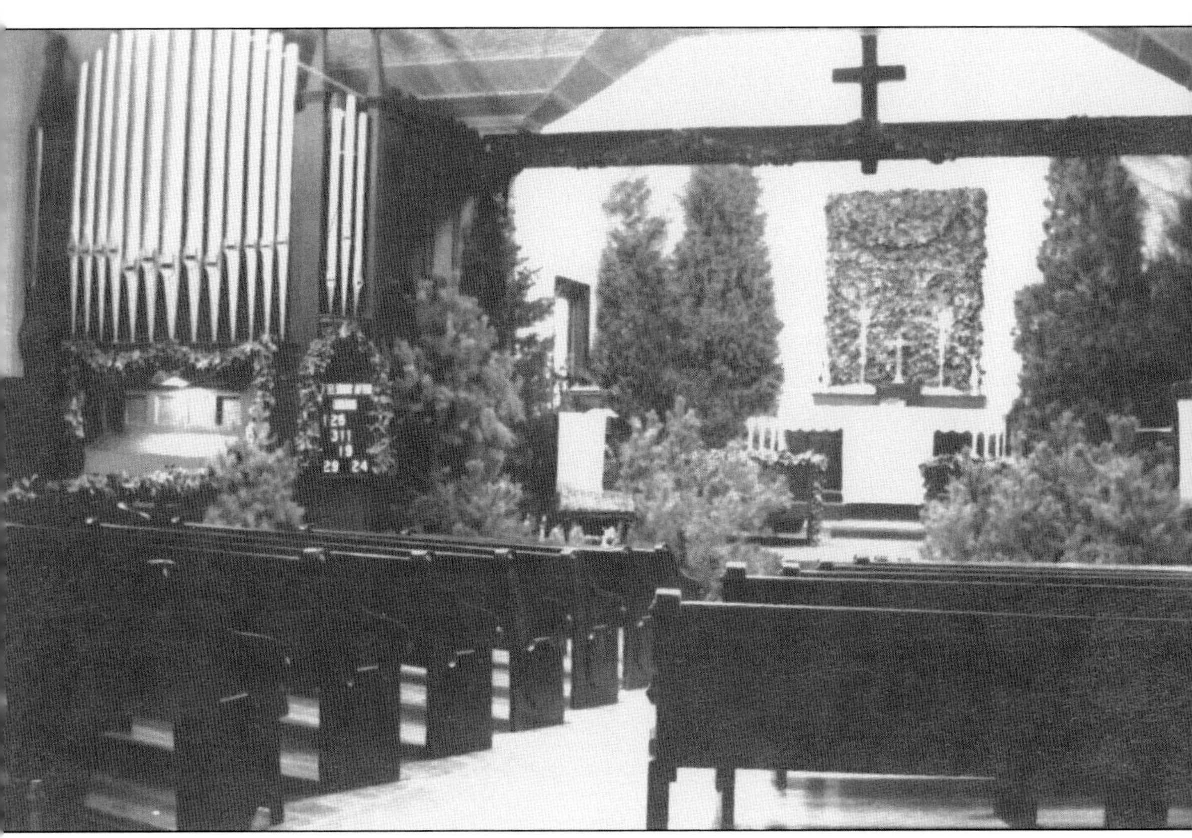

The interior of the Holy Trinity Lutheran Church was decorated with evergreens for Christmas in 1939.

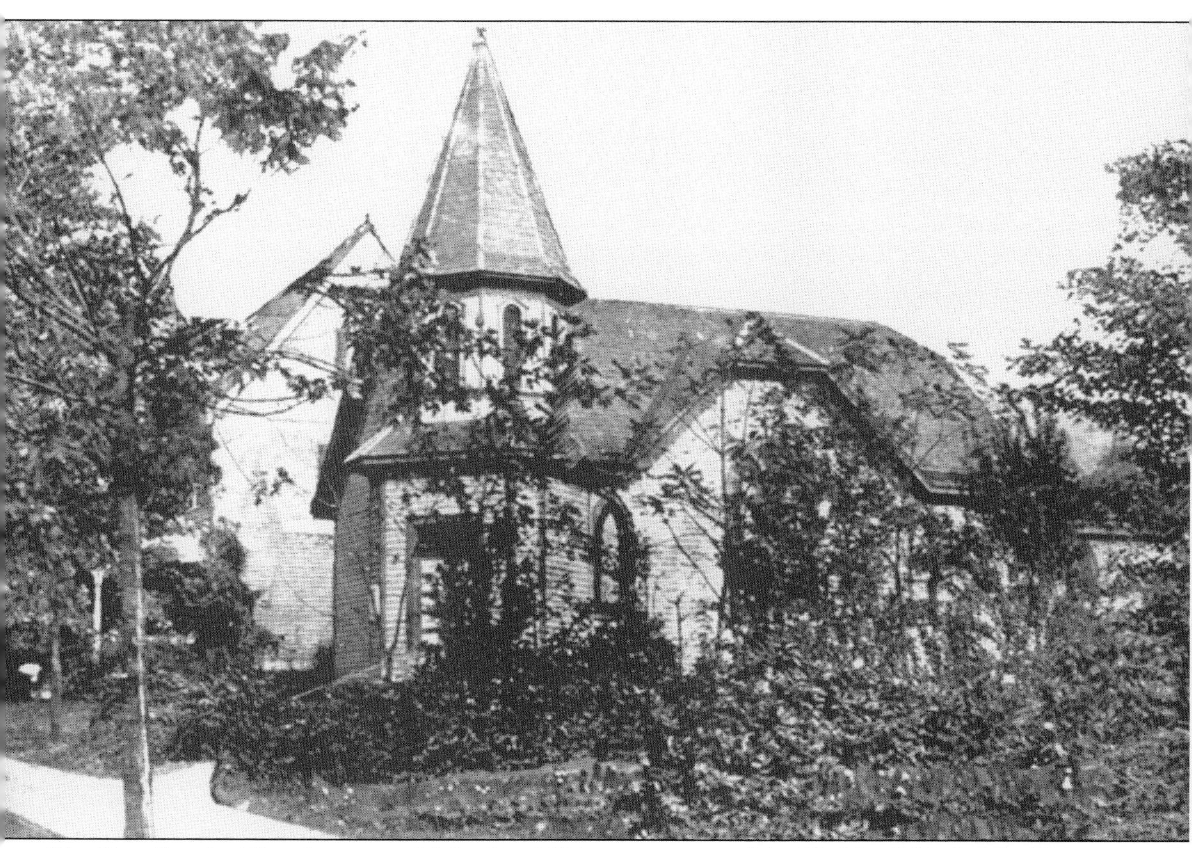

The First Baptist Church was established in 1894 as a mission of the Haddonfield church. The chapel, located on Evesham Road and Camden Avenue, was built for $2,500 under the direction of founding members Frank and Martha Till; Henry, Albert, May and Fannie Charman; Kate Webb; Anna Fougerry; Eliza Clark; and Susie Fish. In 1922, the house of worship was moved on flatbed truck down Camden Avenue to its new home in the 200 block of Lincoln Avenue, where it remains today. Along the way, parishioners held Sunday services by lantern light before the building was settled onto its new foundation. The cost to move the church and dig a new cellar was $750.

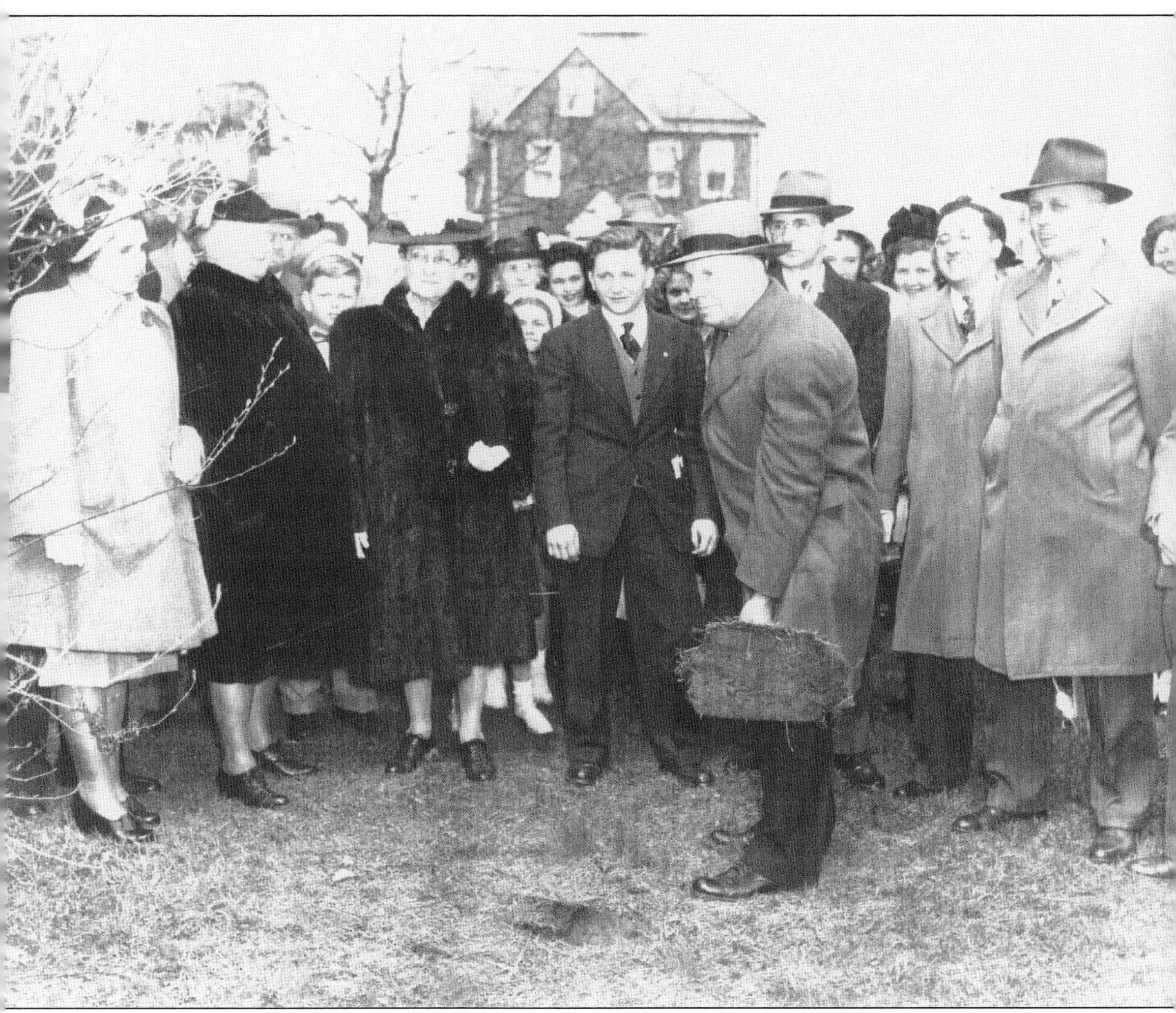

Years later, as the congregation grew, the First Baptist Church built an addition to the original chapel. Dedicated as the Baker Memorial, this undated photograph shows the groundbreaking ceremony.

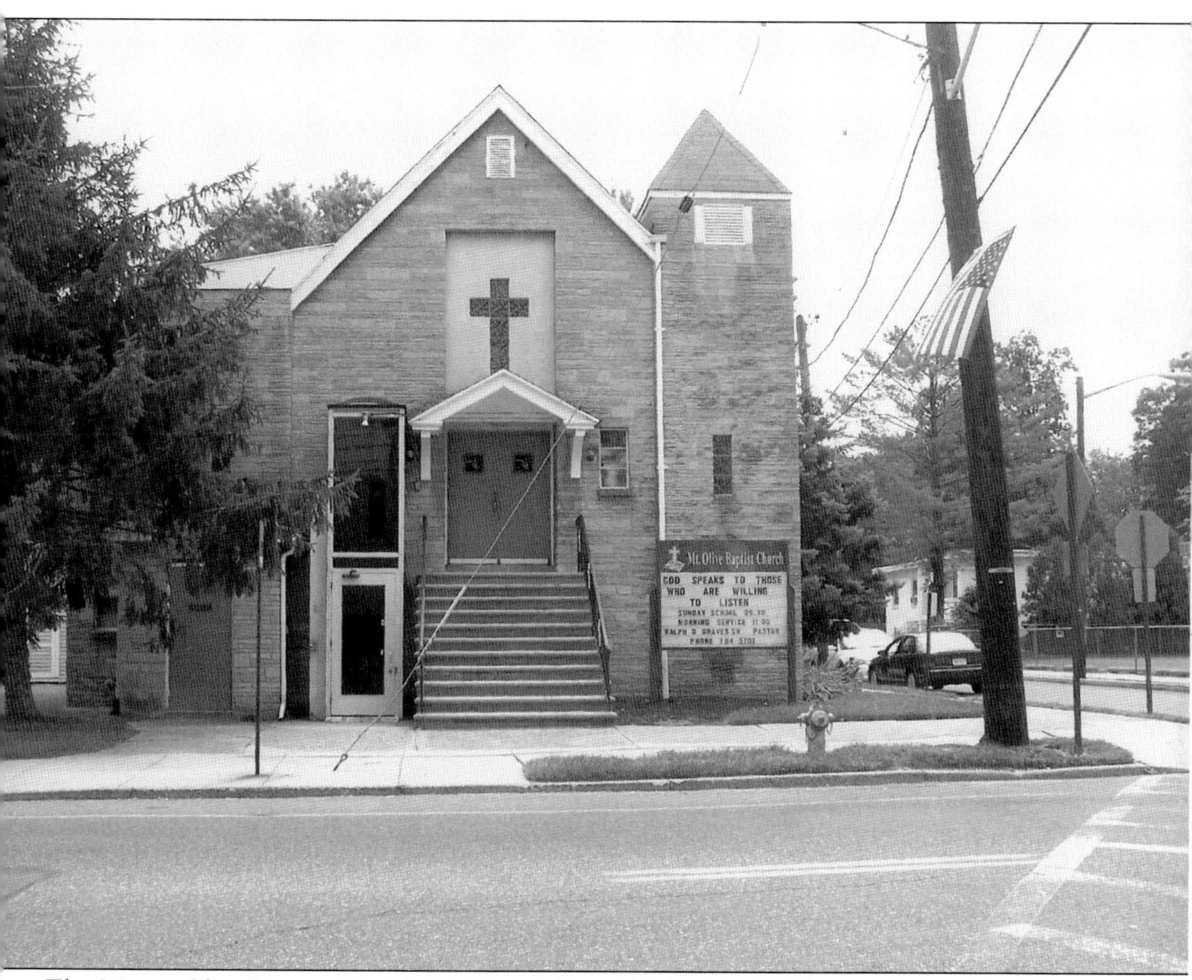

The Mount Olive Baptist Church was originally established as a mission church on Evesham Road by six local families. The founders included the Jordan, Wilson, Chase, Lamett, and Marold families and George Barber.

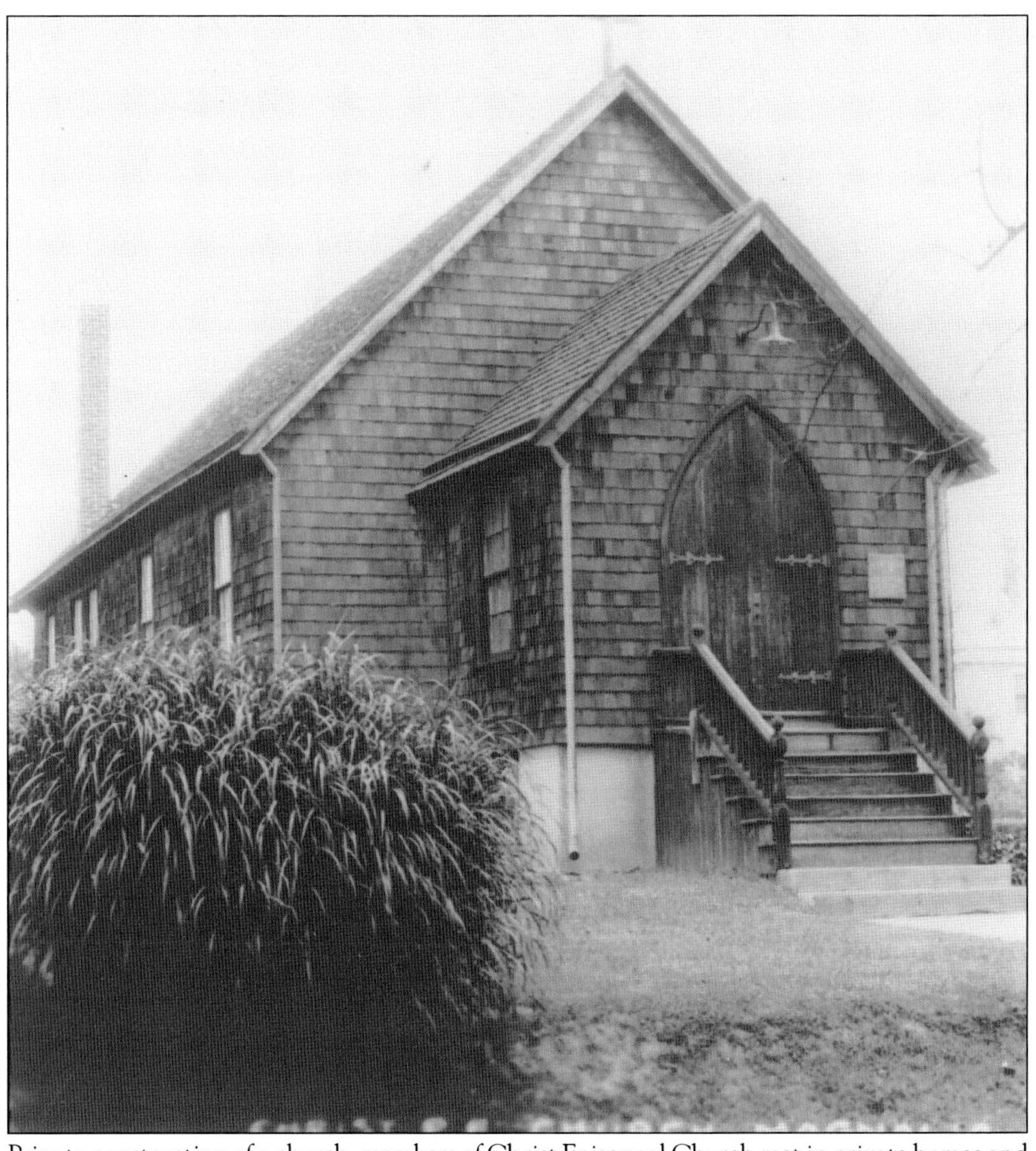

Prior to construction of a church, members of Christ Episcopal Church met in private homes and the firehouse. The church, built in 1914, stands in the 400 block of Evesham Road. Parishioners built an addition to the building in the 1970s.

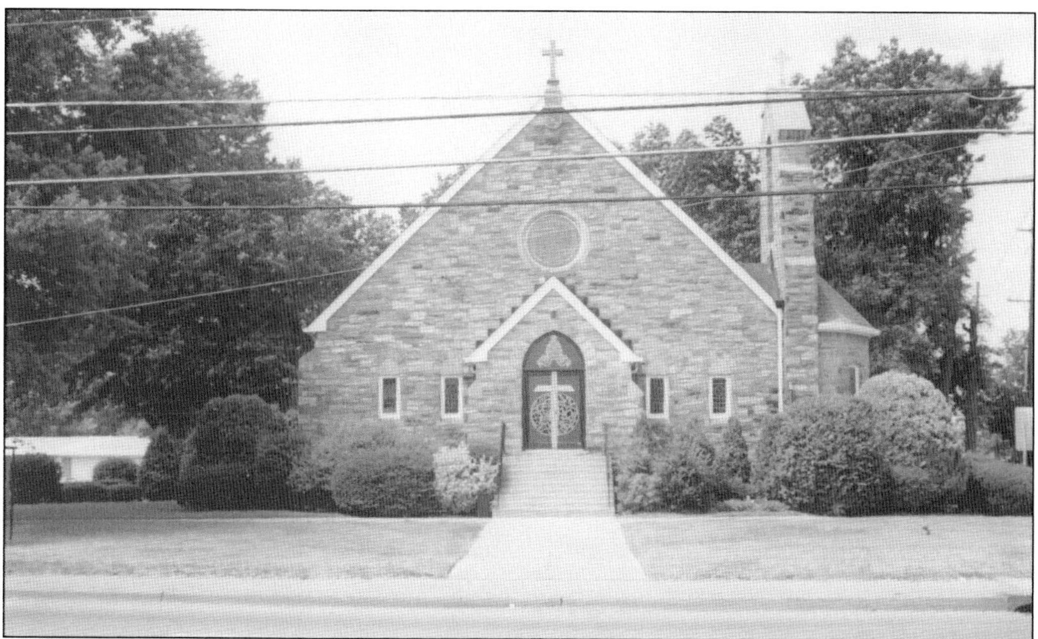

St. Gregory's Catholic Church was constructed in 1951, on land once owned by Magnolia resident Susie Fish, as a mission to St. Rose of Lima in Haddon Heights. An estimated 20 families registered to attend the first mass in the Evesham Road church. In 1953, the rectory was constructed and the mission became a parish.

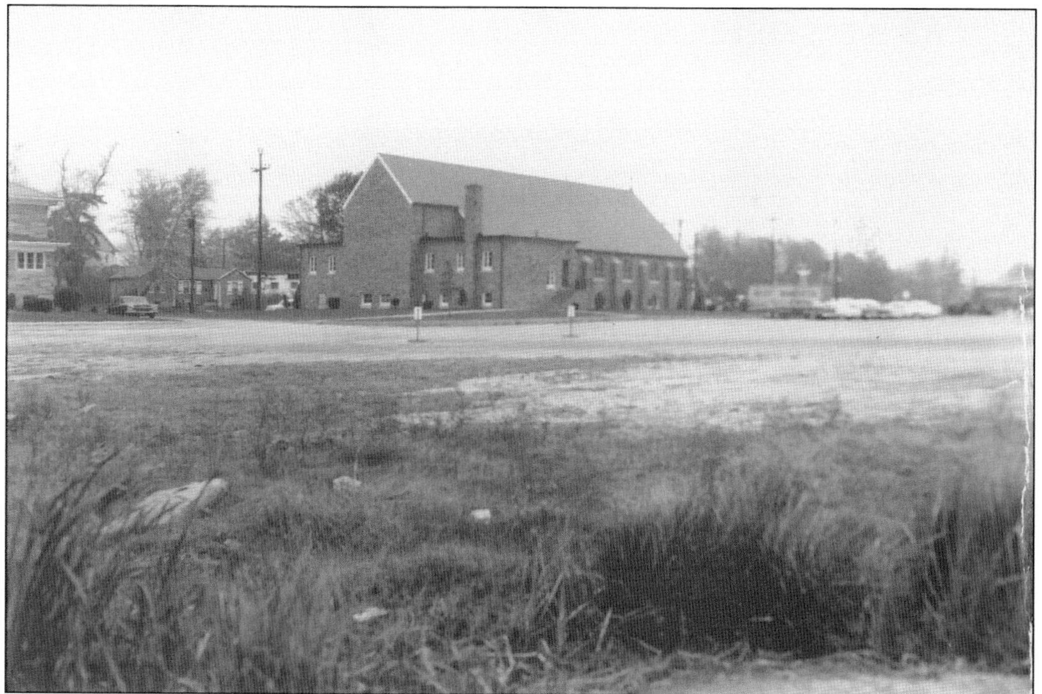

This view of St. Gregory's Catholic Church property shows the grounds before construction of the parish school, looking toward the White Horse Pike. Groundbreaking for St. Gregory's School took place in 1963.

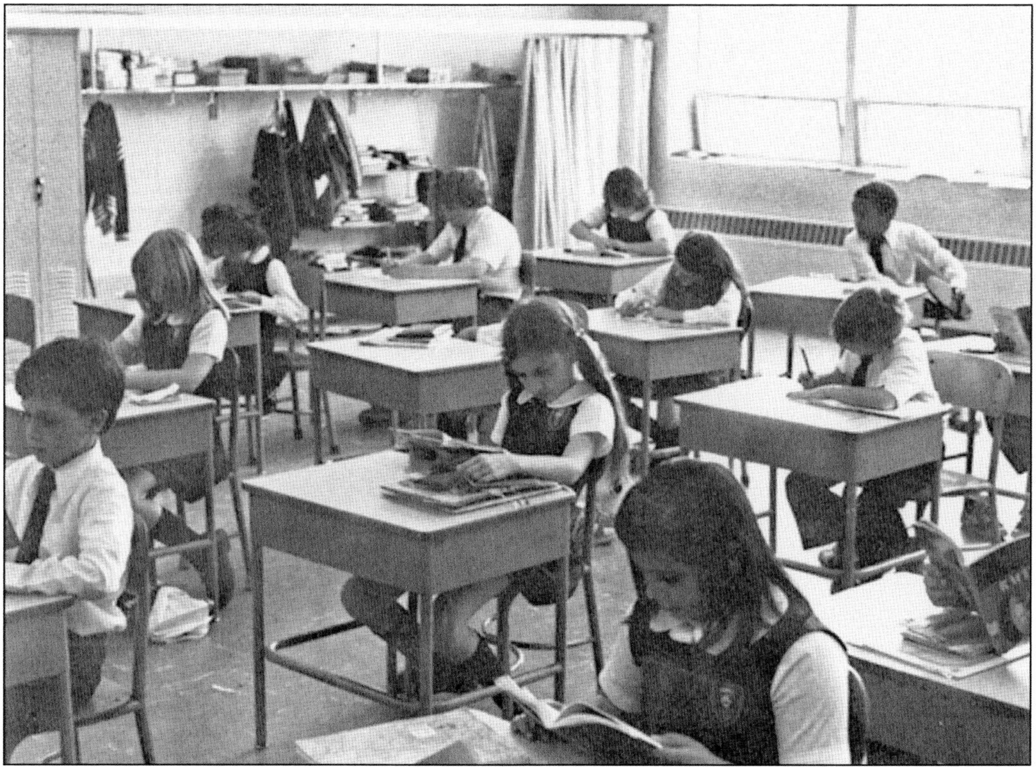

The decision to construct a parish school was linked to community support for a parochial school within the borough and a local fund-raising drive helped support the project. The eight-room school opened with six grades in 1963, and a new class was added annually until the school reached capacity. Pictured above is an unidentified classroom; below are members of the St. Gregory's School PTA. St. Gregory's School closed its doors in 1981.

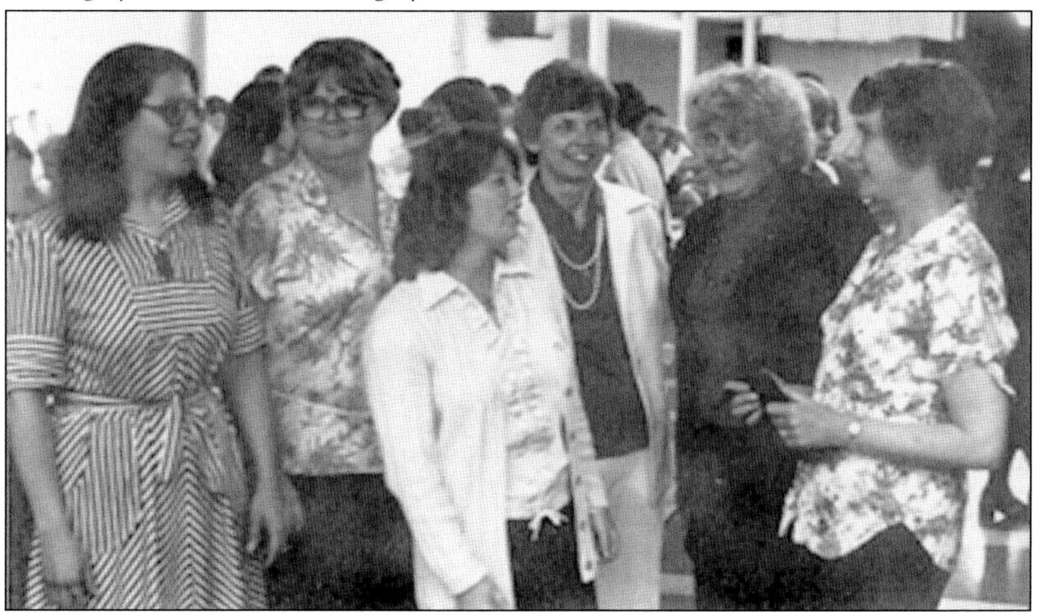

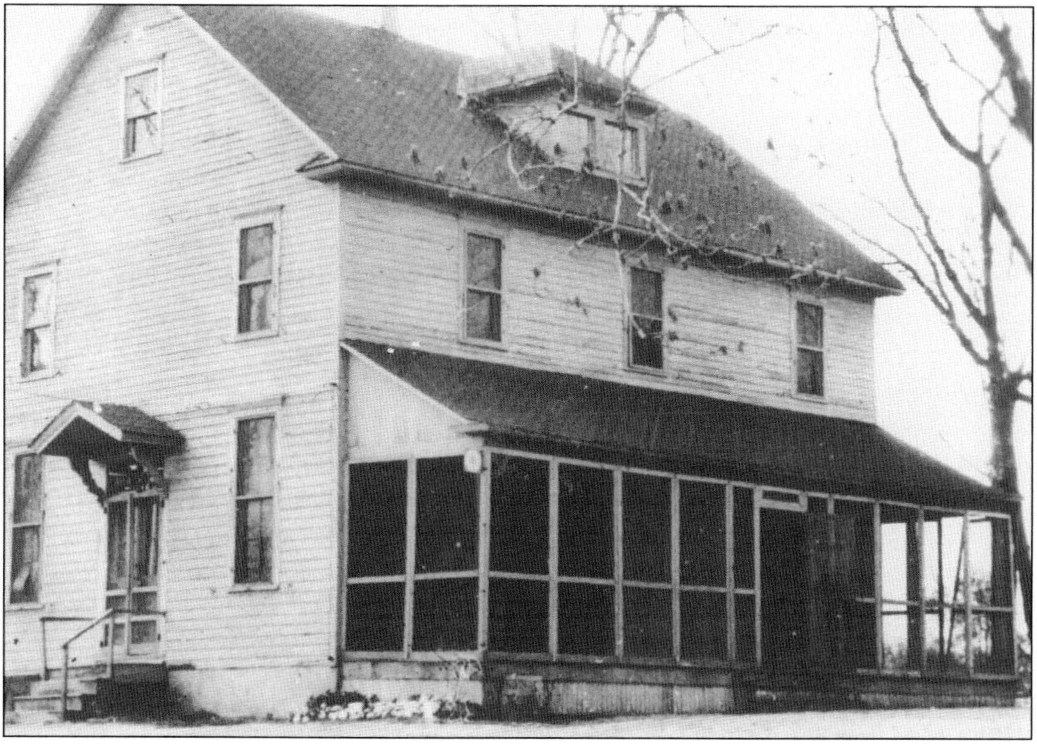

The Greenland School, built in 1855 on Davis Road in what is now Lawnside, accepted students from Audubon to Ashland. The one-room schoolhouse, located where the Acorn Inn later stood, was organized as a result of the New Jersey legislature's ruling, in 1851, that taxes would be collected throughout the state to fund public education.

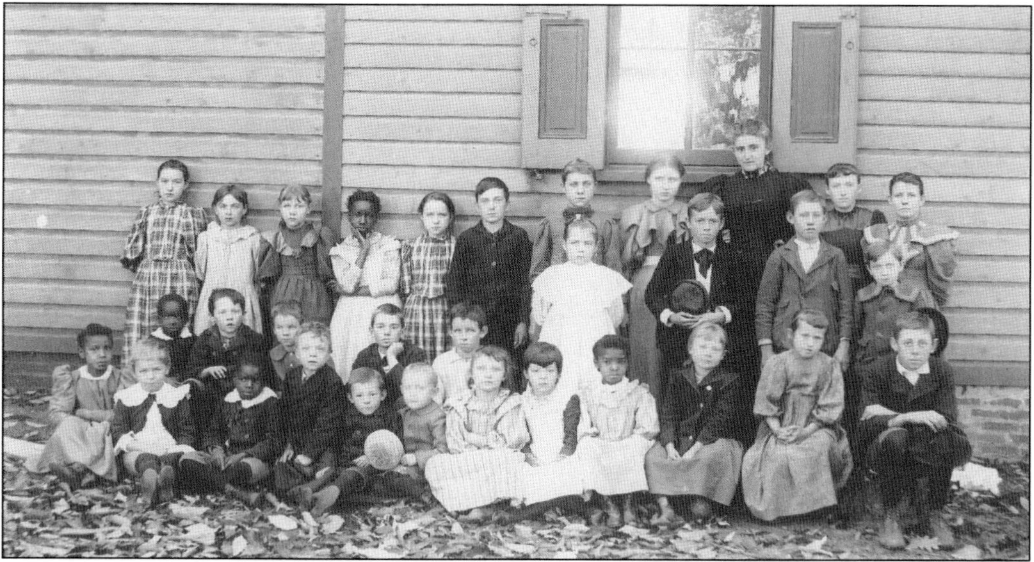

The Greenland School's first class included Lena Buckner (standing to the left of the teacher). Before the schoolhouse was constructed, local Quakers sponsored classes for rich and poor children in the Albertson home. Later a small schoolhouse stood on Evesham Road, where St. Gregory's Catholic Church now stands.

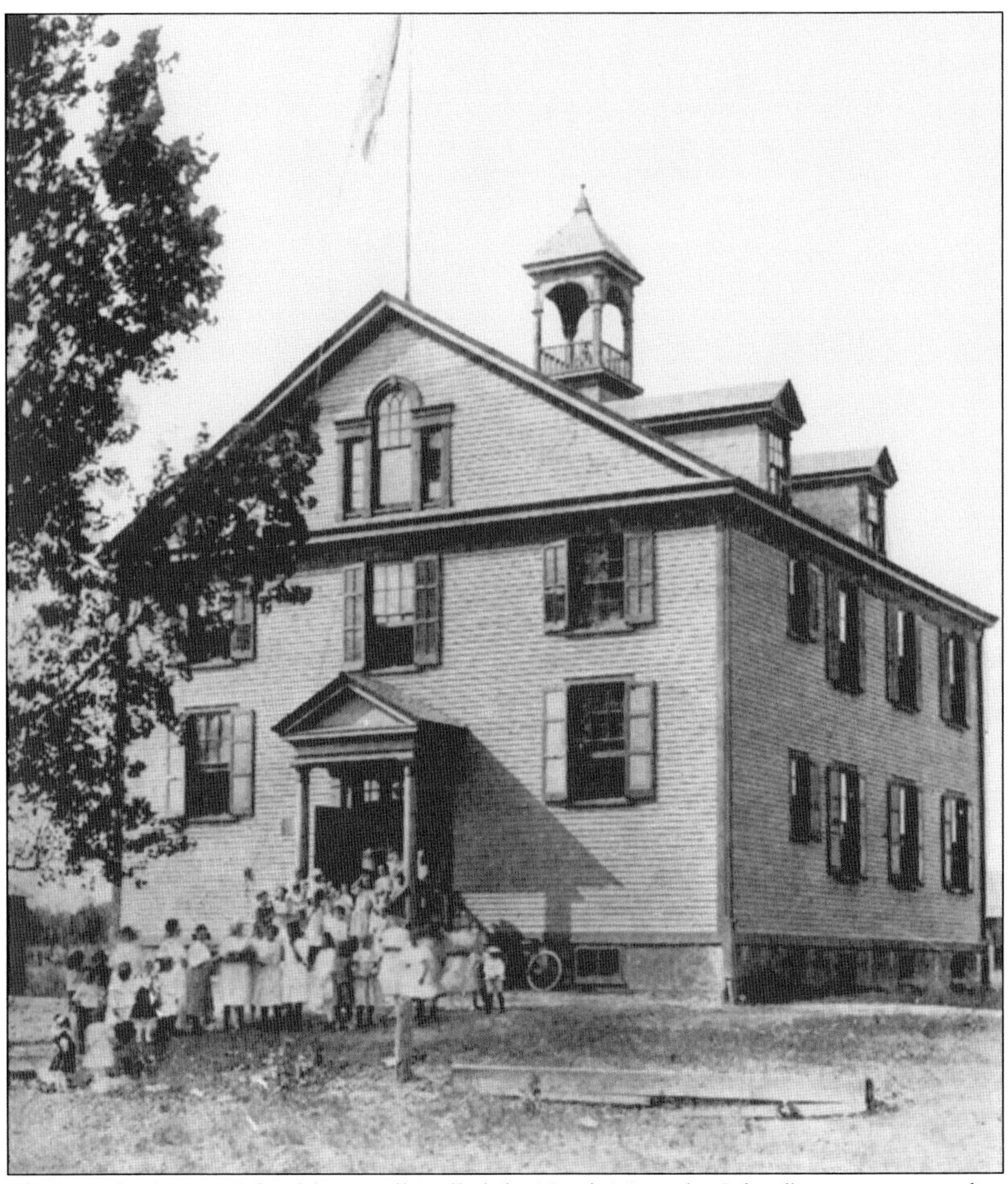

The Lincoln Avenue School (originally called the North Magnolia School) was constructed in 1894 and initially served students who lived on the north side of Evesham Road. Once Magnolia was incorporated, the school served the entire borough, from grades 1 through 4.

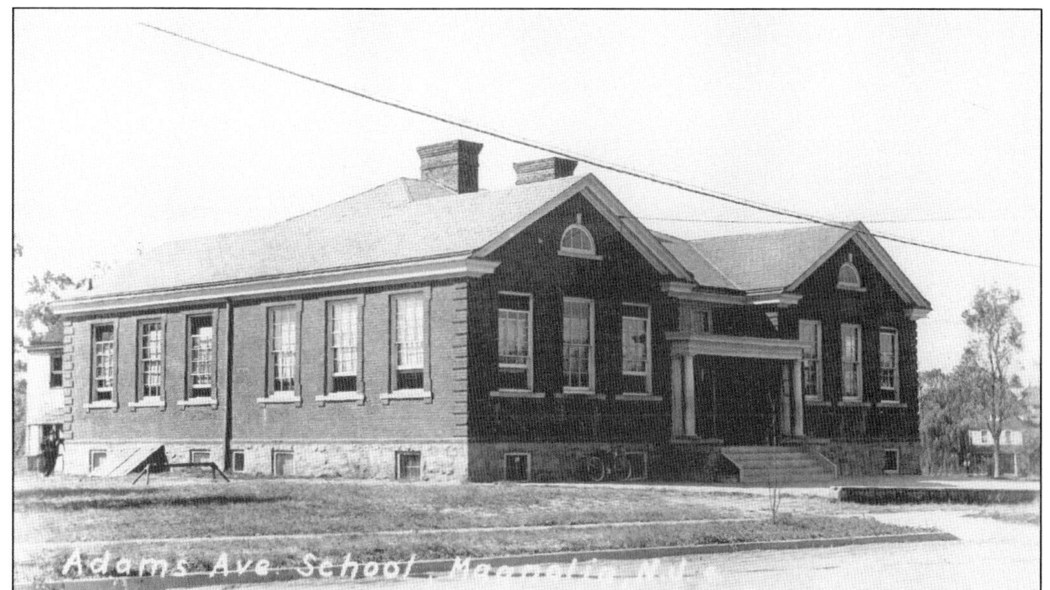

The Adams Avenue School was constructed around 1910 on Warwick Road and served the students on the south side of Evesham Road. Following Magnolia's incorporation, the school served students in grades 5 through 8.

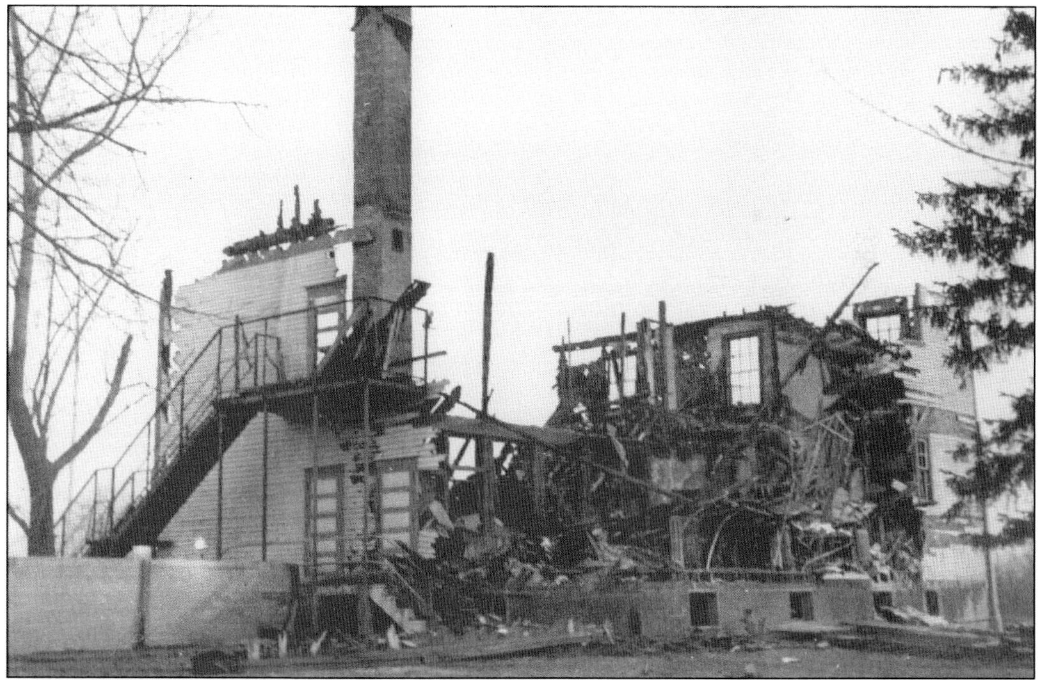

The Lincoln Avenue School burned to the ground on December 13, 1937. Although plans were already underway for the construction of a larger, eight-room schoolhouse, as a result of the fire the school's students were temporary relocated to the Adams Avenue School, and classes were staggered to accommodate the increased population.

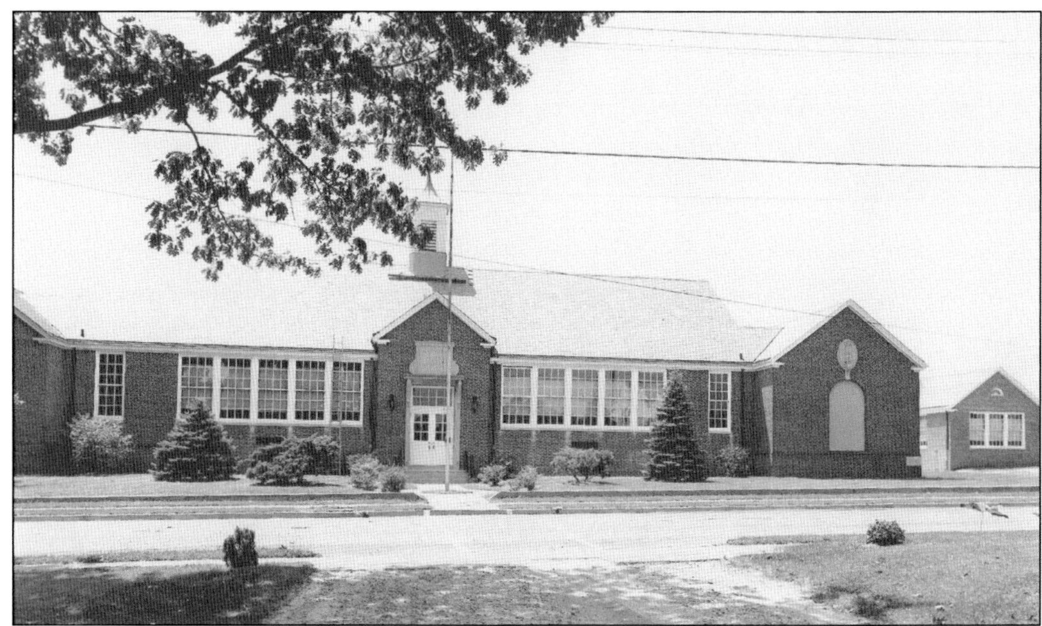

Construction of the new Lincoln Avenue School was completed in 1938, for $70,000. Just 14 years later, four classrooms were added; five years later, in 1957, another 10 classrooms and several offices were constructed. Before students moved into the addition, the school was already overcrowded, and the First Baptist Church rented classroom and auditorium space to the district. Following 17 years of split sessions, eight more classrooms were added in 1968.

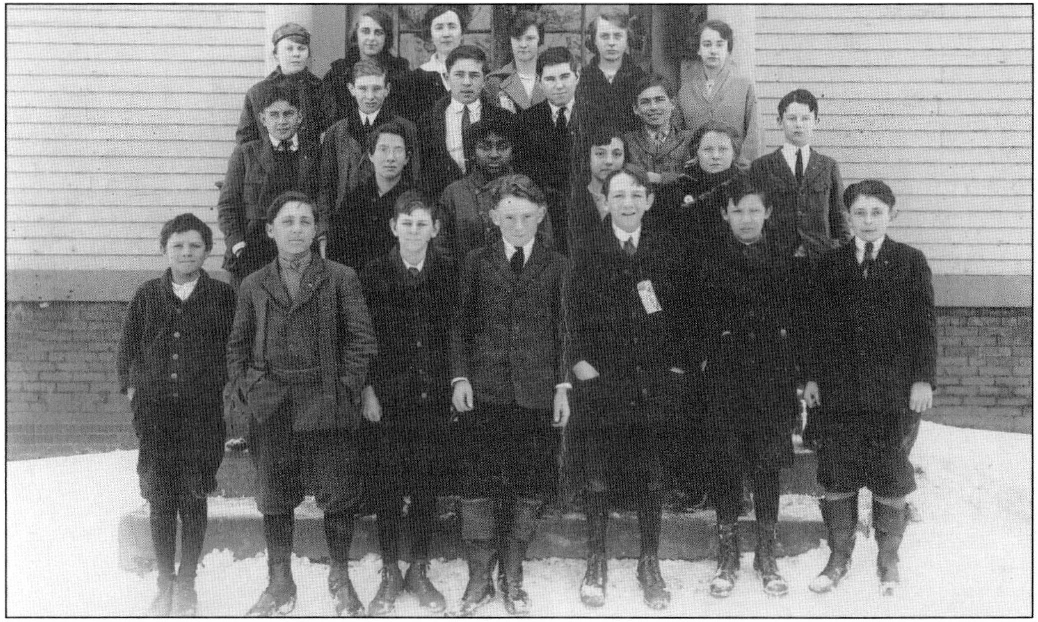

Lincoln Avenue School's 1917 eighth grade graduation class, the second commencement class following the borough's incorporation, included, in no particular order, Marjorie Graham, Mildred Kelly, Walter Hall, Frank Rush, Thomas Mezger, James Finley, Theodosia Walklett, Nellie Rea, Mabel Manigault, John Graham, Charles Watson, Edward Duffield, Edward MacDowell, Nathan Sweeten, and Raymond Pennypacker.

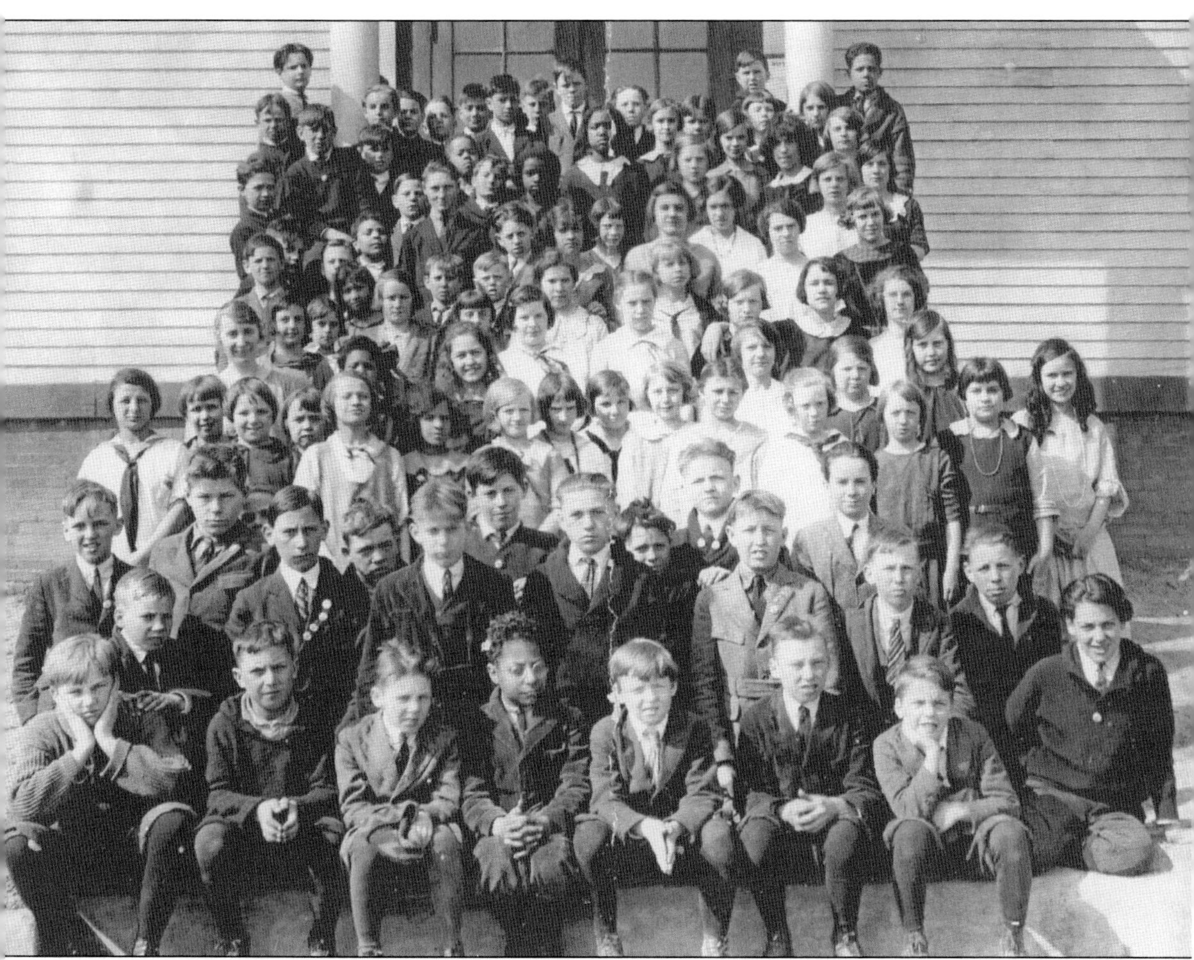

In 1924, Lincoln Avenue School served children in first through fourth grades. The entire school assembled on the two-story schoolhouse's front steps for this photograph.

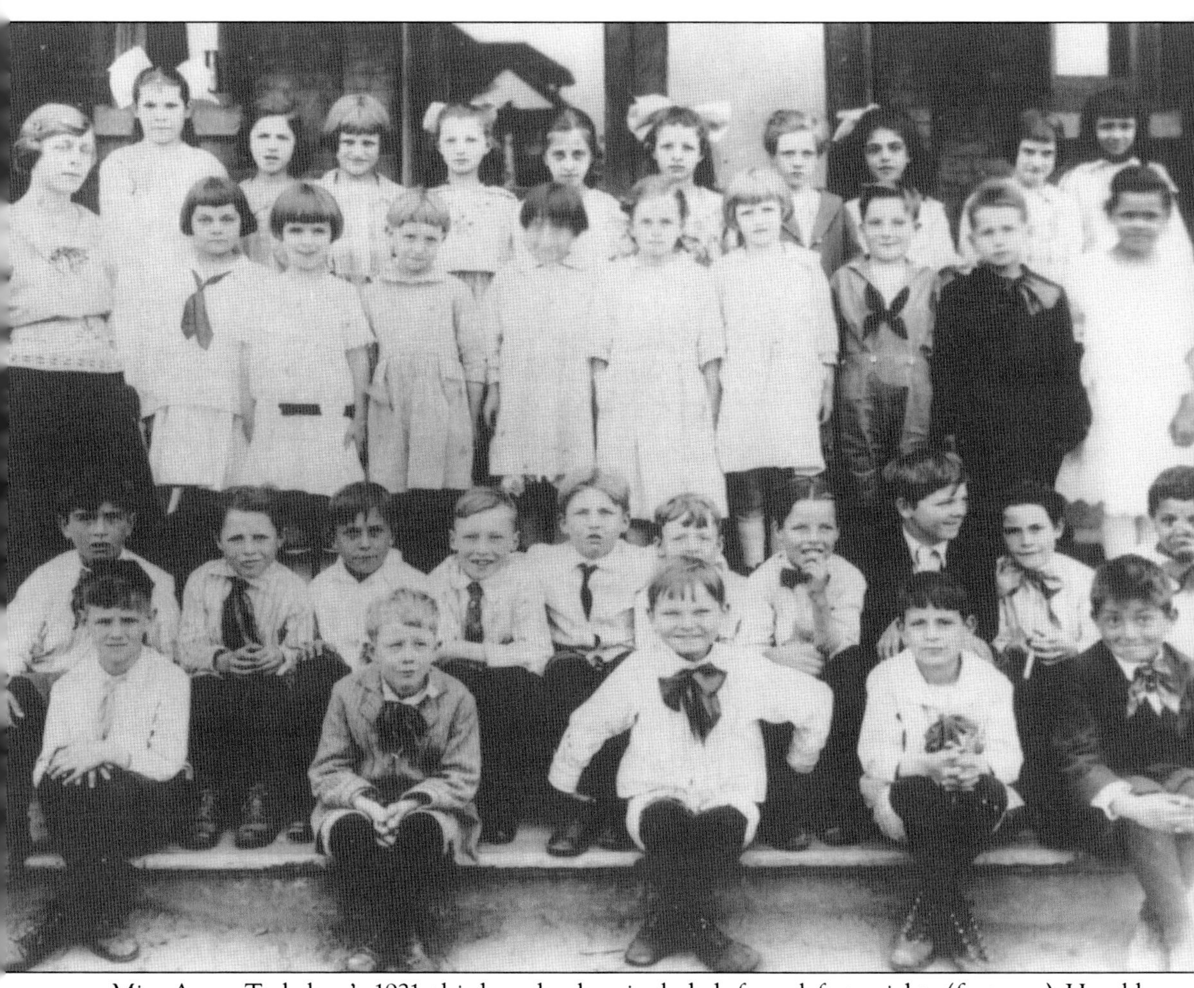

Miss Anna Turkelson's 1921 third grade class included, from left to right, (first row) Harold Stites, ? Wolohan, William Cheesman, William Gloster, and Samuel D'Amico; (second row) Phillip D'Amico, Elwood Laird, George Snell, Charles Klenska, William Graham, Leonard McLaughlin, Leon Wingate, Edward Cheesman, John Ogg Simpson, and Allen Walton; (third row) Miss Turkelson, Edith Broadwater, Dorothy Speakman, Annie or Irene Matthews, Helen Hatz, Beatrice Herrod, Nellie Lindley, George Stoddart, Samuel Priest, and unidentified; (fourth row) Marie Clapp, Evelyn Spiegle, Jean Hutton, Mary Cavallero, Anna Patrella, Joseph Cavellero, Mildred Keetley, Rose D'Amico, Myrtle Hartley Page, and Evelyn Warren.

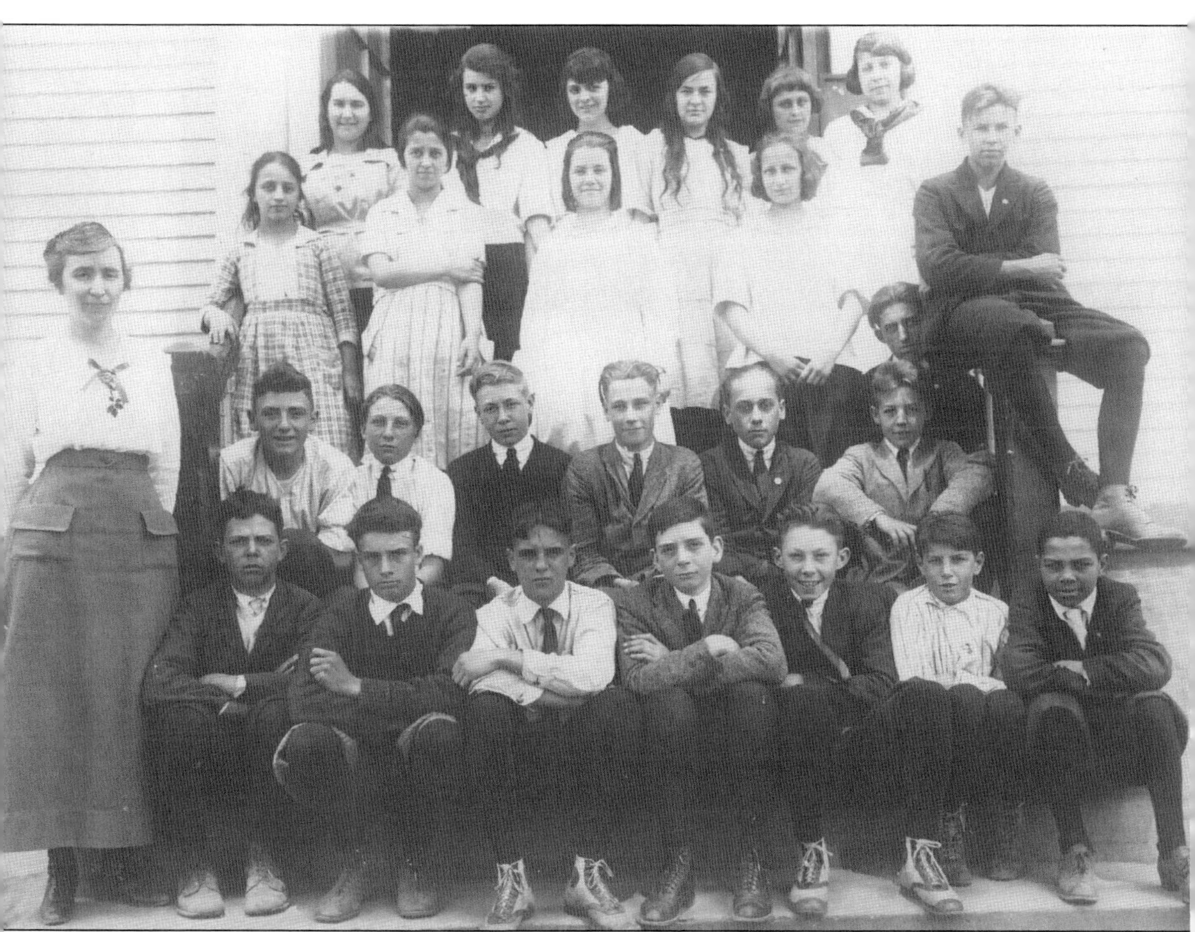

The Lincoln Avenue School class of 1925 included, from left to right, (first row) teacher Mary Marshall, George Cheesman, ? Herod, unidentified, Nelson Euler, Edward Janke, unidentified, and Everett Walton; (second row) Frank McLaughlin, Frederick Buckner, William Allen, Dan Stoddart, Francis Anderson, Henry Maxwell, Harry Taylor, and Raymond Fairbanks; (third row) Beulah Patrella, Angeline Patrella Blanck, Elizabeth Harley Waterfield, and Ruth Wagner; (fourth row) Blanche Spiegle, Virginia Vaughan, Anna Mae Wescott, Edna Harding, Anna Taylor, and Alberta Wingate.

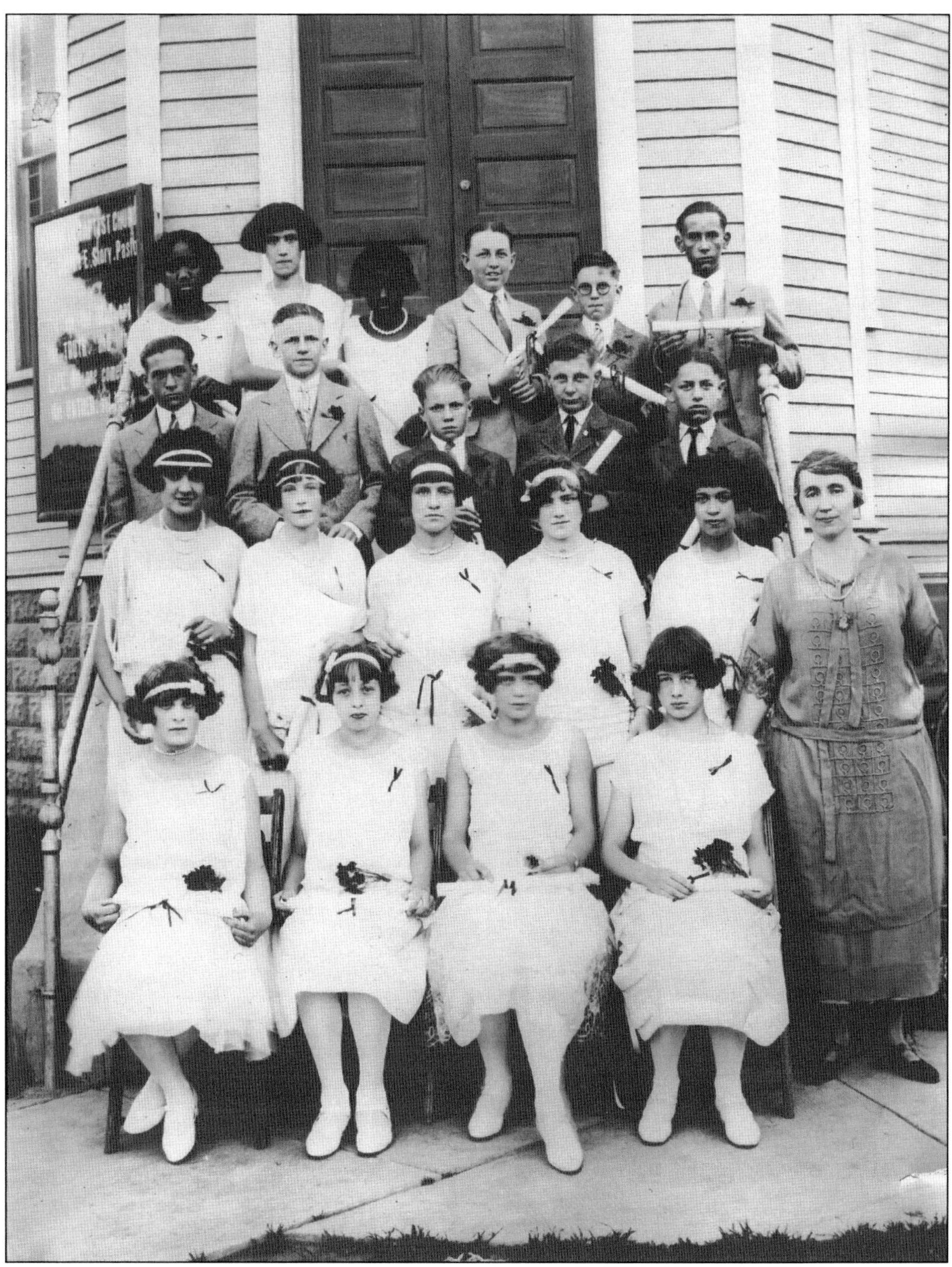

The 1927 Lincoln Avenue eighth grade graduating class included, in no specific order, Orville Hess (valedictorian), Edna Mae Jackson, Gerald Coles, Emily Coble, Catherine Gloster, Howard Hamell, Lewis Lindley, Lemuel Matthews, Elsie Metzer, Benjamin Mezger, Albert Minter, Vito Panebianco, Nellie Ross, Dorothy Ryrie, Hazel Schmick, Leona Watson, Dorothy Mae Warren, Marie White, Katherine White, Rose Ann, and Dorothy Wingate.

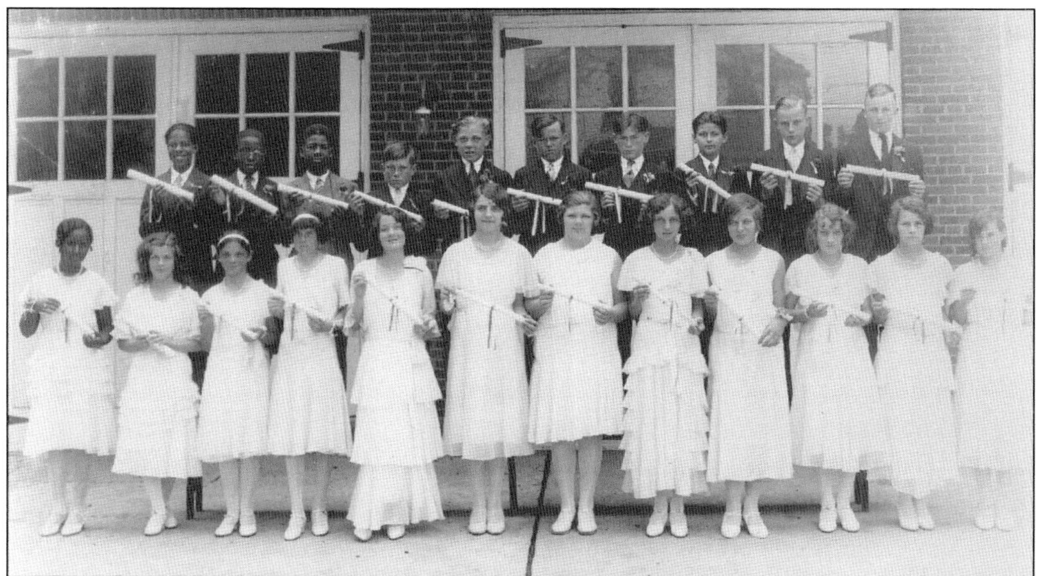

The class of 1931 included, from left to right, (first row) Doris Cooper, Dorothy Yoch, Ruth Davis, Anna Herrod, Elizabeth Stoddart, unidentified, Muriel Kent, Ida Enders, Anna Haitz, Dorothy Marquette, Betty Wilson, and Adlena Laurie; (second row) Charles Farrell, Charles Henderson, George Edgecomb, Ed Johnson, Bill Capie, Archer Myers, Harry Phillips, Elwood Kircher, Stan Ehresmann, and Harry Turner.

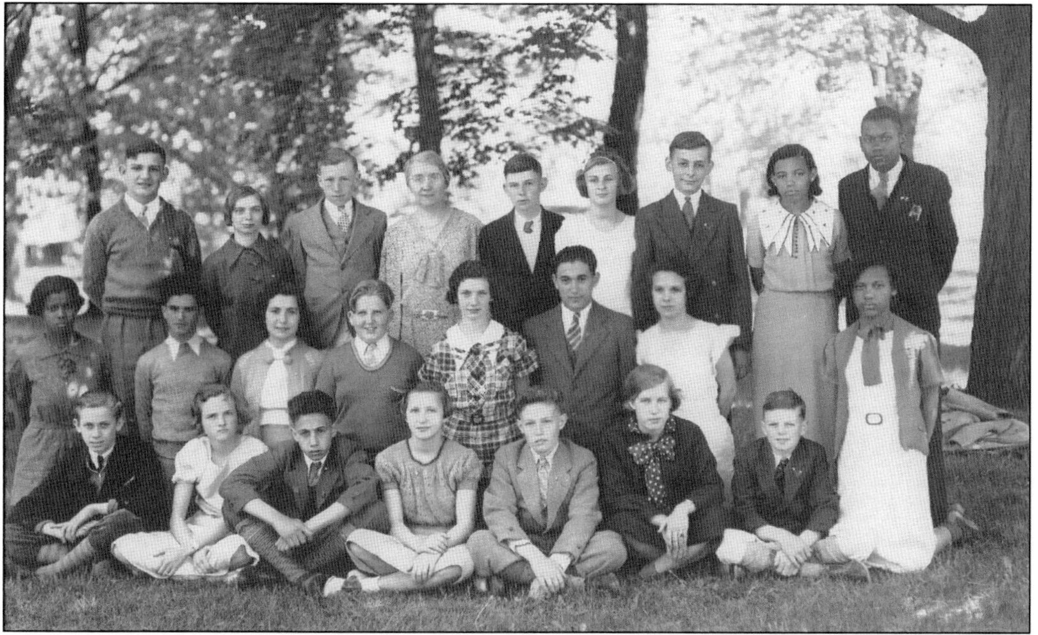

The class of 1935 included, from left to right, (first row) Ed Harder, Mary Hennessy, Ed Cox, Betty Graeff, Martin Cramp, Florence Davis, and Roy Myers; (second row) Mary Flagg, William D'Amico, Gertrude D'Amico, George Johnson, Marian Dean, Ralph Pace, Marian Bowen, and Dorothy Williams; (third row) Jack Hagen, Carolyn Stites, Edwin Cunningham, Mary Marshall (teacher), Harry Myers, Eleanor Arnold, John Christopher, Edna Bryant, and Clifford Hightower.

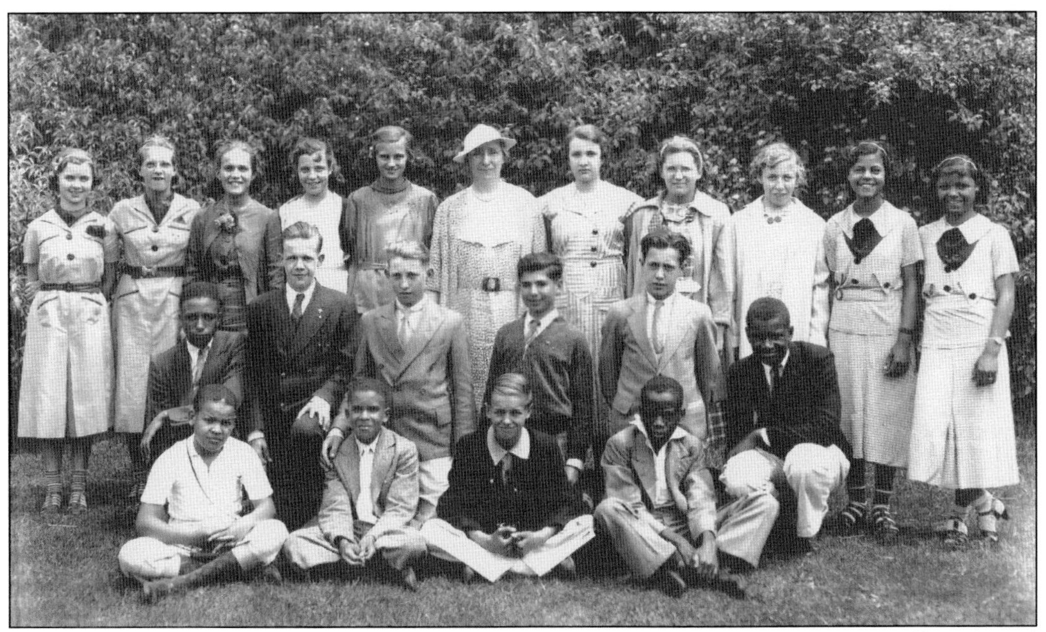

The class of 1936 included, from left to right, (first row) Spencer Moore II, Sylvester Miller, Elwood McAllister, and Lowry Henderson Jr.; (second row) James Travick, Howard Bergstrom, Stanley Brown, Santino D'Amico, Fred Cox, and unidentified; (third row) Ruth Winemore, Velma Rodman, Gertrude Crouthamel, Mary Hall, Mildred Arnold, Mary Marshall (teacher), Lillie Unterbrink, Marian Winterbottom, Evelyn Harper, Wilhemina Gilmore, and Anna Gilmore.

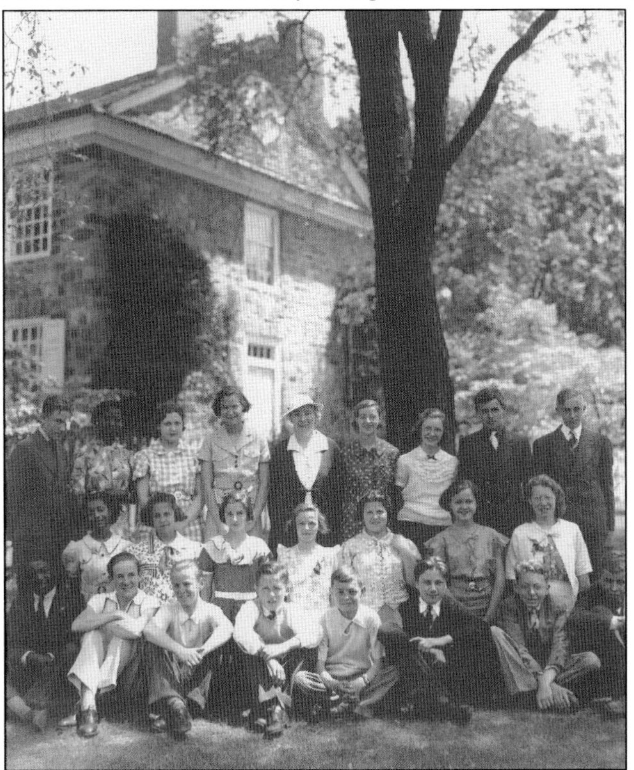

The 1937 eighth grade graduating class included, from left to right, (first row) Harold Brown, Emerson Strang, Clifton Winterbottom, Budd Hineline, Albert McAllister, Joseph Johnson, Warren Patton, and Robert Clermont; (second row) Madalyn Cooper, Agnes Bowen, Doris Grass, Bernice Myers, Thelma Mehl, Mary Bundy, and Evelyn Davis; (third row) Roy Doherty, Betha Hightower, Eugenia Glass, Margaret Christopher, Mary Marshall (teacher), Carolyn Shaw, Louise Dickins, Harry Dean, and Henry Graeff.

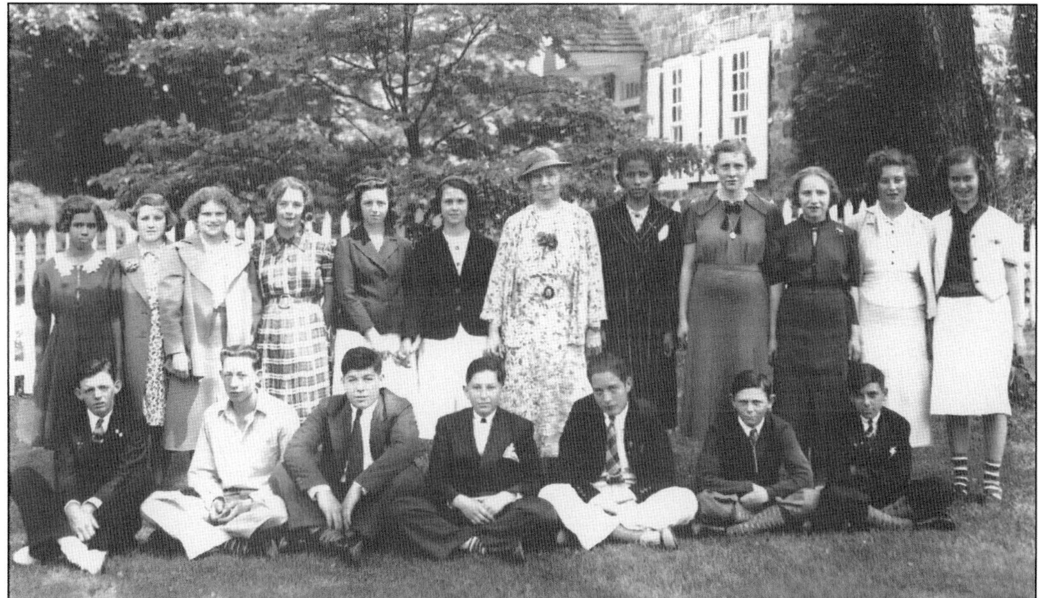

The 1938 eighth grade graduating class, photographed at Valley Forge, included, in no specific order, Audrey Adams, Selig Bascove, Andrew Blanzole, Louise Chatham, Alberta Dainty, Irene Dainty, Edward Davis, Kathryn Gilmore, Donald Graeff, Lois Hickman, Ethel Miller, Frank Miller Jr., Walter Reams, William Reams Jr., Edith Robinson, May Travick, Dorothy Whitall, and Shirley Winnemore.

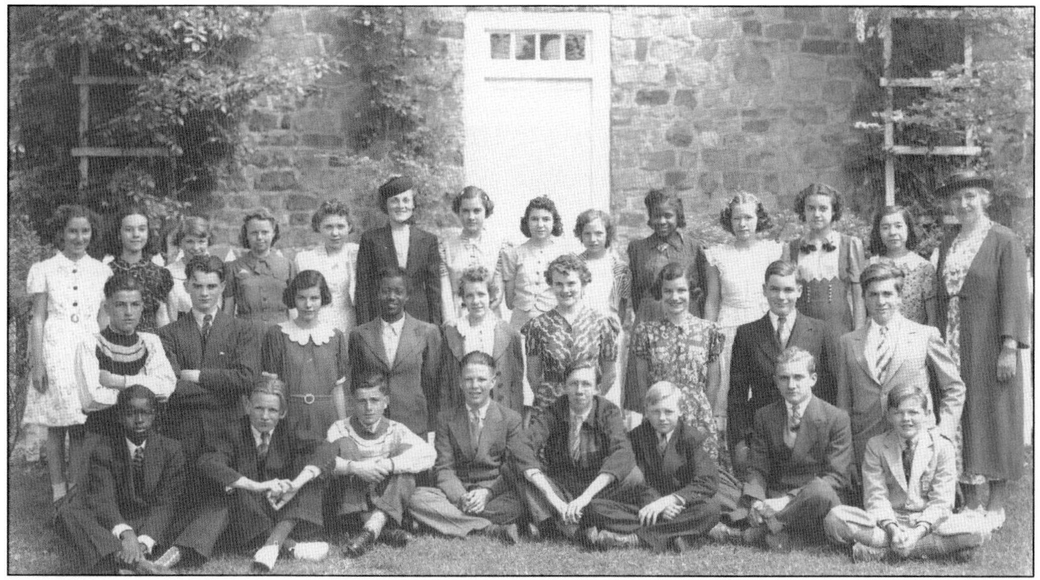

The 1939 graduates included, from left to right, (first row) Henry Brown, James Hennessy, Tony D'Amico, Leon Engle, George Morrow, Harry Callaway, Robert Hagen, and Clayton Myers; (second row) Pete D'Amico, Joseph Money, Dorothy Hunt, Inez Flagg, Elizabeth Bergstrom, Alma Money, Kathryn Hunt, Charles Stoddart, and Rudolph DiPasquel; (third row) Katherine Arno, Gladys Bowen, Virginia Wiser, Evelyn Zimmerman, Maria Bell, teacher Doris Pratt, Elizabeth Johnson, Margaret Gilmore, Elizabeth Hennessy, unidentified, Jane Taylor, Joan Cox, Mary DiPasquel, and teacher Mary Marshall.

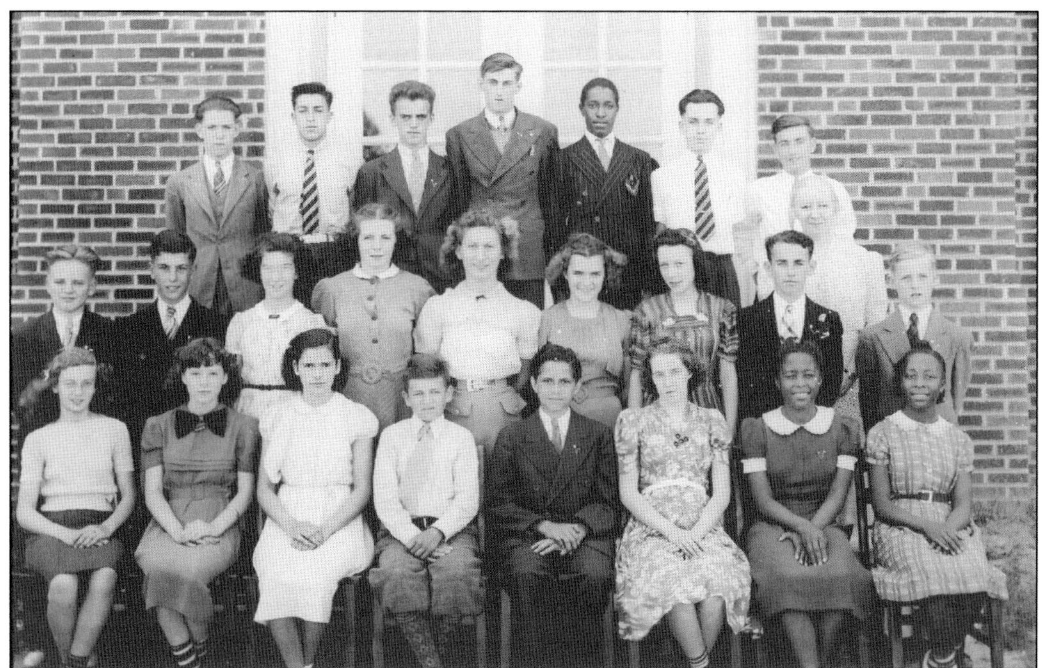

The class of 1940, with their teacher, included, from left to right, (first row) Betty Dean, Marie Schroeder, Dorothy Smith, Joe Mehl, Jim Bundy, Claire Strang, Thelma Wright, and Mae Wright; (second row) Rodman Luckins, Frank D'Amico, Evlyn Myers, Betty Hosey, Martha Delgesso, Betty Winterbottom, Edna Reams, Ellis Holloway, and Bob McAllister; (third row) Ken Stites, Joe Vadurro, Jack Belzer, Curt Arnold, Russell Peynell, Russell Garton Jr., and Joe Brown.

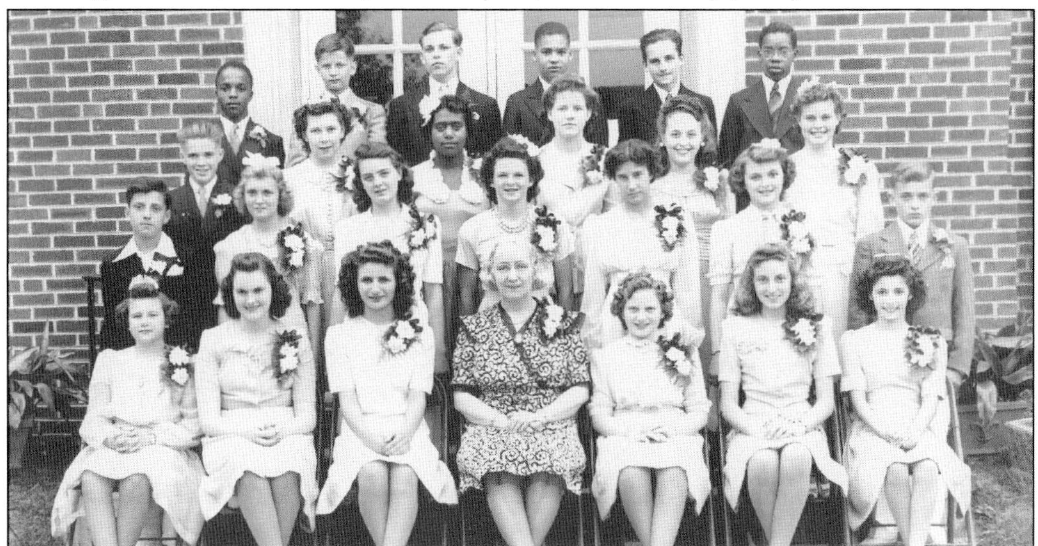

The class of 1942 included, from left to right, (first row) Janet Trueland, unidentified, Theresa Delgesso, teacher Mary Marshall, unidentified, Barbara Dold, and Carolyn Graham; (second row) Maurice Necoechea, Marian Hickman, unidentified, Dolores Myers, Jane Arno, Anna Mae Sickler, and Donald Stoner; (third row) Forrest Wood, Mable Cheesman, unidentified, Elizabeth Money, Camilla James, and Daisy Cook; (fourth row) two unidentified, John Zimmerman, and three unidentified.

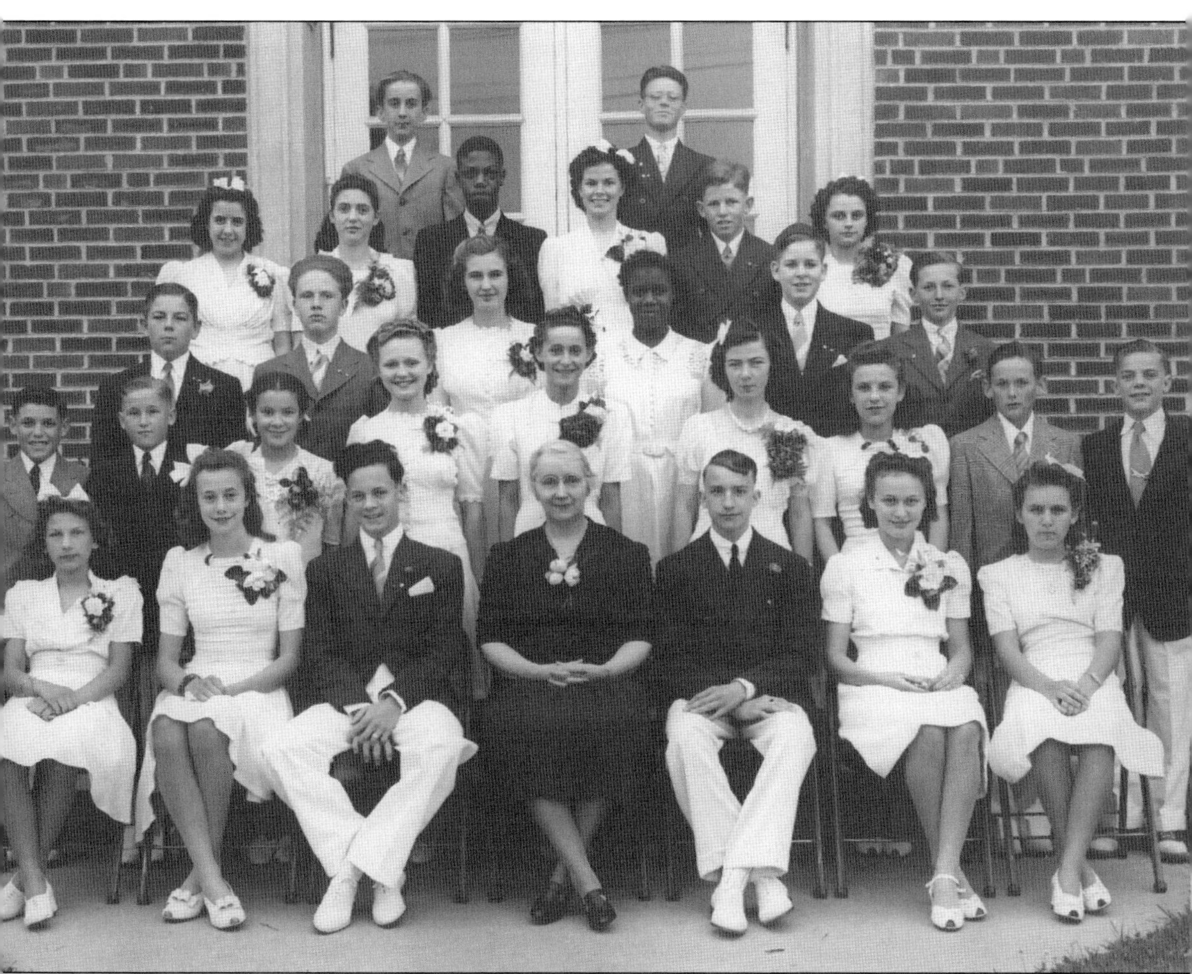

The 1941 class included, from left to right, (first row) June Zimmerman, Frances Murray, Raymond Miller, teacher Mary Marshall, Morgan Wilkerson, Patsy Coss, and Elizabeth Stoner; (second row) Louis Arno, Ervin Trueland, Charlotte Bell, Arlene Luckin, Marian Christopher, Mary Donovan, Elizabeth Bowen, John Hennessey, and James Makin; (third row) Drexel Maxwell, Frank Dold, Lillian Arnold, Lucinda Flage, Harry Wilent, and Harry Horay; (fourth row) Thelma Cox, Mildred Raabe, Albert Mitchell, Kathleen Hosey, Harry Miller, and Dorothy Grau; (fourth row) Walter Unterbrink and Robert Paulson.

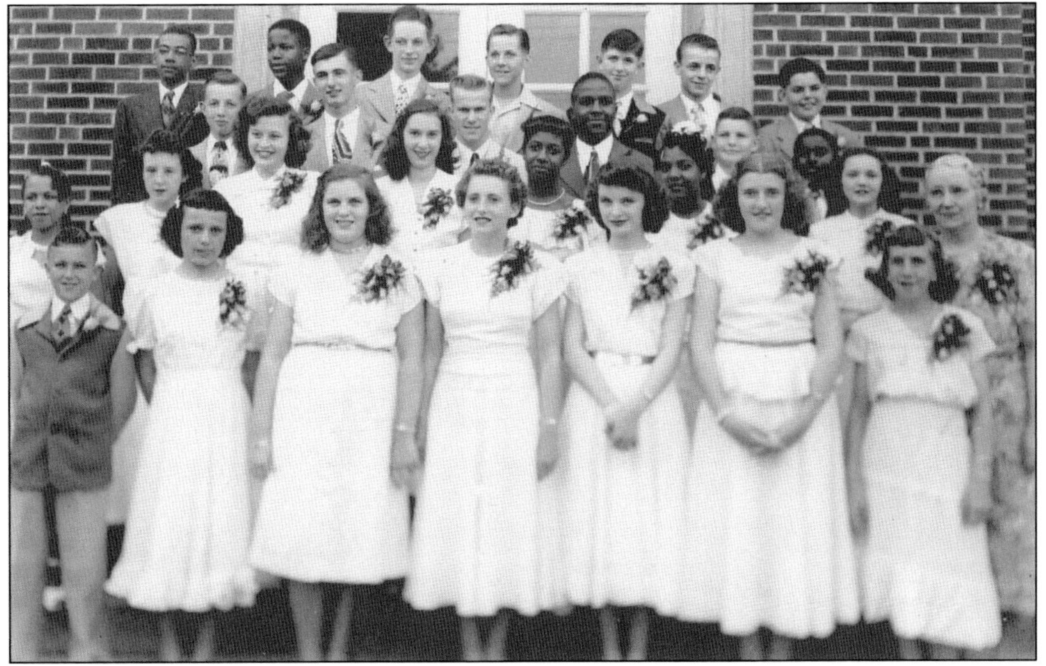

The 1948 class included, from left to right, (first row) Donald Trueland, Barbara Blanck, Lorraine Johnson, Betty Jane Wilson, Jane Bridge, Dot Barton, and Claire Lombard; (second row) Greta Harris, Esther Dolan, Lori James, Mildred Mezger, Alma Flagg, Lillian Darrisaw, Sheila Scott, and teacher Mary Marshall; (third row) Robert Sherwood, Bob Arnold, Jerry Ovepeck, Robert Harris, John Doughter, and Henry Smith; (fourth row) Carrington Jenkins, Robert Dougherty, Charles Shaffer, Donald ?, Howard Rohn, Charles Watson, and Bruce Pearson.

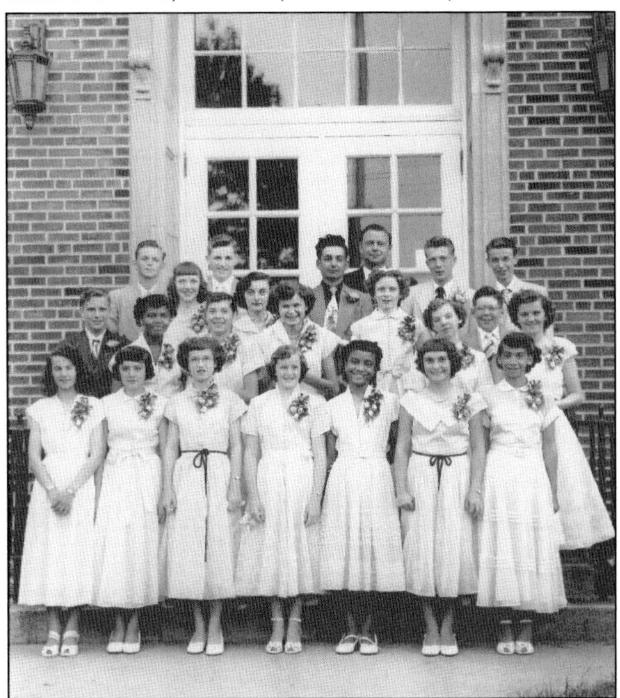

The eighth grade class of 1949 included, from left to right (first row) three unidentified, Joy Trueland, unidentified, Carole Massey, and ? Jenkins; (second row) five unidentified and Beverly Carroll; (third row) unidentified, Evelyn Yost, Anne Marie ?, and unidentified; (fourth row) Billy Dare, Bobby Wisner, ? Pellegrino, ? LaVarge, and Andy James.

Six

Heart and Soul

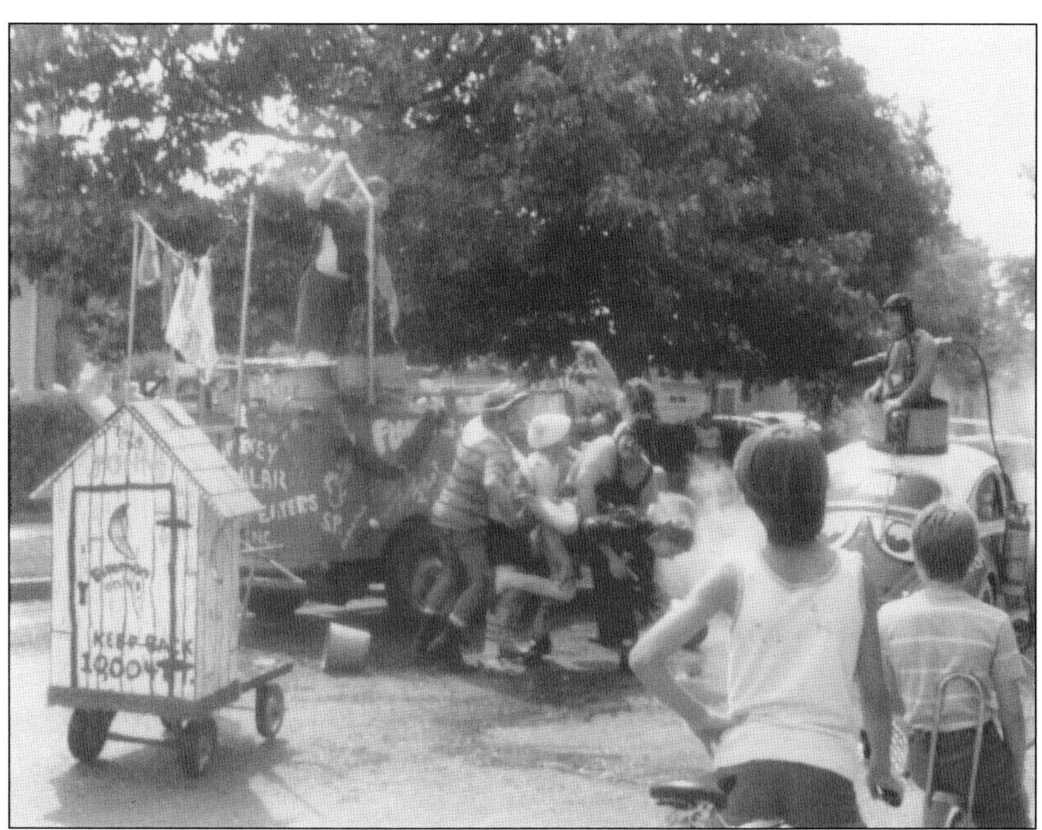

The Magnolia Fire Department's comic unit, the Smokey Holler Smoke Eaters, entertain the crowd during the borough's annual Fourth of July parade in 1976.

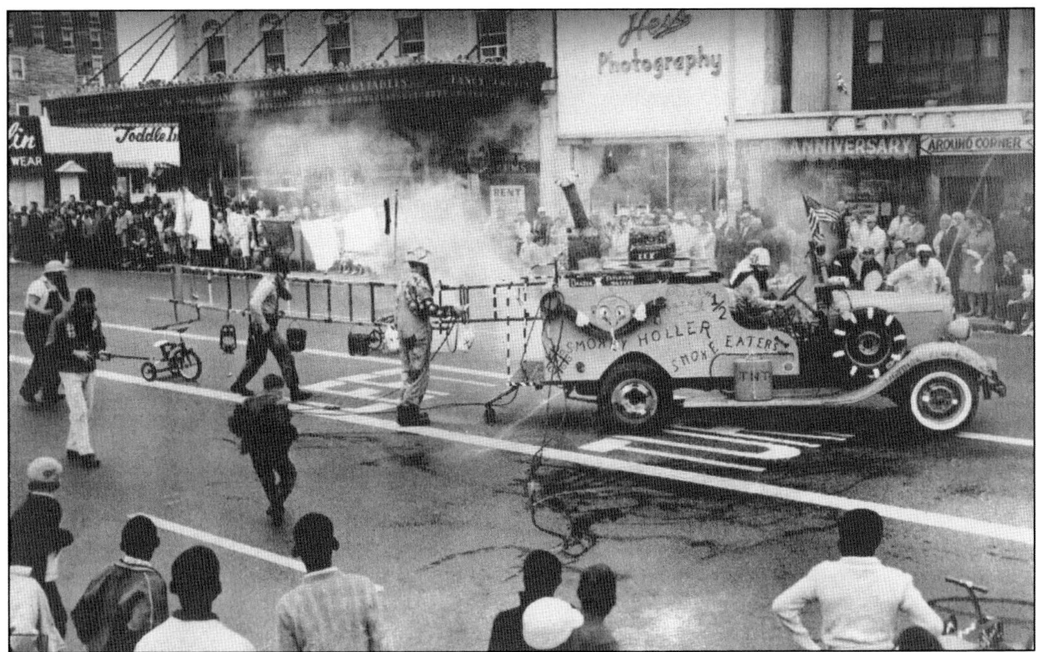

In September 1963, the Smokey Holler Smoke Eaters were a hit on the boardwalk at the Atlantic City Fireman's Convention.

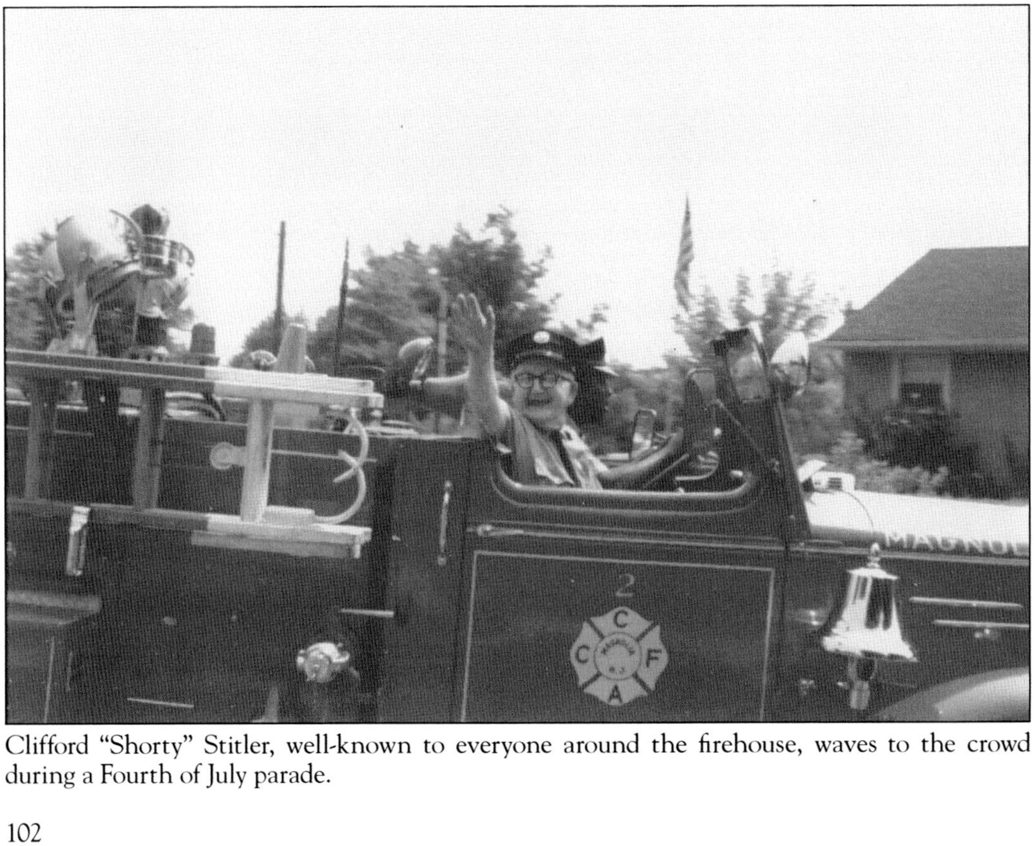

Clifford "Shorty" Stitler, well-known to everyone around the firehouse, waves to the crowd during a Fourth of July parade.

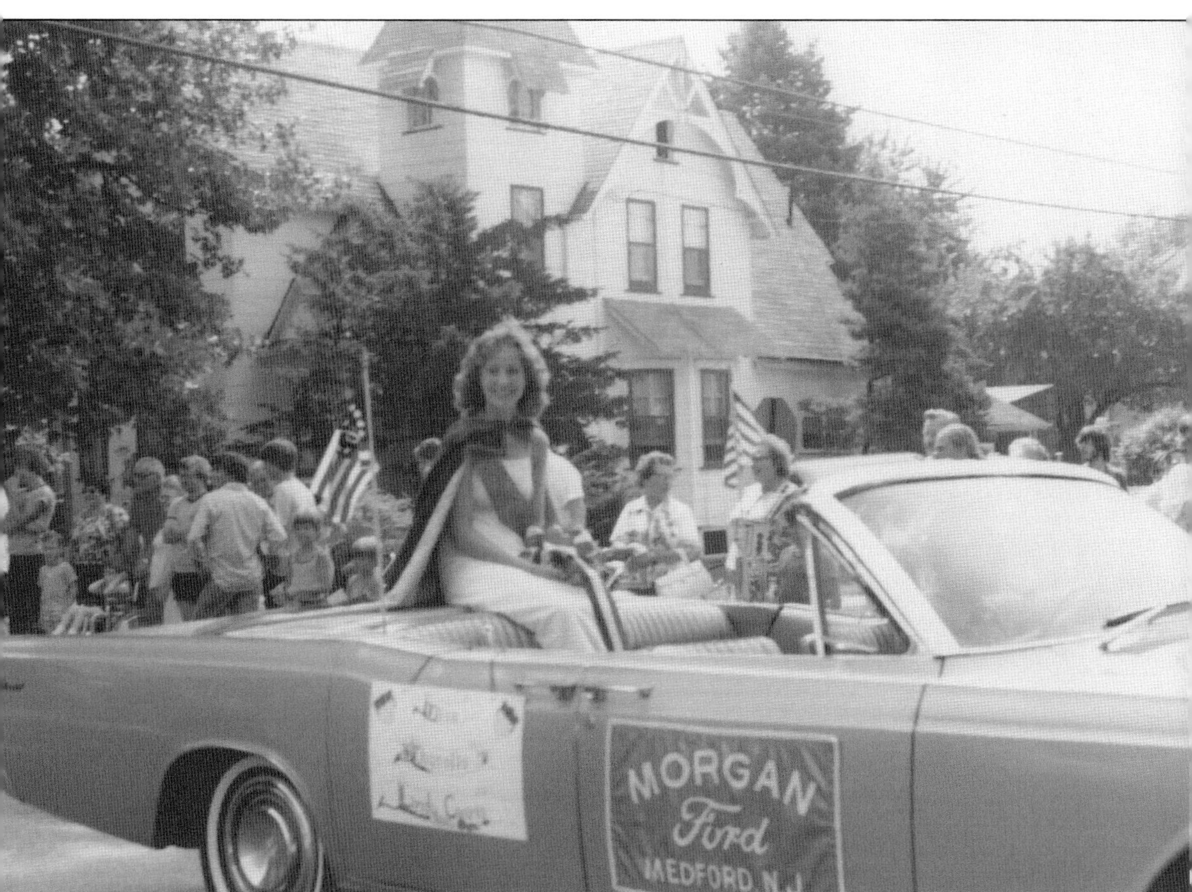

Miss Magnolia 1976, Linda Cassario, rides in the Fourth of July parade. The teen pageant, which has been held sporadically since 1922, has recognized the following borough girls: Frances Charman, 1922; Thelma Rowand, 1925; Joan Pavolich, 1967; Suzanne Harrold, 1968; Bobbie Fetter, 1969; Leona Gills, 1970; Michelle McDonough, 1971; Sandra Hannold, 1972; Linda Cassario, 1976; Lori Benton, 1977; Sandra Negron, 1978; Sheila Hunter, 1979; Lynn Furniss, 1984; Michel DiDino, 1985; Lisa Belli, 1986; Tricia Foster, 1987; Cheri Pfafman, 1988; Kim Baker, 1989; Michele McVeigh, 1990; Maria Carlucci, 1991; Jennifer Kimble, 1992; Heather Hackett, 1993; Kristine Hildebrandt, 1994; Ayesha Cooper, 1995; Allison Neuberger, 2006; and Erin Meagher, 2007.

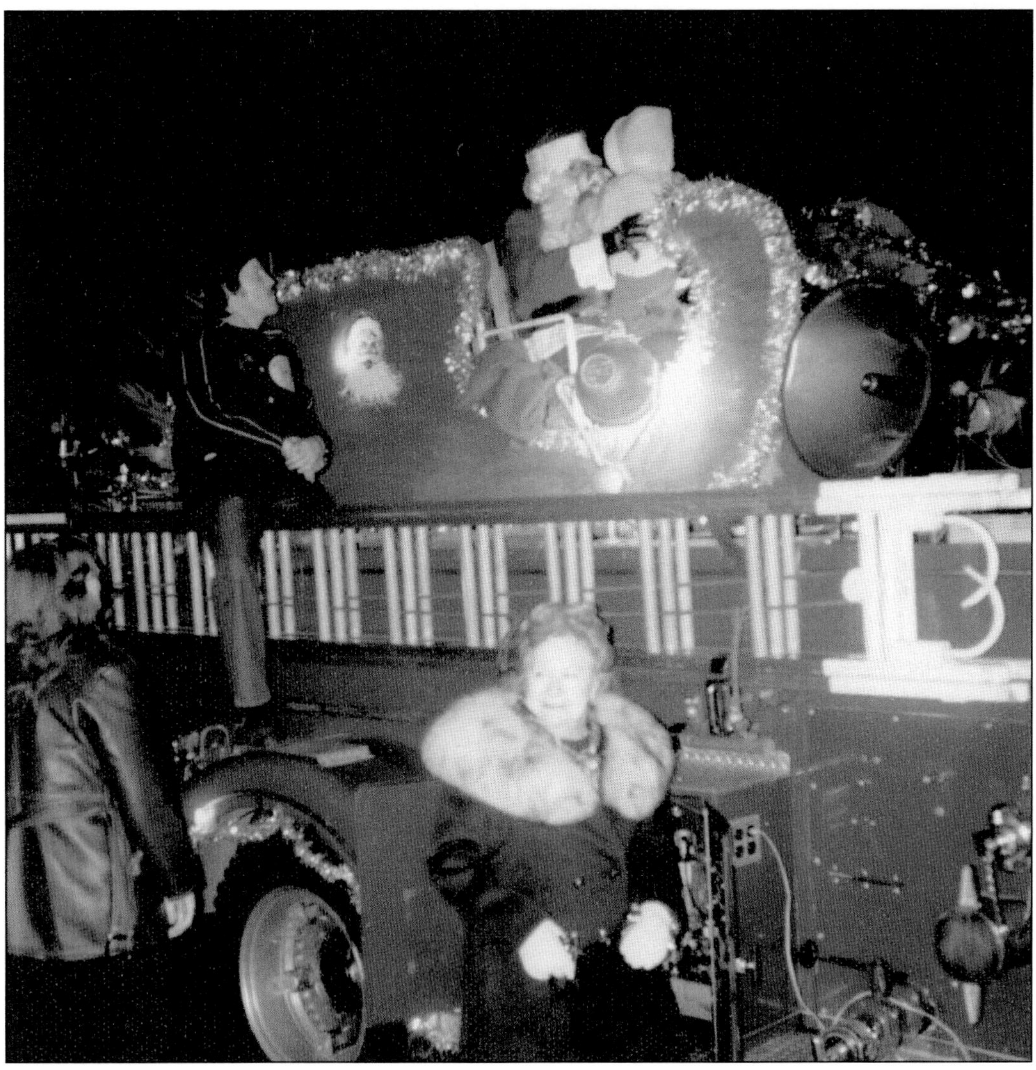

Santa, portrayed by Gil Hymerling, visits with a little one in 1964, during Magnolia's annual Christmas tour through the borough's streets, sponsored by the Magnolia Fire Department. The sound of the fire engine's siren sent children and parents to the streets to anxiously await a glimpse of Santa and a free candy cane from Jimmy Kendall (riding alongside Santa). Thelma Govan stands in front of the engine.

Young workers from the local Bonanza restaurant take part in Magnolia's 1976 bicentennial parade. Seen here are, from left to right, Tim McShane, unidentified, Kathy Carmellie, Toni Tedesco, Kathy Wert, Paul Clark, and Terrie McShane.

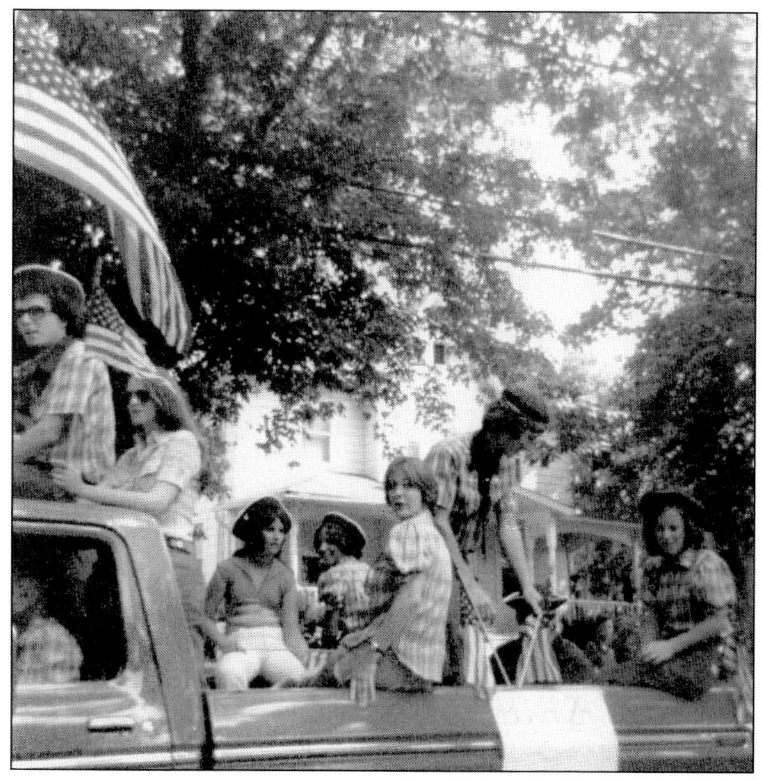

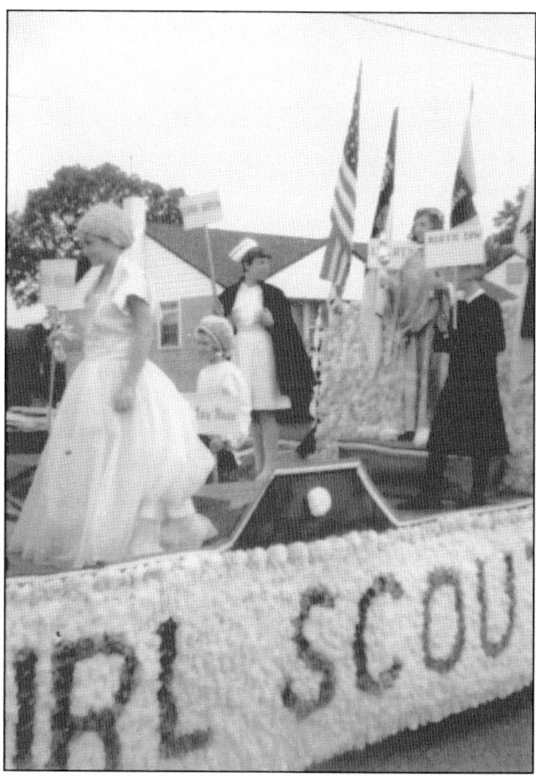

A group of Magnolia Girl Scouts greets the crowds as they cruise down the street on their float during a borough parade.

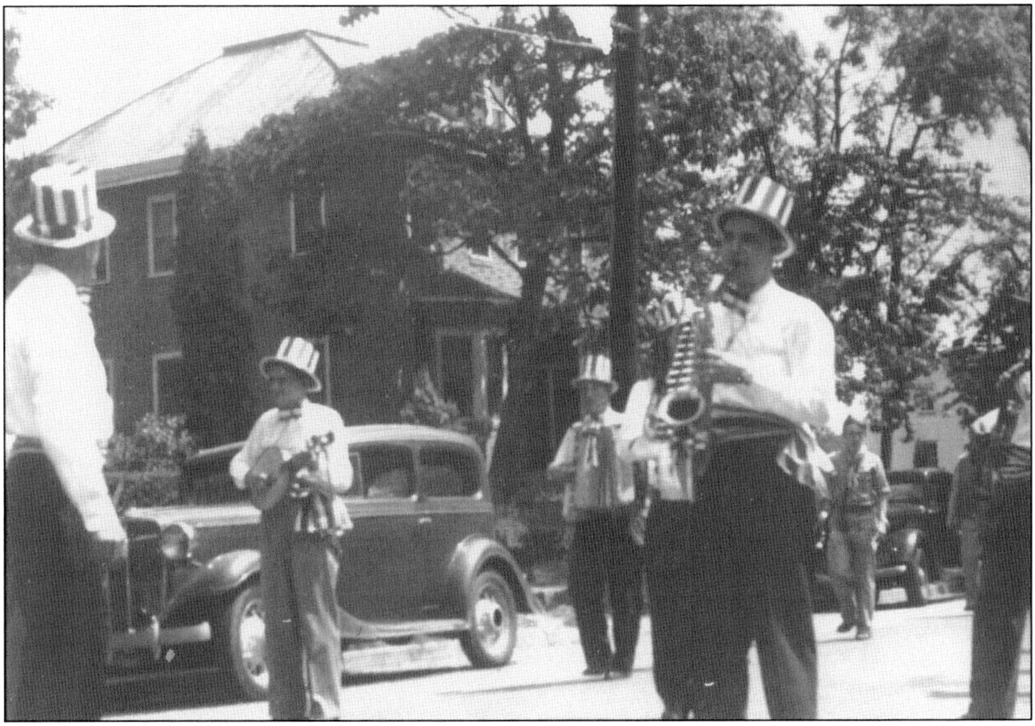

The original Magnolia String Band, sponsored by the American Legion, was formed in 1949 by Harry Stoner, and performed at parades, various regional shows, and for patients at Lakeland Hospital. Members included Donald and Harry Stoner, Walt Nelson, Charles Enders, Bob Arnold, John Hunt, Tom Euler, Hap Turner, John Koch, and Gene Geiger.

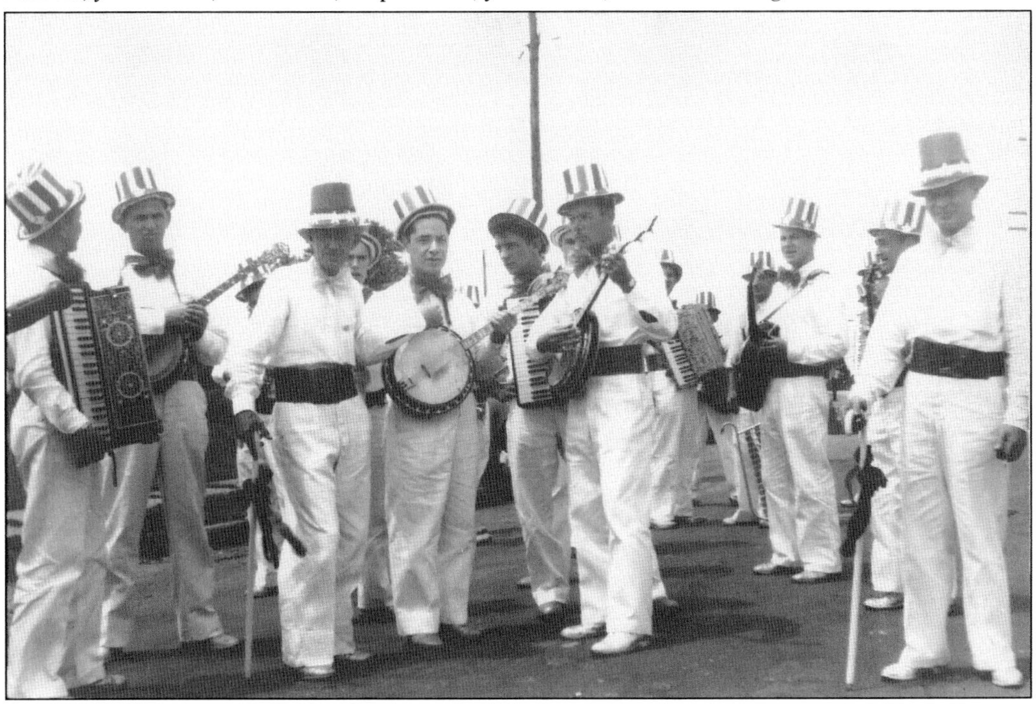

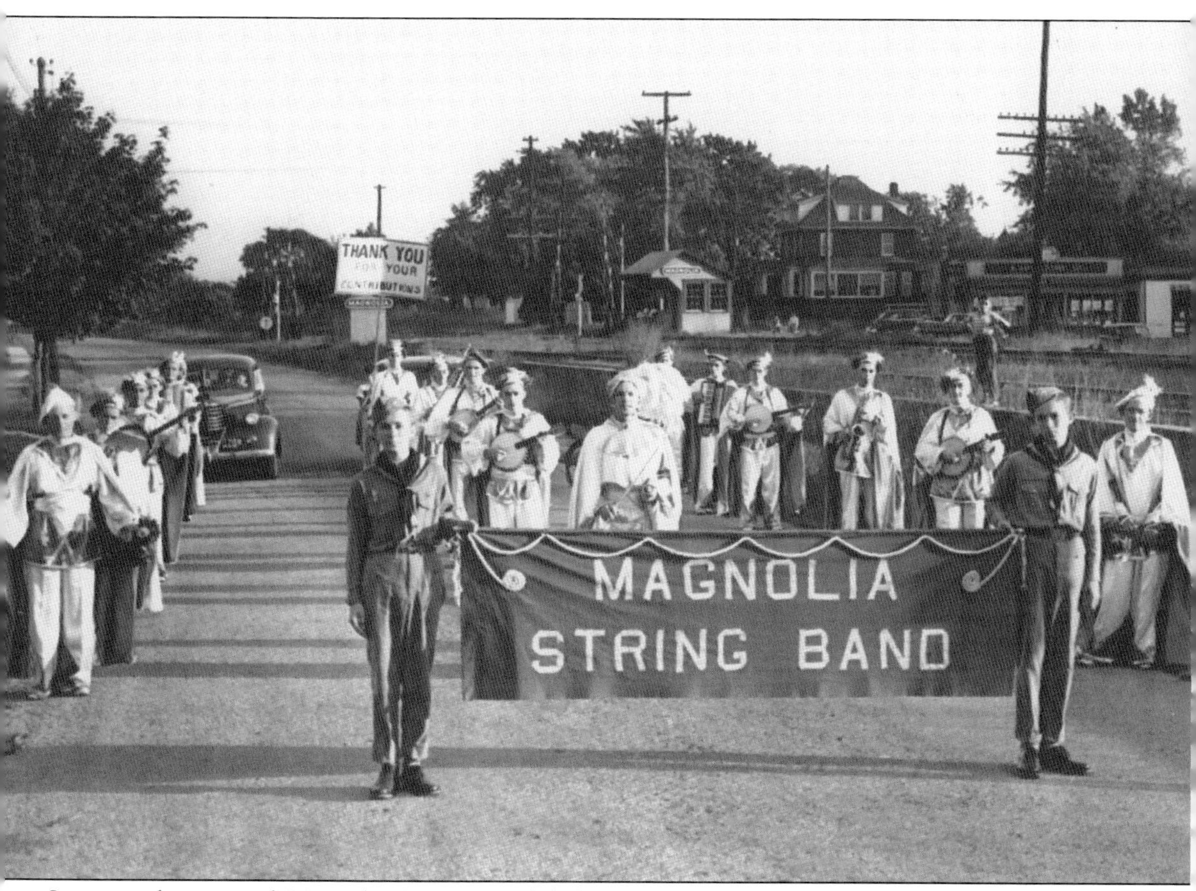

In time, the original Magnolia String Band disbanded, and a second Magnolia String Band, pictured here in this undated photograph, was formed.

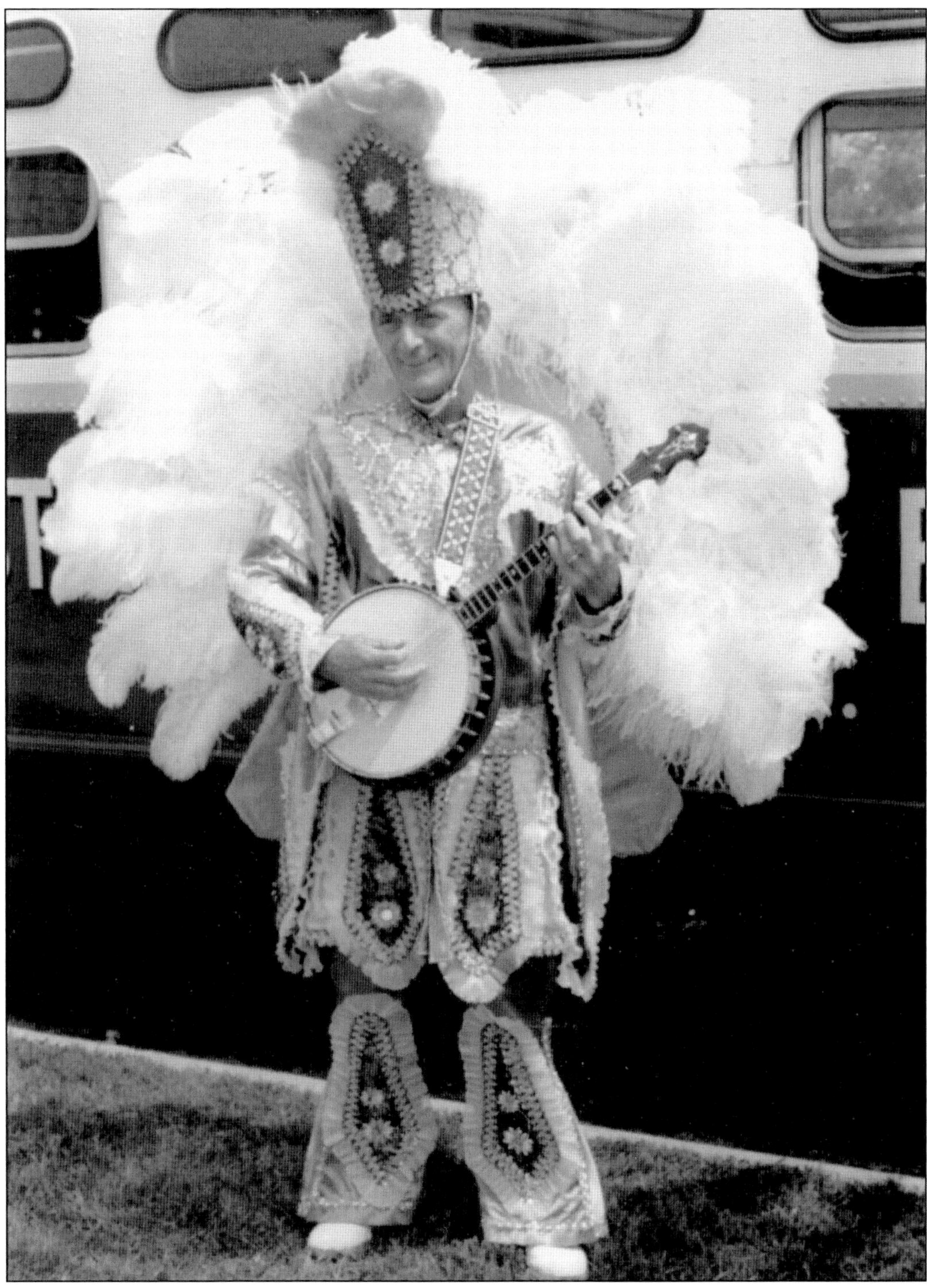

The Sterling String Band was formed in 1965 by Frank Tavener. Jim Hannold (pictured here) was a member of the Sterling group, along with nearly 50 other local musicians, including Richard Young, Ed Thomas, Herb Arnold, Al Parker, Paul Helmridge, Don Stoner, Hap Turner, and Gene Geiger.

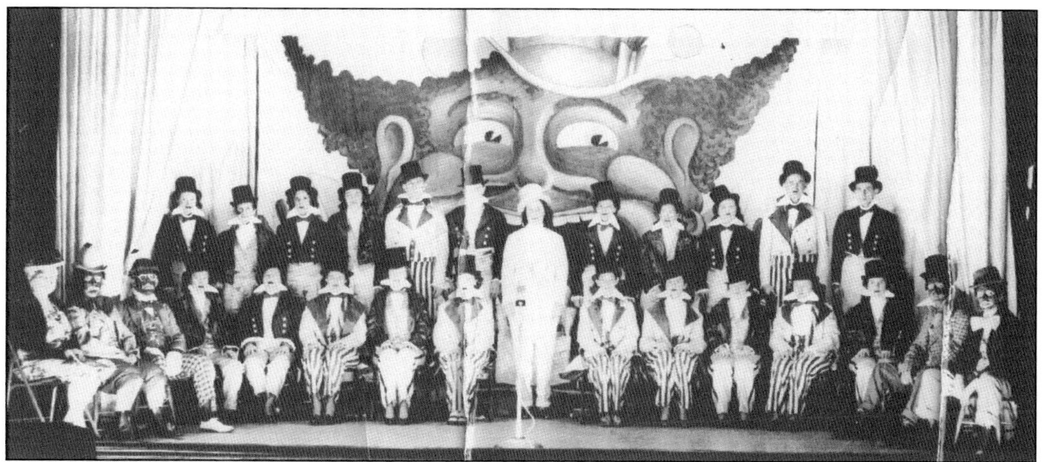

Minstrel shows were frequently held at the Magnolia Fire Hall and Lincoln Avenue School as fund-raising events and drew audiences from around the region. The Magnolia Minstrel Troupe included performers from Philadelphia, Camden, Blue Anchor, and the surrounding communities.

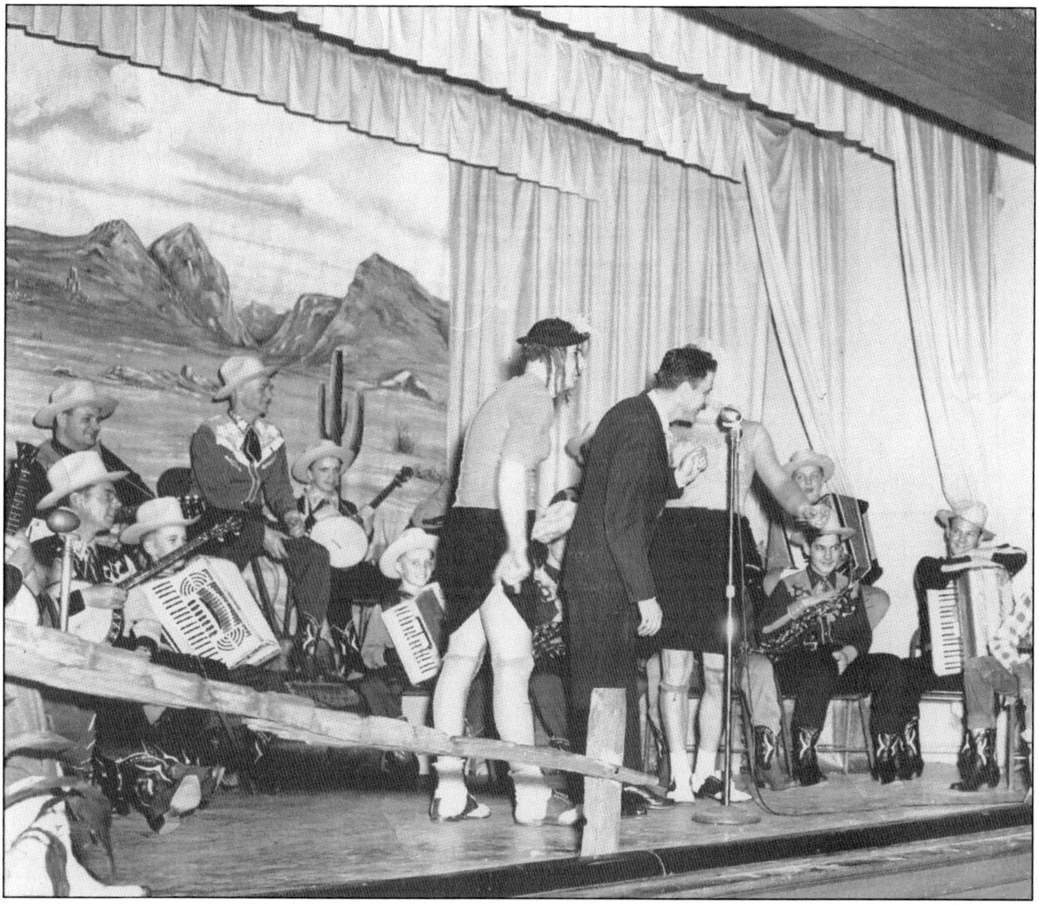

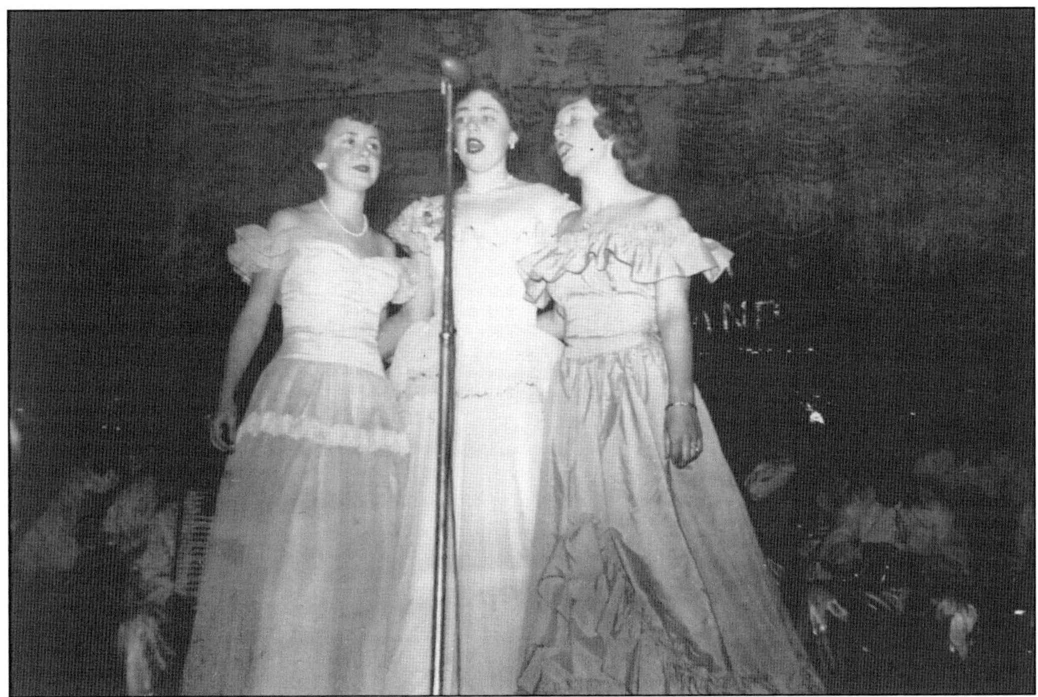

From left to right, Barbara Hewes, Ann Donovan, and an unidentified singer entertain the crowd at a Magnolia Minstrel Show.

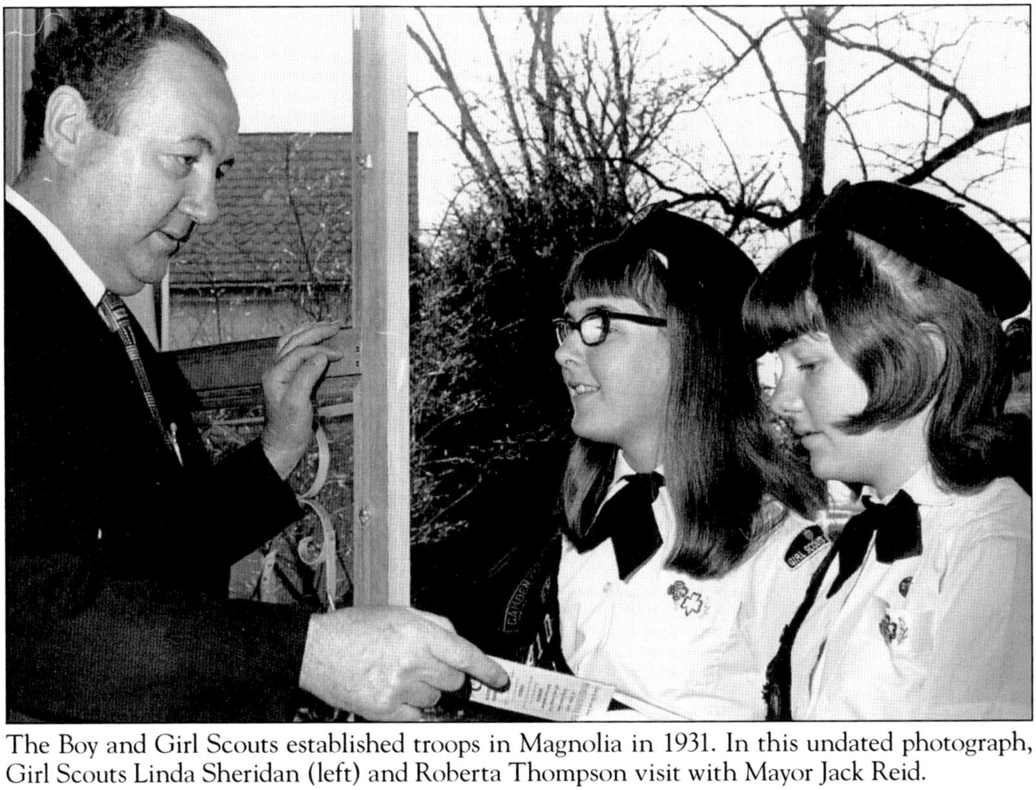

The Boy and Girl Scouts established troops in Magnolia in 1931. In this undated photograph, Girl Scouts Linda Sheridan (left) and Roberta Thompson visit with Mayor Jack Reid.

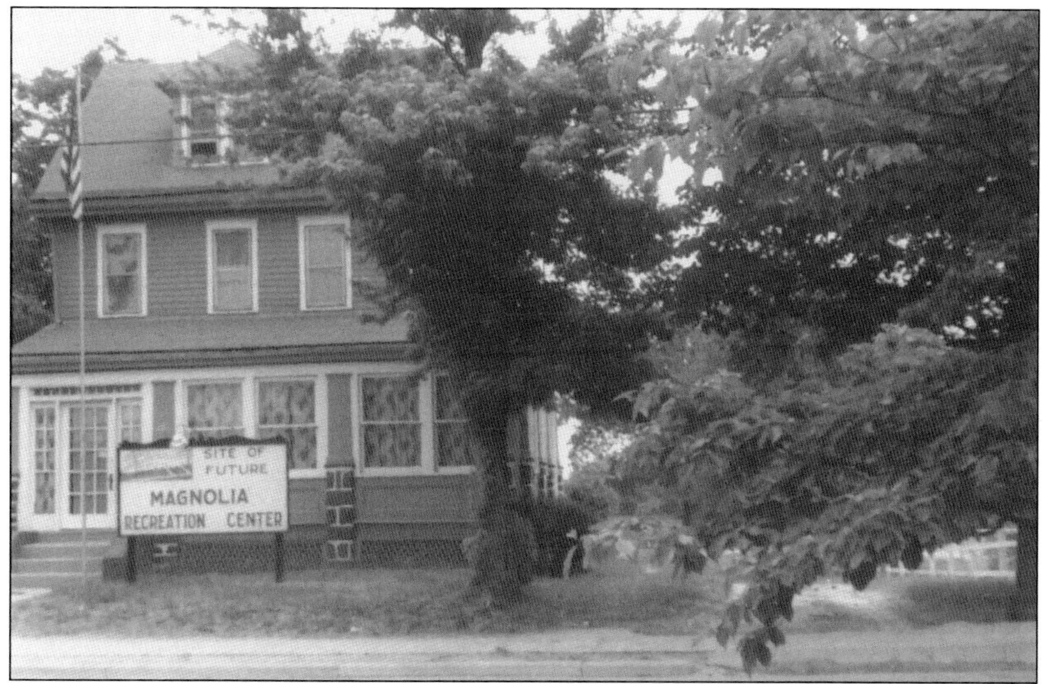

The Marshall home, pictured here, on Warwick Road, was demolished in 1964 to make way for the Magnolia Recreation Center. Organized by Frank Tavener, the center's first president was Robert Young. The organization disbanded in 1972.

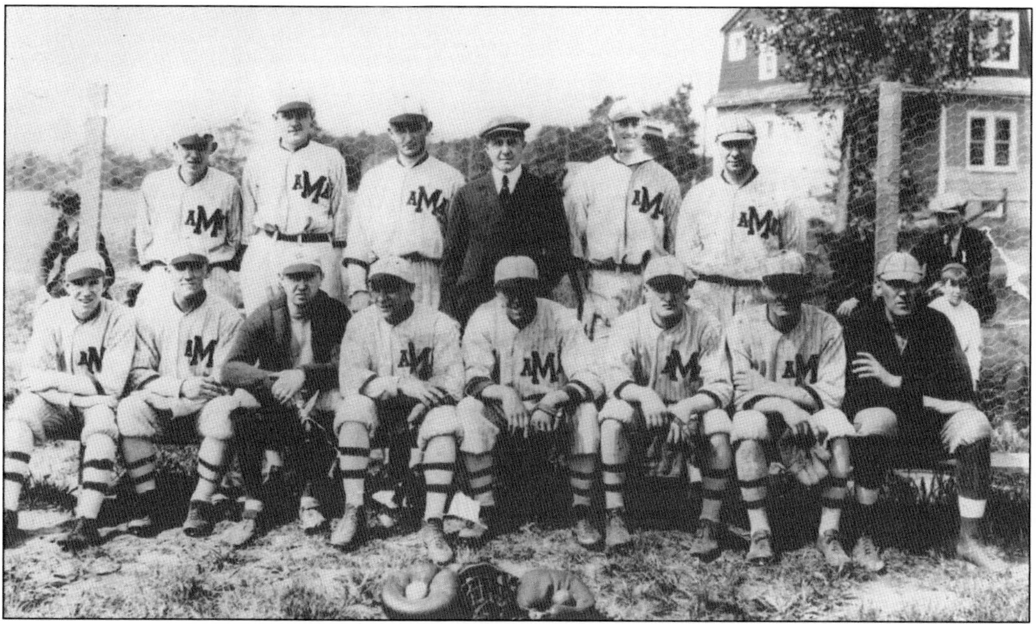

Magnolia's traveling baseball team held home games on the borough ball field at Lafayette and Jefferson Avenues, which later was absorbed by houses. The 1920 team included, from left to right, (first row) unidentified, Eddie McDonnell, Claude Maxwell, unidentified, Sam Olt, Eddie Dold, Frank Dold, and unidentified; (second row) Harry Johnson, Al Strang, Zeb Gayer, Harry Graeff, unidentified, and Walter Unterbrink.

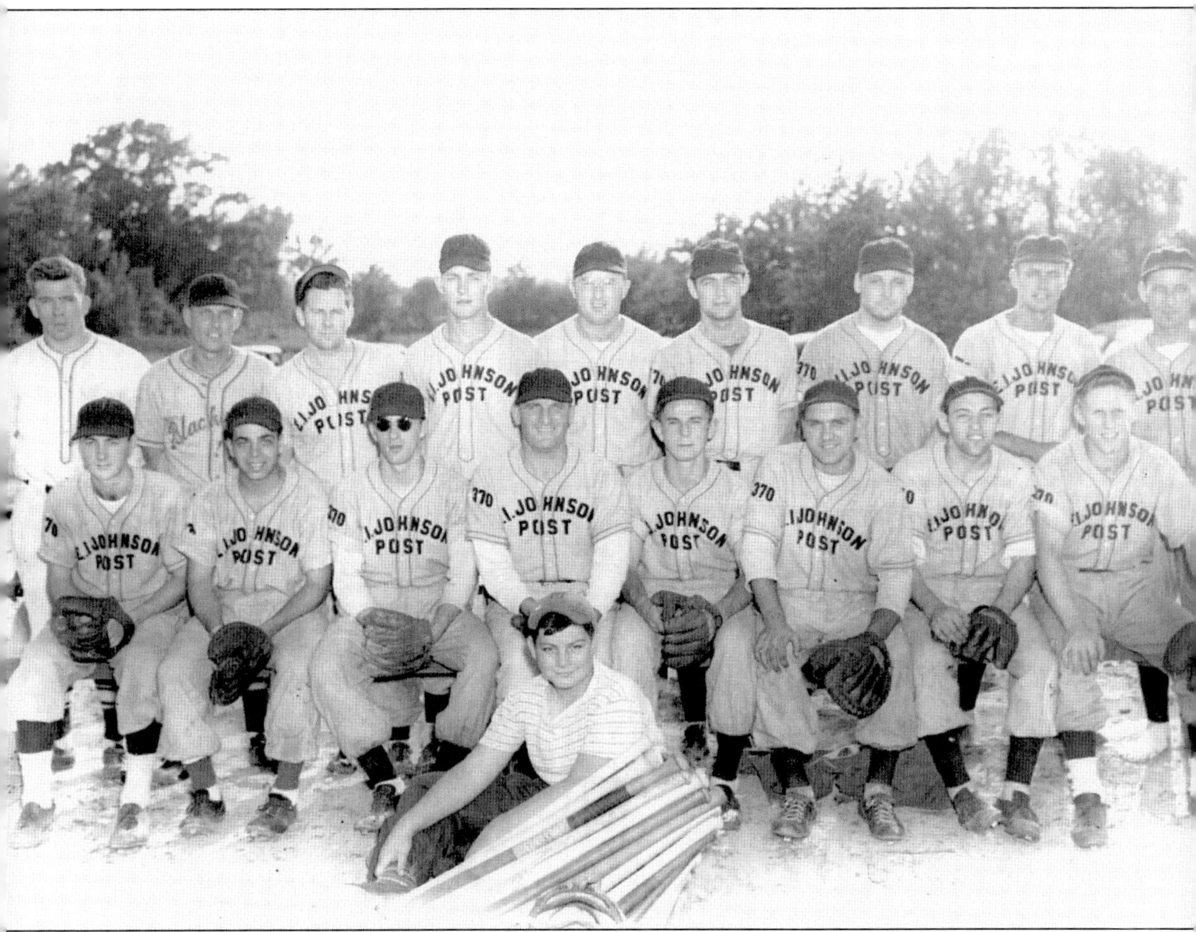

The 1946–47 Magnolia team included, from left to right, (first row) Jack Reid, two unidentified, George Dold, two unidentified, Tony Bezich, and Jack Statton; (second row) unidentified, Ed Connors, Jack Cunningham, Bob McAlister, Harry Turner, Albert McAlister, Ducky ?, Elwood McAlister, and Jack Connors. Bat boy John Hunt sits in front.

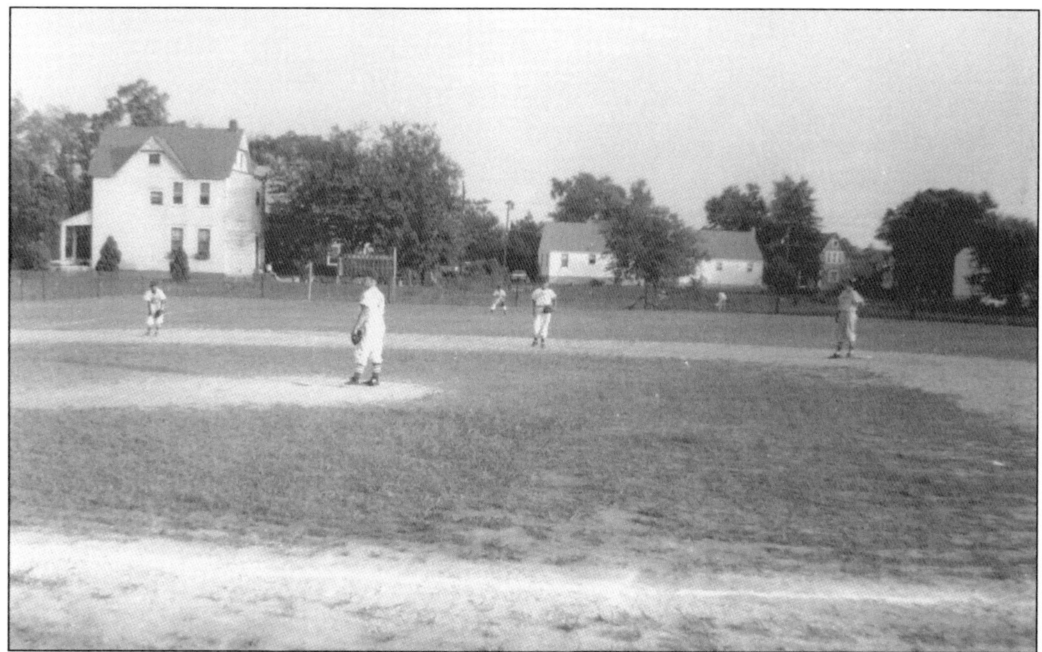

Organized baseball for the younger set began in the 1950s on the school grounds and evolved into an official Little League program in 1955, when the Albert G. Wise Memorial Field was dedicated on Barrett Avenue. At first, the borough's teams played without official uniforms, wearing t-shirts with names like Civic, Alchester, and Vaughan for identification. In this 1964 photograph, a Magnolia Little League team works the outfield during a game.

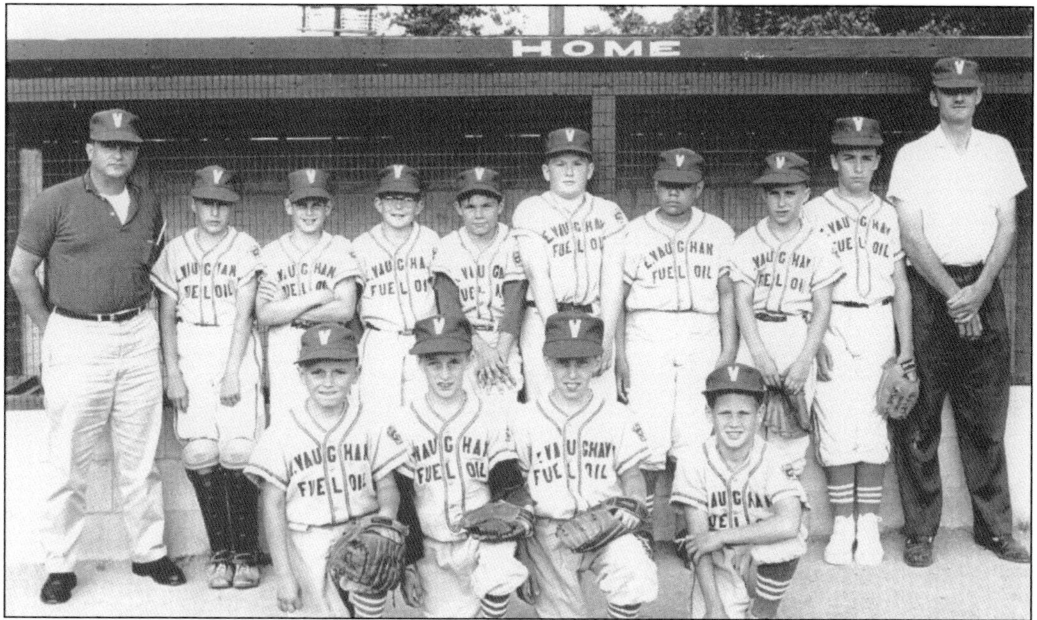

In 1962, the Vaughan Oil Cardinals Little League team included, from left to right, (first row) Glenn Bowman, Charles Keil, Rob Vaughan, and unidentified; (second row) coach Bob Houser, Gary Kalber, Bob Labascio, Steven Houser, four unidentified, Joe Vadurro, and coach Harry "Bink" Johnson.

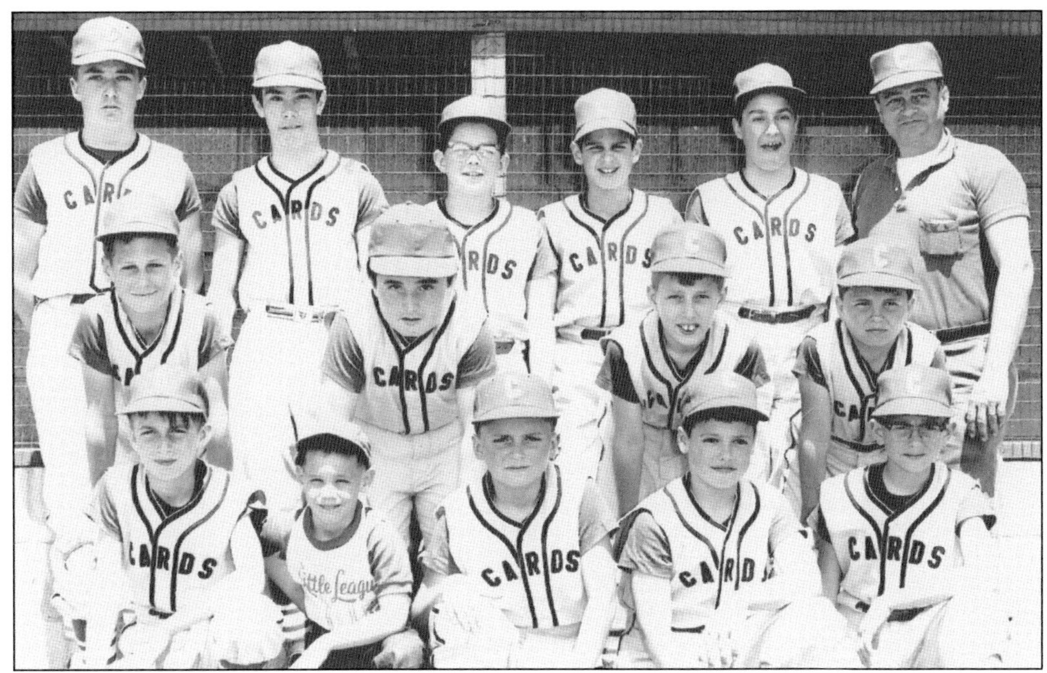

The 1963 Vaughn Oil Cardinals team included, from left to right, (first row) Charles Keil, David Greenway, Glenn Bowman, Charles O'Kane, and David Jiulanti; (second row) Kim Kline, Dennis Stoddart, Rob Vaughan, and Dave Trueland; (third row) Joe Vadurro, Danny Stoddart, Steven Houser, Robert Labascio, and Gary Kalber. The coach was Bob Houser.

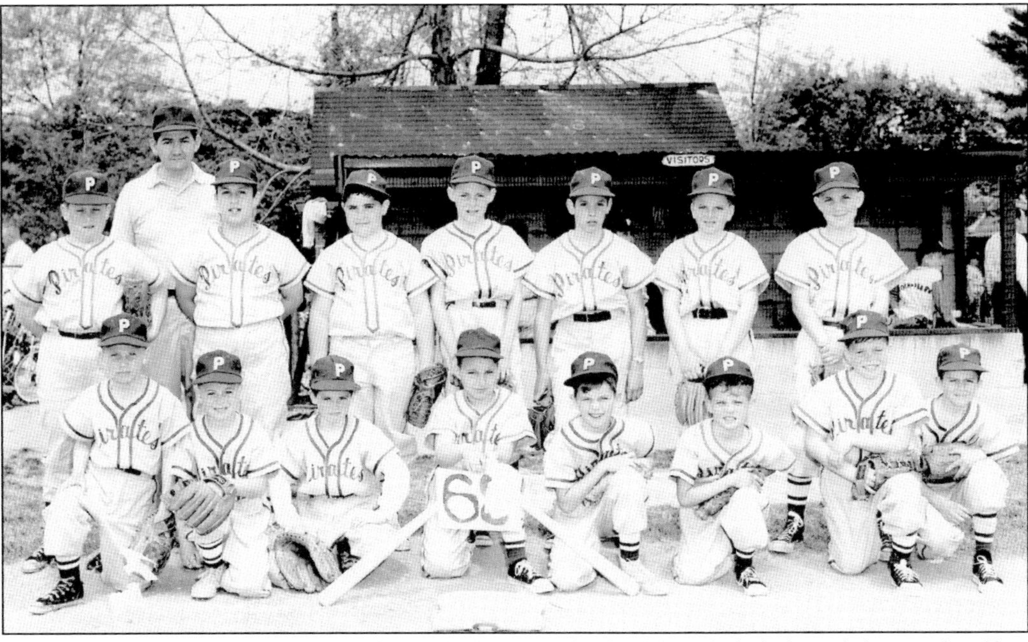

The 1968 Pirates, coached by Frank Duffy (seen in the back) included, from left to right, (first row) Don Petrelli, Joe McNally, Kevin Kirk, Scott James, Dan Willier, unidentified, Randy Campbell, and unidentified; (second row) unidentified, Mike Sweeney, Brian Myers, unidentified, Ron Pino, unidentified, and Bob Brady.

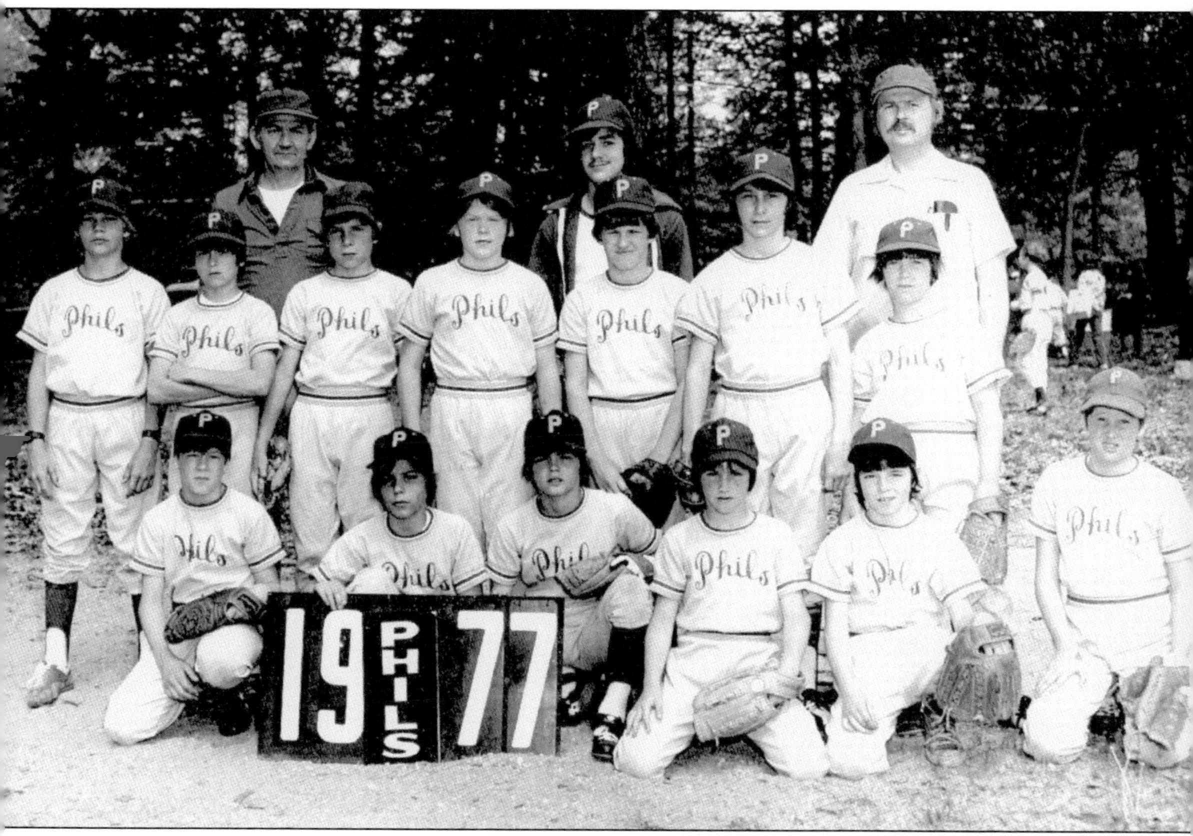

The 1977 Phils won the state championship in a best of three series. The championship team included coaches Nelson Yingst, John ?, and Frank Duffy. The team players included, from left to right, (first row) Rob Doyle, Tom Reeb, Curtis Palimeno, Darren Patnode, Mark Gervasi, and Ron Baldwin; (second row) Rich Michielli, Mike DiGacamo, John Lewis, Eric Paulson, Kurt Hohing, Billy Johnston, and Rick Foster.

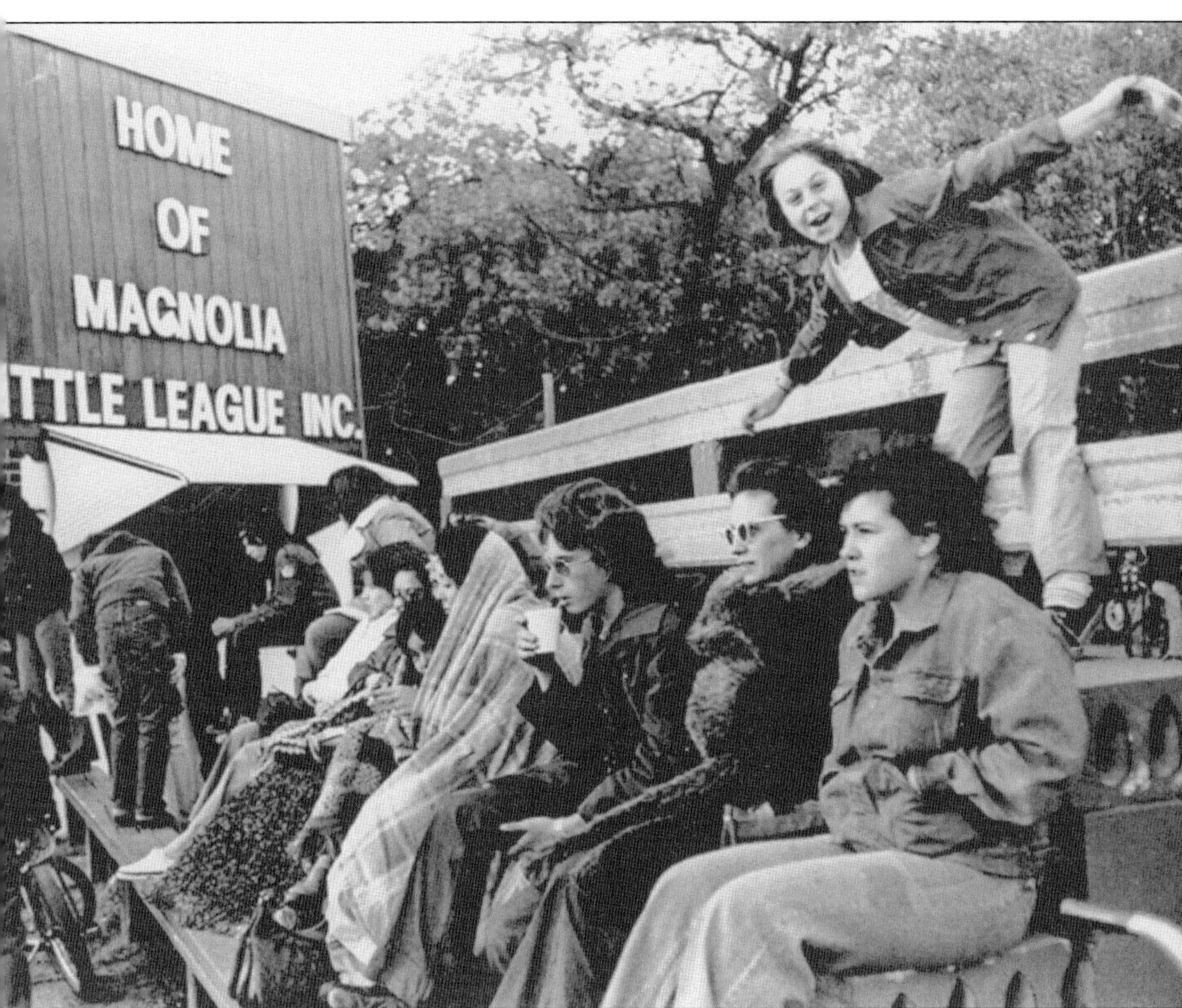

Local supporters watch the Phils play in 1976. Pat Stearne is visible wrapped in the blanket, with Nicloe Montlena peaking out from behind. When local Little League first began, resident Orie Johnson, president of the league's ladies auxiliary, kept the crowd cool by using her own wagon to haul ice and supplies to make snow cones. In 1956, she convinced the women to purchase a snow cone machine and launch the snack bar, which is visible in the background of this photograph. In addition to Johnson, Margaret Wright, Vivien Turner, Dot Rambo, Betty McAlister, Marian Greenaway, Madeline Jiulanti, Flossie Oliver, and Dot Kiel took turns manning the snack station.

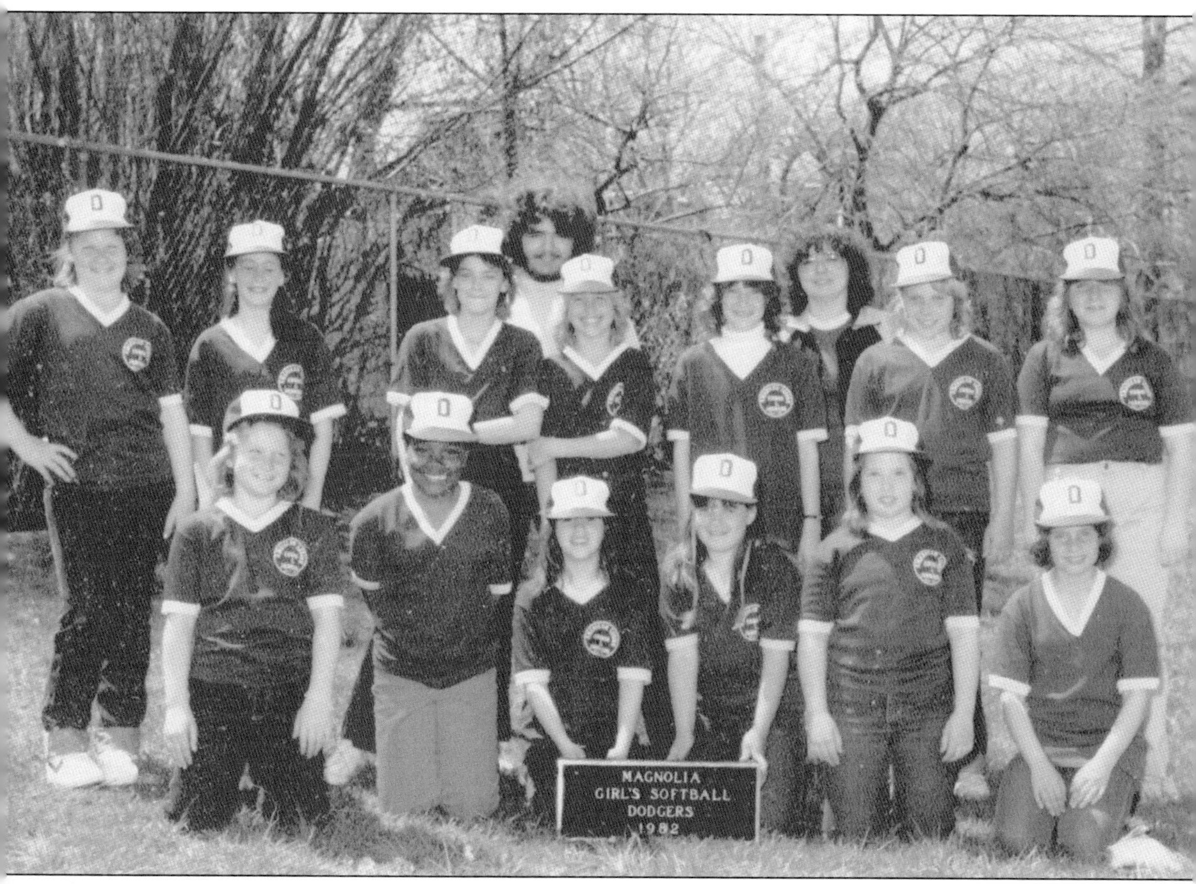

The 1982 Dodgers girls softball team included, from left to right, (first row) Kim Nicholas, Karen Shaw, Theresa ?, Bobbie Jean Ritter, Chantel Clark, and Tracy Zebrowski; (top row) Kathy Nicholas, Margie Schroeder, Terri Law, coach Craig ?, Patti Phillips, Heather Grabowski, unidentified, Pam Piper, and Alicia Gilmen.

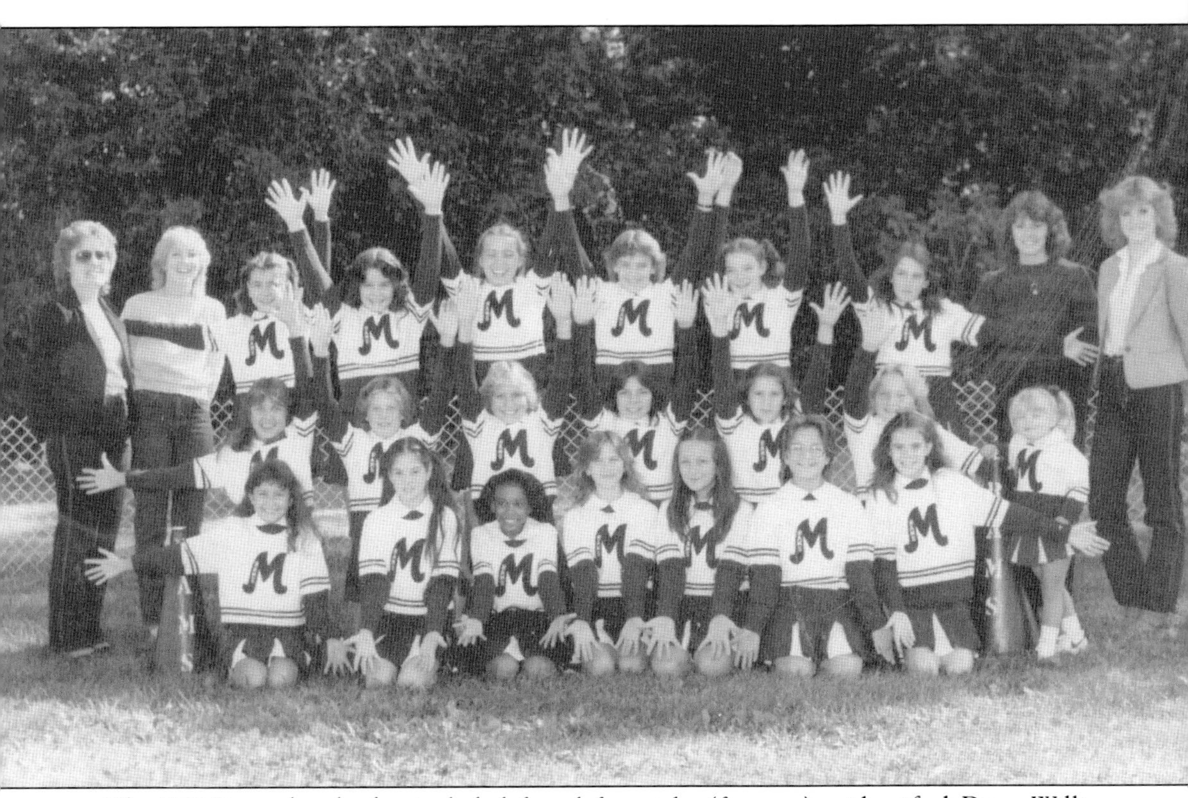

The 1983 Rams cheerleaders included, from left to right, (first row) unidentified, Dawn Williams, unidentified, Stacy Encin, and four unidentified; (second row) Marlene Dougherty, Tina Curry, Patti Phillips, Carol Rutkowski, unidentified, and Kim Nicholas; (third row) Michele Rutkowski, unidentified, Heather Volkmann, Terri Law, Denise Lavigne, and unidentified. The four women are unidentified.

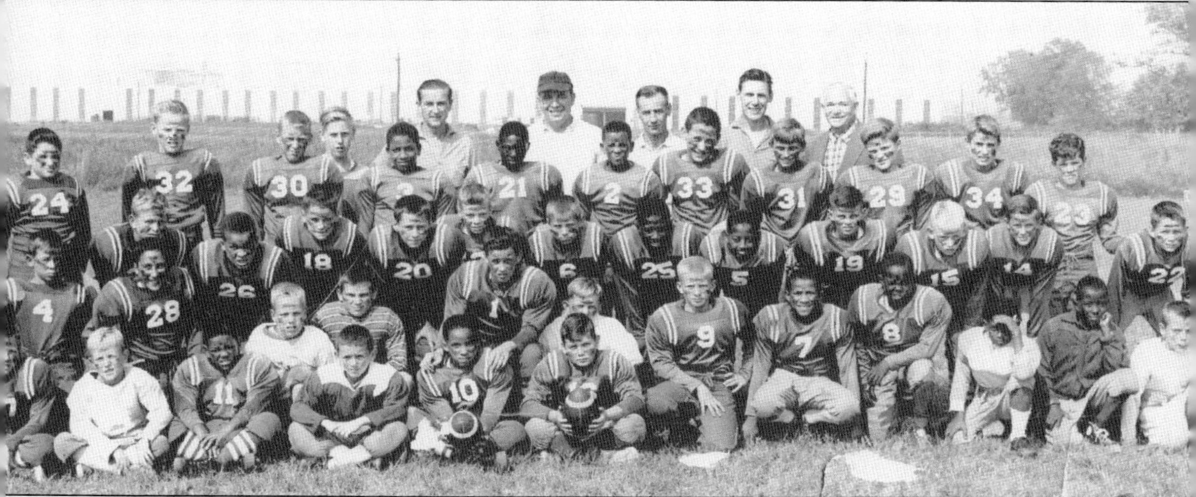

Joseph Foster launched the Magnolia Rams in 1959, with the help of Donald Craig Sr., Bud Chapman, Ozzie Bass, John Jones, and John Cunnion, and incorporated the team into the Philadelphia Interstate League in 1962. Doris Orr, who founded the Rams Women's Auxiliary, served as the team's first president.

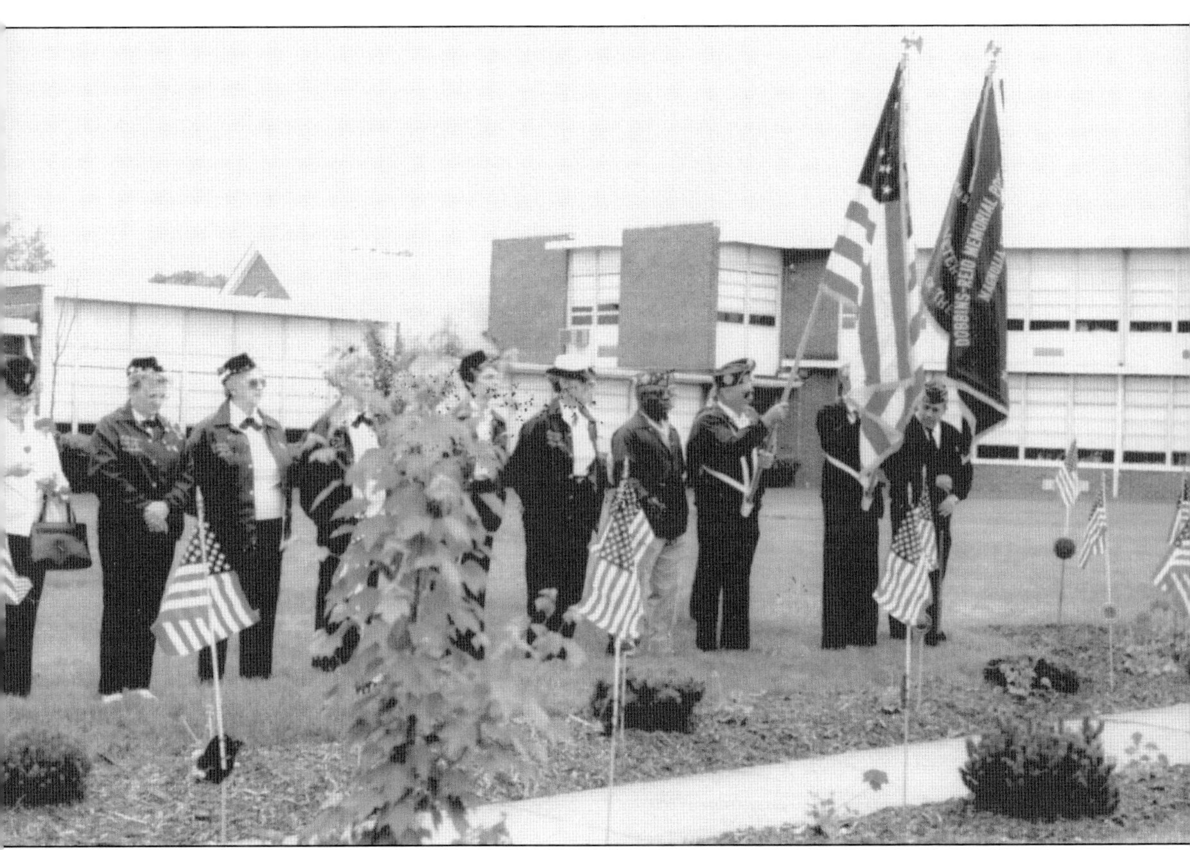

Members of the Edwin I. Johnson American Legion Post No. 370 Auxiliary remember fallen service members during a Memorial Day service at the Legion Hall in 1987. Seen here are, from left to right, Vivien Turner, Marie Bracken, Betty Hoffman, Helen Gallagher, Ruth Shinn, Jane McKenna, Aaron Tart, Frank Hannhen, Matt Thistlewood, and Dick Massey.

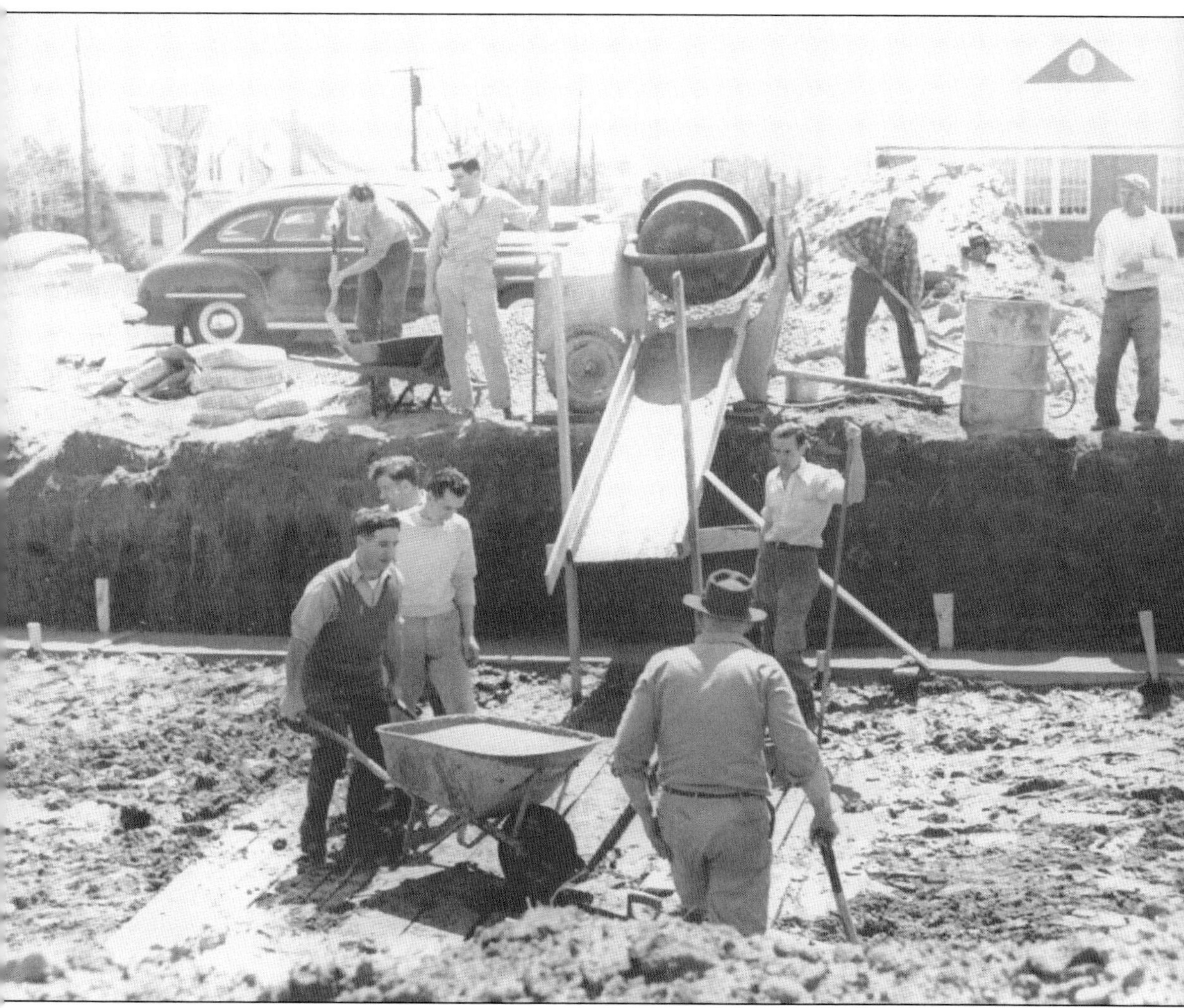

The post was founded in 1946, following the death of Magnolia resident Edwin I. Johnson in World War II. For the first four years, members met in the fire hall, until the post could be constructed on Warwick Road. The borough donated the land for the building, and private donations of time and money, as well as fund-raisers sponsored by the local Mothers Service Club, covered the construction costs. The foundation is well underway in this 1949 photograph.

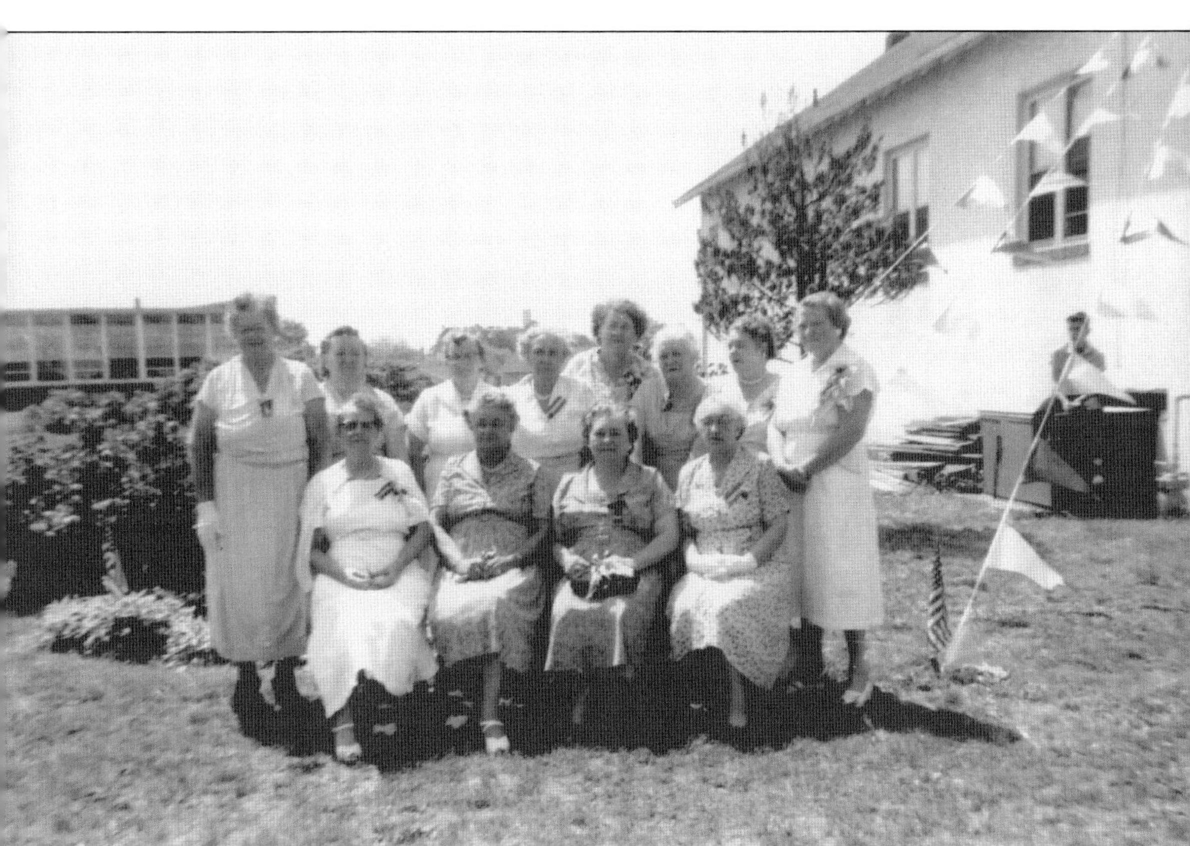

Local American Gold Star Mothers stand at the American Legion Post in this undated photograph. The American Gold Star Mothers was founded in 1929 as a support and community service organization for women who lost a child in World War I and was later extended to include casualties of other wars. Among the Magnolia residents gathered here are Lillian Shoemaker, Nellie Stites, Myrtle Quigley, and Sadie McAlister.

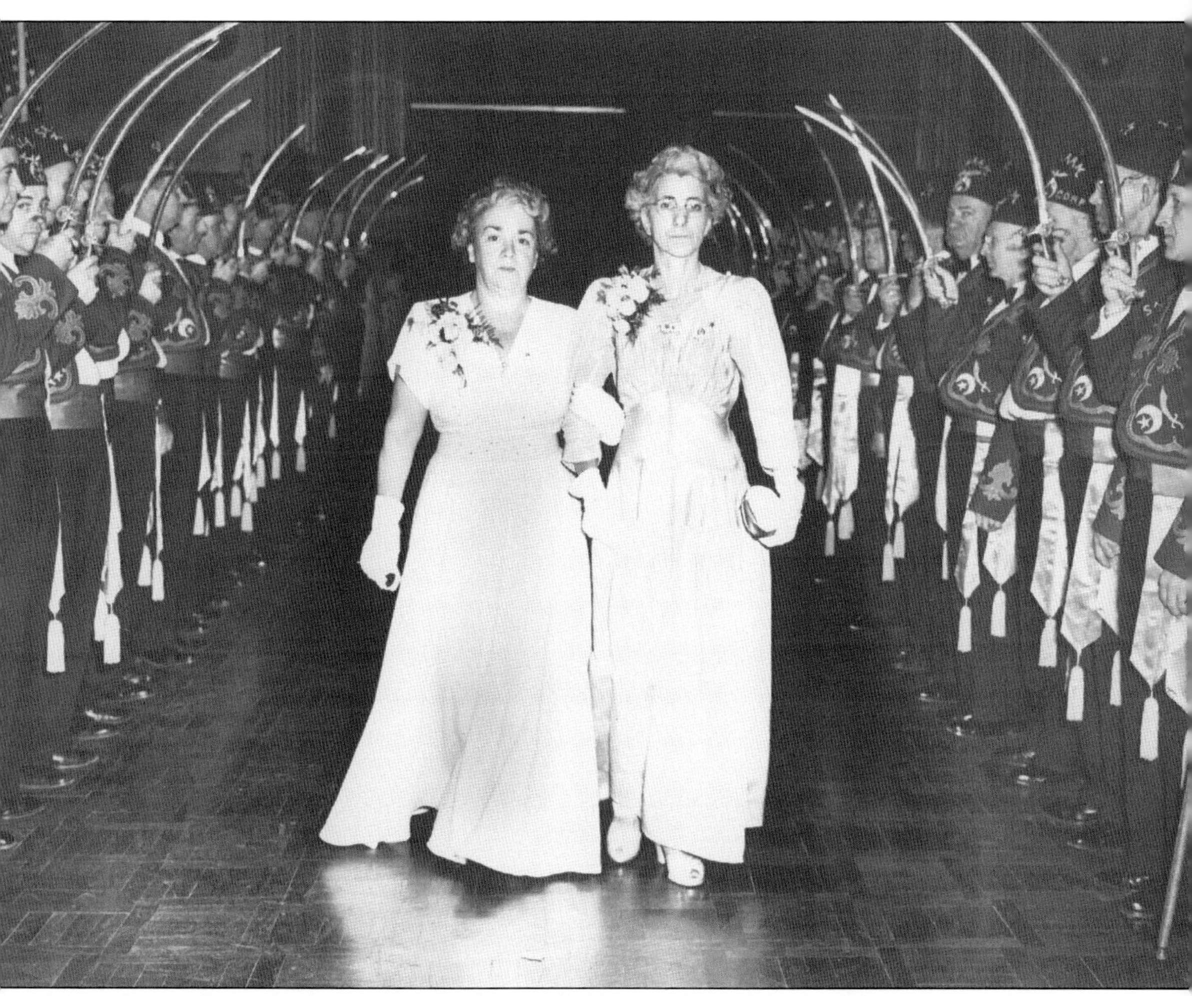

Magnolia resident Charlotte "Lottie" Johnson (left), president of the Camden County Chapter of the American Gold Star Mothers, is honored along with an unidentified Gold Star officer during a national convention in this undated photograph.

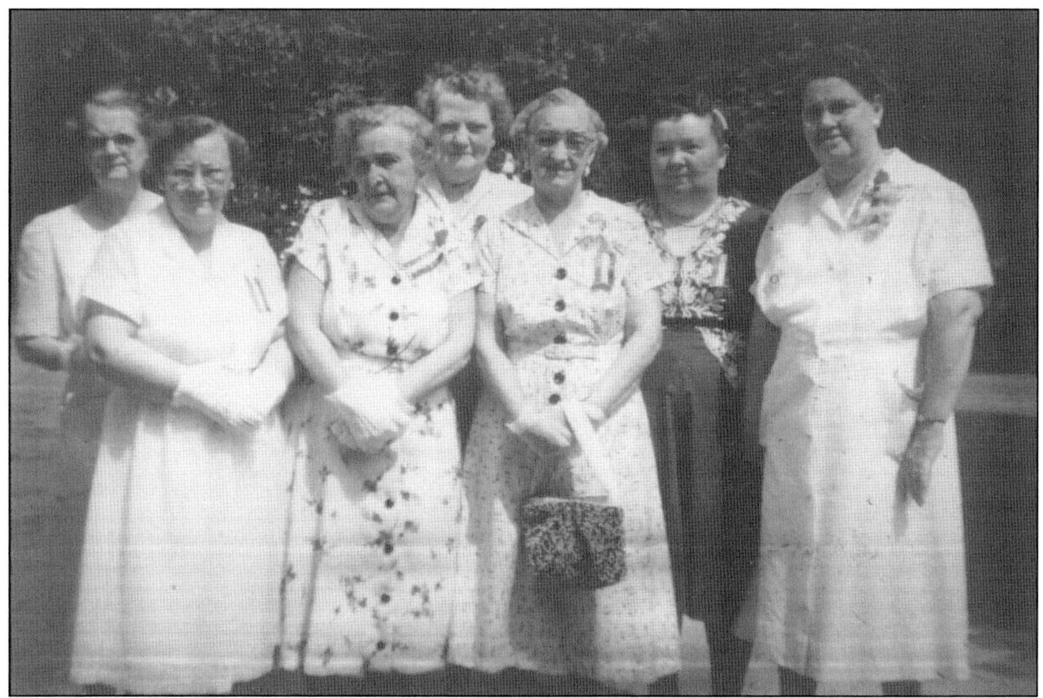

Magnolia's Mothers Service Club regularly held fund-raising events to collect enough cash to send a bit of spending money to local service members during World War II. The 1942 club included, from left to right, Sadie McAlister, Bessie Turner, Myrtle Engler, Myrtle Quigley, Haddie Hillman, Nellie Stites, and Lillian Shoemaker.

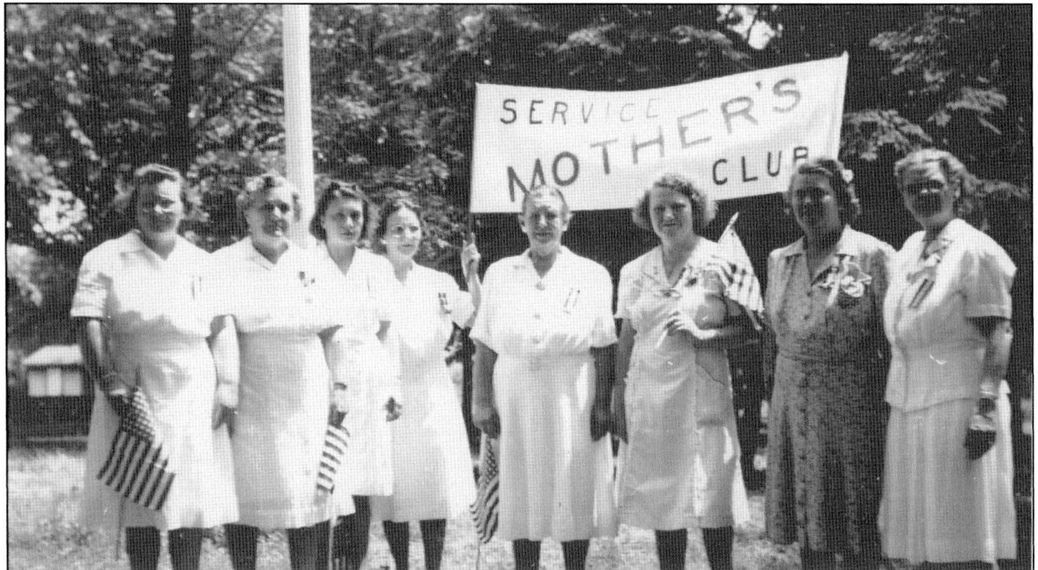

The 1943 club included, from left to right, Bessie Turner, Myrtle Engler, unidentified, Anna Castor, Sarah Weidemann, Myrtle Quigley, Daisy Cook, and Sadie McAlister.

Magnolia N.J.
12/15/43.

Mothers Service Club:
Magnolia, N.J.

att: Mrs. Mc Allister.

Dear Mrs. Mc Allister,

I would like to express my sincere appreciation to the members of the mothers service club. for their gift of $2.50 and also the christmas gift of $5.00 which I recieved recently.

Sincerely,
Jack. Reid.

Like all of Magnolia's boys serving during World War II, Jack Reid, who would one day serve as Magnolia's mayor, wrote a thank you note to the Mothers Service Club after receiving a total of $7.50 from the women. The Magnolia Historical Society has the complete collection of service letters, as well as a scrapbook of servicemen's photographs, available for public viewing.

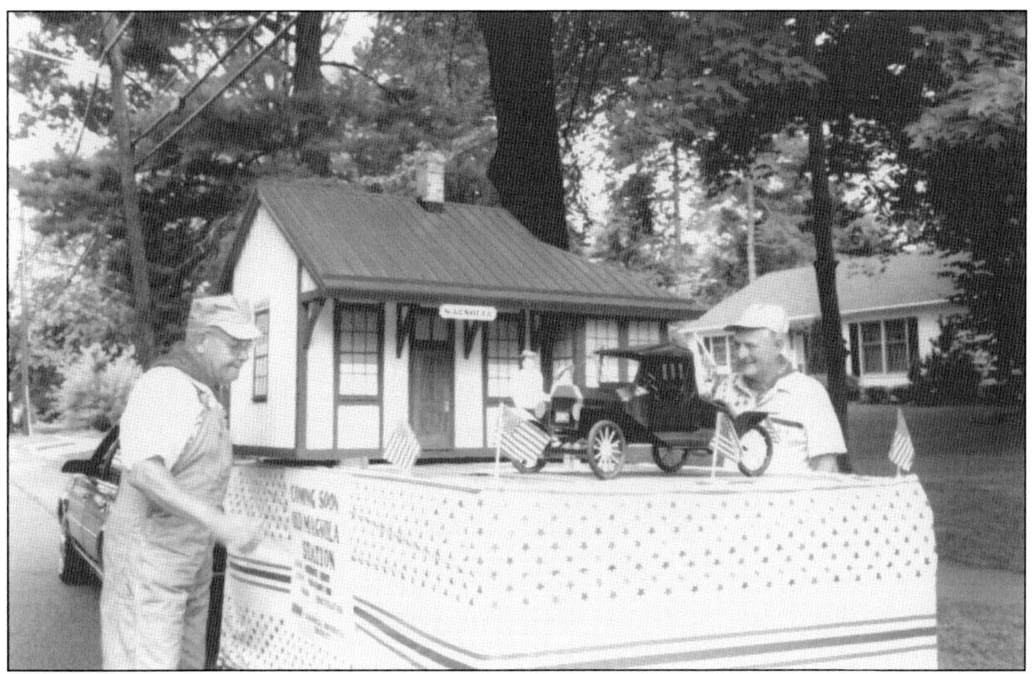

The Magnolia Historical Society unveiled plans to reconstruct the borough's train station at its original location in 1995 and establish the building as the society's headquarters. Land along the railroad tracks was acquired with the support of the borough council. Showing off a replica of the future station at the Fourth of July parade in 1995, is Spencer C. Moore (left) and Jim Hannold. The model was built by Ted Deusch.

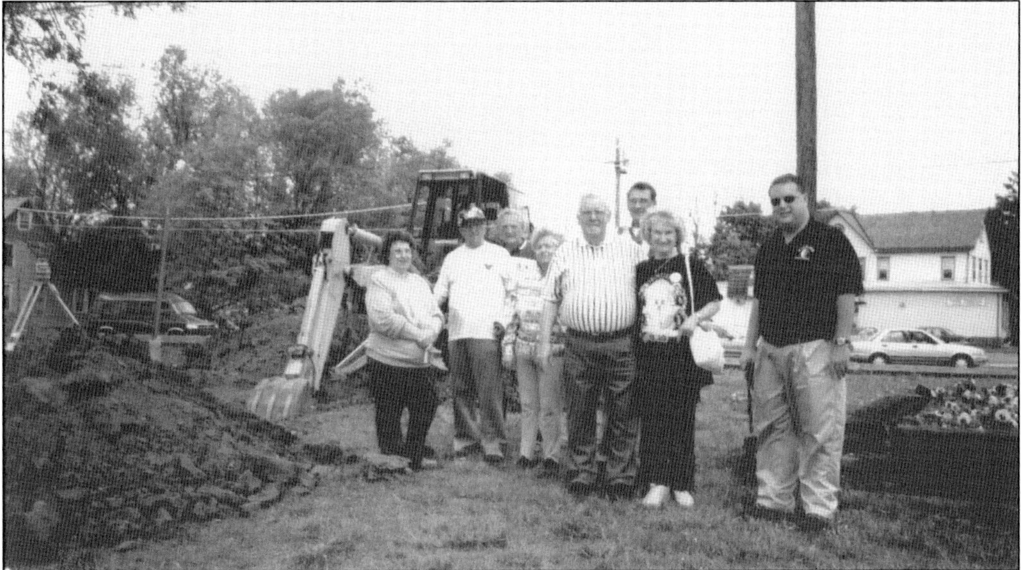

Following nearly four years of planning, groundbreaking for the train station took place in the spring of 1999. Checking out the progress are, from left to right, historical society members Helen and Tom Bradley, Jim and Mary Hannold, Ken and Joyce Stites with John O'Kane behind, and Tony DePrince. The project was financed through grants, donations of labor and money, and fund-raising events.

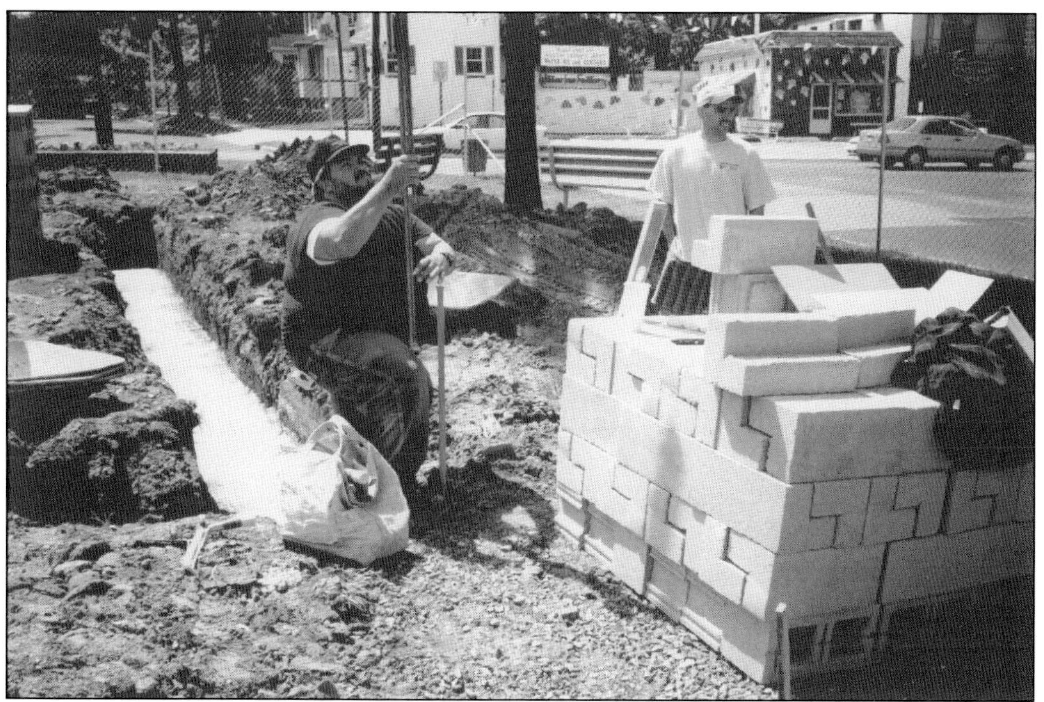

Tom Vadurro (left) works on the foundation of the train station in May 1999.

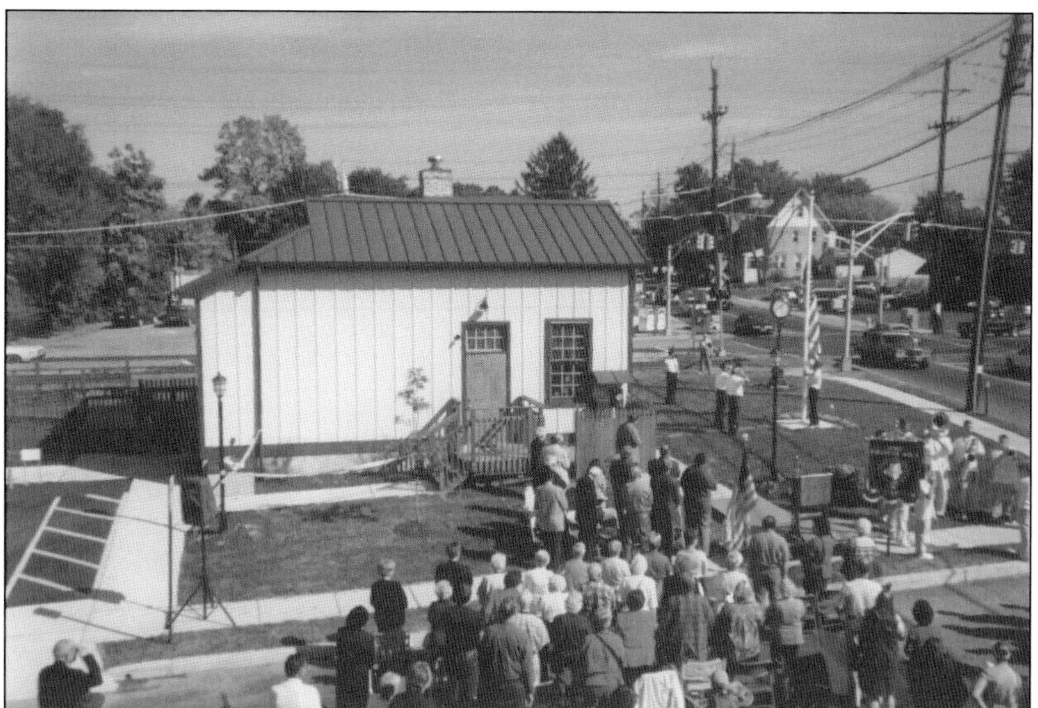

The Magnolia Train Station was completed and opened to the public in the fall of 2000, and the adjacent park was officially dedicated the following year. Turnout for the train station's opening ceremony drew a large crowd of local supporters.

Across America, People are Discovering Something Wonderful. *Their Heritage.*